Sams **Teach Yourself**

Node.js

in **24** **Hours**

SAMS   800 East 96th Street, Indianapolis, Indiana, 46240 USA

Sams Teach Yourself Node.js in 24 Hours

ISBN-13: 9780672335952
ISBN-10: 0672335956

Library of Congress Cataloging-in-Publication Data:

Printed in the United States of America

First Printing September 2012

Trademarks

All terms mentioned in this book that are known to be trademarks or service marks have been appropriately capitalized. Sams Publishing cannot attest to the accuracy of this information. Use of a term in this book should not be regarded as affecting the validity of any trademark or service mark.

Warning and Disclaimer

Every effort has been made to make this book as complete and as accurate as possible, but no warranty or fitness is implied. The information provided is on an "as is" basis. The author and the publisher shall have neither liability nor responsibility to any person or entity with respect to any loss or damages arising from the information contained in this book or from the use of the programs accompanying it.

Bulk Sales

Sams Publishing offers excellent discounts on this book when ordered in quantity for bulk purchases or special sales. For more information, please contact

U.S. Corporate and Government Sales
1-800-382-3419
corpsales@pearsontechgroup.com

For sales outside of the U.S., please contact

International Sales
international@pearsoned.com

Editor-in-Chief
Mark Taub

Acquisitions Editor
Laura Lewin

Development Editor
Sheri Cain

Managing Editor
Kristy Hart

Project Editor
Anne Goebel

Copy Editor
Geneil Breeze

Indexer
Tim Wright

Proofreader
Sarah Kearns

Technical Editor
Remy Sharp

Publishing Coordinator
Olivia Basegio

Interior Designer
Gary Adair

Cover Designer
Anne Jones

Senior Compositor
Gloria Schurick

Contents at a Glance

Table of Contents

About the Author

George Ornbo is a UK-based JavaScript and Ruby developer. He has been creating web applications for more than eight years, first as a freelancer and more recently working at pebble {code} in London. He blogs at http://shapeshed.com and can be found in most of the usual places around the Web as @shapeshed.

.

Dedication

This book is dedicated to my wife, Kirsten.
Without your support, this book would not have been possible.

Acknowledgments

Thanks to Trina MacDonald and the team at Pearson for giving me the chance to write this book. Your encouragement and guidance was invaluable.

Thanks to Remy Sharp, the technical editor on the book. You picked up numerous mistakes and oversights over the course of the reviews. I owe you a beer! Any mistakes left in the book are, of course, my own.

Thanks to my colleagues at pebble {code}. From the start, you were right behind me writing the book. I am very grateful for the flexibility around big projects that allowed me to finish the book.

We Want to Hear from You!

As the reader of this book, you are our most important critic and commentator. We value your opinion and want to know what we're doing right, what we could do better, what areas you'd like to see us publish in, and any other words of wisdom you're willing to pass our way.

We welcome your comments. You can email or write to let us know what you did or didn't like about this book—as well as what we can do to make our books better.

Please note that we cannot help you with technical problems related to the topic of this book.

When you write, please be sure to include this book's title and author as well as your name and email address. We will carefully review your comments and share them with the author and editors who worked on the book.

Email: errata@informit.com
Mail: Addison-Wesley/Prentice Hall Publishing
         ATTN: Reader Feedback
         1330 Avenue of the Americas
         35th Floor
         New York, New York, 10019

Reader Services

Visit our website and register this book at informit.com/register for convenient access to any updates, downloads, or errata that might be available for this book.

Introduction

The ability to use JavaScript on the server allows developers who are familiar with JavaScript to add server-side development to their curriculum vitae. Node.js is much more than that, though. It rethinks network programming in the context of the modern Web where an application may rely on reading and writing data from many different places and may have millions of concurrent users.

JavaScript is often seen as a toy language by developers who have traditional computer science degrees. But, JavaScript has survived numerous challenges and is now integral to the direction of the Web both in the browser and with Node.js on the server-side too. There has never been a better time to write JavaScript, especially on the server!

Node.js represents a development platform that can respond to creating applications for the modern Web. This includes

- ▶ Real-time applications
- ▶ Multiplayer games
- ▶ Single-page applications
- ▶ JSON-based APIs

It is focused on speed and scalability and can handle thousands of concurrent users without needing expensive hardware. The Node.js project recently became the most watched project on GitHub and is now being used by companies like EBay, LinkedIn, and Microsoft.

Node.js is much more than JavaScript on the server. It is a fully featured network programming platform for responding to the demands of modern web programming.

Who Should Read This Book?

This book makes few assumptions about programming experience, but it is helpful to have some basic experience with JavaScript. As Node.js is primarily run from the terminal, it is helpful to understand what a terminal is and how to run basic commands. Finally, because Node.js is primarily a network programming tool, it helps to understand a little of how the Internet works, although this is not essential.

Why Should I Learn Node.js?

If you are interested in creating applications that have many users, deal with networked data, or have real-time requirements, then Node.js is a great tool for the job. Furthermore, if you are creating applications for the browser, Node.js allows your server to be JavaScript, making it much simpler to share data between your server and client. Node.js is a modern toolkit for the modern Web!

How This Book Is Organized

This books starts with the basics of Node.js, including running your first Node.js program and using npm (Node's package manager). You then are introduced to network programming and how Node.js uses JavaScript callbacks to support an asynchronous style of programming.

In Part II of the book, you learn how to create basic websites with Node.js first by using the HTTP module and then using Express, a web framework for Node.js. You also learn how to persist data with MongoDB.

Part III introduces tools for debugging and testing Node.js application. You are introduced to a number of debugging tools and testing frameworks to support your development. You learn how to deploy your Node.js applications to a number of third-party services, including Heroku and Nodester.

Part IV showcases the real-time capabilities of Node.js and introduces Socket.IO. You learn how to send messages between the browser and server and build full examples of a chat server and a real-time Twitter client. Finally you learn how to create JSON APIs with Node.js.

Part V focuses on the Node.js API and explores the building blocks for creating Node.js applications. You learn about processes, child processes, events, buffers, and streams.

Part VI introduces areas that you may want to explore once you get beyond the basics. You learn about CoffeeScript, a JavaScript pre-compiler, how to use Middleware with Node.js, and how to use Backbone.js to create single-page applications with Node.js. Hour 22 also introduces how to write and publish your own Node.js modules with npm.

Code Examples

Each hour in this book comes with several code examples. These examples help you learn about Node.js as much as the text in this book. You can download this code at http://bit.ly/nodejsbook-examples, and they are also available as a GitHub repository at https://github.com/shapeshed/nodejsbook.io.examples.

Conventions Used in This Book

Each hour starts with "What You'll Learn in This Hour," which includes a brief list of bulleted points highlighting the hour's contents. A summary concluding each hour provides a bit of insight reflecting on what you as the reader should have learned along the way.

In each hour, any text that you type appears as **`bold monospace`**, whereas text that appears on your screen is presented in `monospace` type.

`It will look like this to mimic the way text looks on your screen.`

Finally, the following icons introduce other pertinent information used in the book:

BY THE WAY

By the Way presents interesting pieces of information related to the surrounding discussion.

DID YOU KNOW?

Did You Know? offers advice or teaches an easier way to do something.

WATCH OUT

Watch Out! advises you about potential problems and helps you steer clear of disaster.

PART I

Getting Started

Introducing Node.js

What You'll Learn in This Hour:

▶ What Node.js is and why it was created

▶ Examples of applications that you can create with Node.js

▶ Creating and running your first Node.js program

What Is Node.js?

On November 8, 2009, Ryan Dahl delivered a speech to jsconf.eu, a conference on JavaScript, introducing Node.js to the JavaScript community. He had become frustrated that concurrency (doing more than one thing at once) is difficult in many programming languages and often leads to poor performance. He wanted to make it easier to write networked software that is fast, supports many users, and uses memory efficiently. So he created Node.js.

Around the same time that Ryan Dahl was exploring ways to approach the problem, companies like Apple and Google started to heavily invest in browser technologies.

With Google relying on browsers for the delivery of products like Gmail, Google's engineers created V8, a JavaScript engine for the Google Chrome web browser. This is a highly optimized piece of software designed specifically for the Web. Google wanted to encourage the development and adoption of V8, so it was open sourced under a Berkley Software Distribution (BSD) license.

Ryan Dahl decided to use the V8 engine to create a JavaScript server-side environment. This made sense for many reasons:

▶ The V8 engine is extremely fast.

▶ V8 is focused on the Web, so it is proficient at things like Hypertext Transfer Protocol (HTTP), Domain Name System (DNS), and Transmission Control Protocol (TCP).

▶ JavaScript is a well-known language on the Web, making it accessible to most developers.

At its core, Node.js is an event-driven server-side JavaScript environment. This means that you can create server-side applications with JavaScript in the same way that you can with languages like PHP, Ruby, and Python. It is particularly focused on networks and creating software that interacts with networks.

What You Can Do with Node.js

Node.js is a programming platform, so you are limited only by your imagination and programming skills. You can create small scripts to do things on a file system or large-scale web applications to run entire businesses. Because of the way Node.js is designed, it lends itself well to multiplayer games, real-time systems, networked software, and applications that have thousands of concurrent users.

Some companies using Node.js are

▶ LinkedIn

▶ eBay

▶ Yahoo!

▶ Microsoft

Some examples of applications that you can create with Node.js are

▶ Real-time multiplayer games

▶ Web-based chat clients

▶ Mashups that combine data sources from around the Web

▶ Single-page browser applications

▶ JSON-based APIs

BY THE WAY

What Is Server-Side JavaScript?

Most web developers are familiar with using JavaScript to manipulate and interact with the content of web pages in a browser. This is commonly known as client-side JavaScript as it happens in the browser or client. Server-side JavaScript occurs on the server before the page is sent to the browser. It is the same language, though, of course!

Installing and Creating Your First Node.js Program

Enough talk! It's time to see Node.js in action and write your first Node.js program. First, you need to install Node.js. Installers for Windows and OSX are available on the Node.js home page at http://nodejs.org/. To install Node.js on these platforms, simply download the relevant file and double-click the installer. If you are on Linux or want to manually compile Node.js, you can find instructions at https://github.com/joyent/node/wiki/Installation.

Verifying That Node.js Is Correctly Installed

After you install Node.js, it is time to verify that it is correctly installed. You need to use a terminal to interact with Node.js. If you are on OSX, you can find the terminal application in Applications > Utilities > Terminal. If you are on Windows, you can start a terminal by holding down the Windows key and pressing r and then typing **cmd**. In Linux, the terminal application is usually called Terminal.

TRY IT YOURSELF ▼

Follow these steps to check Node.js is successfully installed:

1. Open a terminal and type **node**.

2. You should see a prompt.

3. Type **1 + 1**. You should see a 2 returned (see Figure 1.1).

FIGURE 1.1
Checking that Node.js is successfully installed

Creating Your "Hello World" Node.js Program

Now it is time to create a Node.js program that starts a web server displaying Hello World.

▼ TRY IT YOURSELF

Follow these steps to run a Hello World server:

1. Open the text editor that you use to write software and create a new file.

2. Copy the code shown in Listing 1.1 into the file. (If you downloaded the code for this book, this listing is available as hour01/example01.)

Listing 1.1   Hello World Server

```
var http = require('http');
http.createServer(function (req, res) {
  res.writeHead(200, {'Content-Type': 'text/plain'});
  res.end('Hello World\n');
}).listen(3000, "127.0.0.1");
console.log('Server running at http://127.0.0.1:3000/');
```

3. Save the file to your computer as server.js.

4. Run the program from the terminal:

   ```
   node server.js
   ```

   You should see `Server running at http://127.0.0.1:3000`. This means that the server has started.

5. Open a web browser and visit http://127.0.0.1:3000. If you see Hello World, you successfully created your first Node.js program (see Figure 1.2).

6. To stop the server run, go back to the terminal and press Ctrl+C. This kills the Node.js process and stops the server.

You just ran server-side JavaScript!

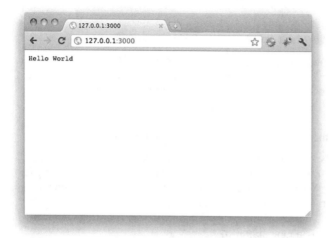

FIGURE 1.2
Your first Node.js program!

Summary

Hurray! You just created and ran your first Node.js program. You are probably not going to retire as an Internet millionaire just yet, but you will build on this simple example in future hours to create more complex applications, including a chat server and a real-time Twitter client.

Apart from creating a simple server, this first hour taught you that Node.js runs on top of the V8 engine, an open source JavaScript engine developed by Google. You also learned that Node.js can be used for many purposes and excels at creating networked applications with thousands of concurrent users.

In the next few hours, you explore what makes Node.js different from other programming languages and frameworks, specifically the features that make it fast and how you can write code to take advantage of it.

Q&A

Q. **Can I use JavaScript on the server? Isn't JavaScript just for the browser?**

A. JavaScript can absolutely be used on the server, and many features of JavaScript make it an excellent choice. Writing server-side JavaScript has many benefits, particularly when it comes to concurrency. If you have experience writing JavaScript with a framework like jQuery, you will see similar patterns used in Node.js.

Q. **Is Node.js better than PHP, Python, .NET, or Ruby for creating web applications?**

A. Assessing which programming language is the best is like trying to say which city is the best in the world. It depends. The type of application you are going to create informs your choice. But it is fair to say that Node.js is capable of most things that other programming languages can do and excels in areas that other languages and platforms do not.

Q. **Should I be worried that Node.js is a new platform?**

A. Node.js is relatively young in terms of programming platforms. The speed of development is moving fast, and new libraries are being created every day by developers around the world. The advantage of using Node.js is that you have access to a platform that is on the cutting edge and has learned from other programming languages. Now is a great time to become involved with the Node.js community.

Q. **Do I need to be an expert JavaScript programmer to use Node.js?**

A. You need to use JavaScript to write Node.js applications, but by no means do you need to be an expert. One of the reasons for the success of JavaScript as a language is that it is accessible. At its core, JavaScript is a simple language, so there is no need to feel intimidated. Furthermore, Node.js uses a number of patterns that you will soon become familiar with. You explore these patterns in the rest of this book.

Q. **Should I believe the hype surrounding Node.js?**

A. If you purchased this book, you have probably heard a little about Node.js. Maybe you read blogs that say things like, "Node.js is the next Ruby on Rails," or "Node.js is the new hotness." Take this with a grain of salt. Node.js is a programming platform that excels at many things, but other programming languages and platforms will continue to thrive. After reading this book, you can make up your own mind on what Node.js can offer you.

Workshop

Now that you know more about Node.js, here are a few questions to help you cement your new-found knowledge.

Quiz

1. What is the JavaScript engine that Node.js is based on?

    A. V8 JavaScript engine

    B. SpiderMonkey

    C. SquirrelFish

2. Who created Node.js?

    A. Ryan Adams

    B. Sophie Dahl

    C. Ryan Dahl

3. Extra credit: In relation to Node.js, what does concurrency mean?

    A. Running programs at the same time

    B. The ability to do more than one thing at a time

    C. That you can only perform one operation at a time

Quiz Answers

1. A. Node.js is built on top of the V8 JavaScript engine. This was created by Google and open sourced under a BSD license.

2. C. Although it would be lovely if Node.js were created by a British model or an American musician, Ryan Dahl created it. You can find out more about Ryan by visiting his home page at http://tinyclouds.org/.

3. B. A round of applause if you got this question correct! You learn more about concurrency in the next few hours because it is a key feature of Node.js.

Exercises

1. Modify the Hello World example to change the text displayed to "I am programming in Node. js!".

2. Modify the Hello World example to change the port number that the server starts on.

3. Using the Hello World example, get used to starting and stopping Node.js from the terminal by typing `node server.js` and then stopping the program with Ctrl+C.

HOUR 2
npm (Node Package Manager)

What You'll Learn in This Hour:

▶ Installing modules for Node.js with npm

▶ Finding modules for your Node.js applications

▶ Using modules in your Node.js applications

▶ Finding documentation on Node.js modules

▶ Using a package.json file

What Is npm?

npm (Node Package Manager) is a package manager for Node.js. It allows developers to create, share, and reuse modules in Node.js applications. It can also be used to share complete Node.js applications. Modules are simply libraries of code that can be reused in different projects. If you have programmed in other languages, npm is similar to RubyGems in Ruby, CPAN in Perl, pip in Python, or PEAR in PHP.

Typical examples of modules include

▶ A library for interacting with a database

▶ A library for validating input data

▶ A library for parsing yaml files

Using Node.js modules is a great way for an inexperienced developer to get started by leaning on the expertise of more experienced developers.

Whatever you do with Node.js, you should be familiar with npm and the libraries that it can offer you.

Most Modules Are Open-Source

The Node.js community publishes most modules under open-source licenses. This generally means modules are free to install, modify, and distribute.

Installing npm

If you installed Node.js from one of the installers at http://nodejs.org, npm is installed already. If you compiled Node.js from source installation, instructions for npm can be found at http://npmjs.org/. After you complete the installation, check that it was successful by opening a terminal and typing **npm** (see Figure 2.1). You should see some help text returned.

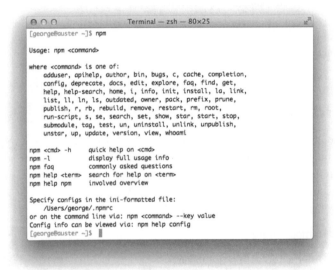

FIGURE 2.1
Checking that npm is successfully installed

Using sudo

If you are on a UNIX system (Mac OSX or Linux), it is strongly encouraged that you install npm without sudo privileges for security reasons.

Installing Modules

After you install npm, you can begin installing modules from the terminal:

```
npm install [module_name]
```

This command sends a request to the npm registry server to download the latest version of a module to your computer. You see an output to confirm that the files have been successfully downloaded:

```
module_name@1.2.0 ./node_modules/module_name
```

The output tells you three things:

▶ The name of the module that has been downloaded

▶ The version of the module

▶ Where the module has been downloaded

BY THE WAY

Make Sure That You Are Connected!

Because the npm registry and the source files for modules are hosted on the Internet, you need to be connected to the Internet to install modules via npm.

Using Modules

To use modules in your Node.js applications, you must require them after they have been downloaded. Requiring a module in your application looks like this:

```
var module = require('module');
```

Now when you run your application, it will look for the source files for the library and include it in your application. Normally, you want to use the module so it is assigned to a variable.

TRY IT YOURSELF ▼

If you downloaded the code examples for this book, this code is available as hour02/example01.

To use third-party modules in Node.js, follow these steps:

1. Open your text editor and write the following:

```
var _ = require('underscore');
_.each([1, 2, 3], function(num){
  console.log("underscore.js says " + num);
});
```

2. Save your file as follows:

```
foo.js
```

3. Install the underscore module using your terminal:

```
npm install underscore
```

WATCH OUT

Check Your Directory

For npm to install modules in the right place, you must be within your project folder when you run the command.

4. Run the program from your terminal:

```
node foo.js
```

The program should use the underscore module to count to 3 (see Figure 2.2):

```
underscore.js says 1
underscore.js says 2
underscore.js says 3
```

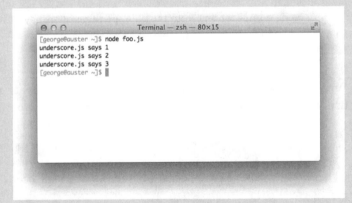

FIGURE 2.2
Using the underscore library to count to 3

How to Find Modules

Now that you can install Node.js modules, you probably want to explore what is available to you. Node.js has a vibrant developer community, and modules are being created and maintained every day.

Official Sources

There are a number of places that you can search for modules. First, there is an official npm web-based search tool at http://search.npmjs.org/ (see Figure 2.3). This is the canonical resource for finding third-party modules. Try searching for "irc". You should see a number of modules available relating to irc with a short summary of what the module does.

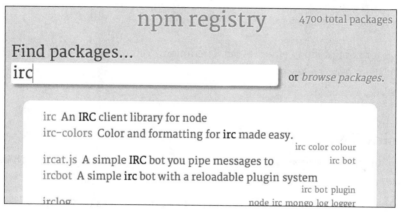

FIGURE 2.3
Searching for modules at http://search.npmjs.org/

Once you find the module you are looking for, install it from the command line as before.

You can also search for Node.js modules directly from the npm command-line tool in your terminal (see Figure 2.4):

```
npm search irc
```

Note that the first time this command is run, it may take some time as the index is created.

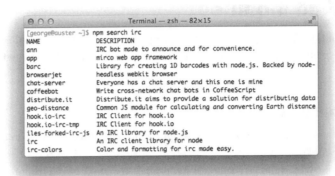

FIGURE 2.4
Searching for modules via the command line

This searches for not just module names but descriptions. You can also search across keywords by placing a space between keywords:

```
npm search socket connect
```

Unofficial Sources

A number of unofficial sources also are available for searching for npm modules. These use the official registry data but add some additional information on modules.

Blagovest Dachev created a site at http://blago.dachev.com/modules that provides information on the number of watchers, forks, and issues a project has on GitHub (see Figure 2.5). This is extremely useful for seeing how active a project is and when it was last updated.

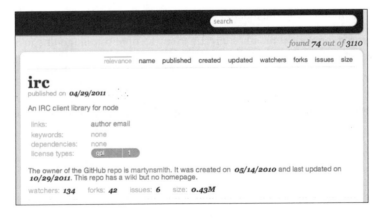

FIGURE 2.5
Searching for modules at http://blago.dachev.com/modules

Eirik Brandtzæg created a similar tool at http://eirikb.github.com/nipster/ that is also popular within the Node.js community. This ranks projects by the number of forks on GitHub, which is a good indication of how popular a project is (see Figure 2.6).

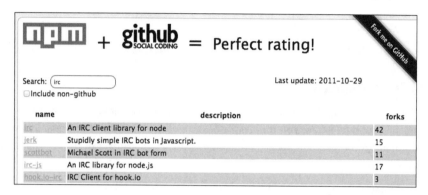

FIGURE 2.6
Searching for modules on Nipster

Another excellent search tool can be found at http://toolbox.no.de/.

WATCH OUT

A Note on Using Modules

Even though a module is available via npm, it does not mean that it is well tested or stable. Use the number of downloads a module has and the number of issues on a project as a rough guide of how reliable and mature a module is.

Local and Global Installation

You can install modules with npm in two ways, and understanding how they work is important.

Local Installation

A local install means that the library will be installed locally for your project in a folder called node_modules (as you saw when you installed the underscore library). This is the default behavior, so expect this to happen whenever you run

```
npm install [module_name]
```

If your Node.js application is called foo.js, this results in the following folder structure:

```
- foo.js
- node_modules/
   - module_name
```

This is the most common and recommended way of installing Node.js modules.

Global Installation

Some modules have executables that you may want to run wherever you are on your filesystem. An example of a module where you might want to use a global install is Express. Express is a web development framework for Node.js and comes with a generator that allows you to create a skeleton site.

To install modules globally, simply add the -g flag when you install it.

```
npm install -g express
```

Installing a module globally means that it can be run wherever you are on your filesystem.

BY THE WAY

Anyone Can Author Node.js Modules

The npm registry is open to anyone in the world to submit modules. There is no approval process, and it is easy to submit code to the registry so that it can be shared with other developers.

How to Find Module Documentation

Now that you know how to install and find modules, you need to find out how to use them. Generally, Node.js modules are well documented, and you can view documentation for modules in a browser by running

```
npm docs [module_name]
```

This opens a browser with the documentation page as provided by the module author. Often, this is a link to a README file on GitHub. To view the documentation on underscore.js, run

```
npm docs underscore
```

It is also possible to view the bugs on a project by running

```
npm bugs underscore
```

This opens a browser with the issues page as provided by the module author.

As you become more experienced, you may find that reading the source code of a module is the quickest way to understand what it does.

```
npm edit underscore
```

A "gotcha" here is that this command needs to be run from the root of a Node.js project folder, and the module must already be downloaded in the node_modules folder.

BY THE WAY

You Can Update Documentation

Most npm modules are hosted on GitHub, and module authors greatly appreciate contributions to module documentation. If you find something missing in the documentation, consider helping the author to improve the documentation.

Specifying Dependencies with package.json

As you develop Node.js applications, you will undoubtedly make use of modules. Installing each module one by one can be time consuming and prone to error. What if you forget to install a module, for example?

Thankfully, npm allows developers to specify the modules that they want to use in their application using a package.json file and then to install them with a single command:

```
npm install
```

This has many advantages:

▶ You do not have to install modules one by one.

▶ It is easy for other developers to install your application.

▶ Your application's dependencies are stored in a single place.

Returning to the example where we installed the underscore module, we can now add a package.json file to the project. A package.json file just contains information about the project in a specified format. A minimal package.json looks like this:

```
{
  "name": "example02",
  "version": "0.0.1",
  "dependencies": {
    "underscore": "~1.2.1"
  }
}
```

You learn about the details of a package.json file in a later hour, but for now, the key section here is dependencies. We specify that our application needs the underscore module.

▼ TRY IT YOURSELF

If you have downloaded the code examples for this book, this code is available as hour02/example02.

Follow these steps to use a package.json file for dependencies:

1. Open your text editor and write the following:

```
var _ = require('underscore');
_.each([1, 2, 3], function(num) {
  console.log("underscore.js says " + num)
});
```

2. Save your file as follows:

```
foo.js
```

3. Create a new file called package.json and add the following content:

```
{
  "name": "example02",
  "version": "0.0.1",
  "dependencies": {
    "underscore": "~1.2.1"
  }
}
```

4. Save your file as follows:

```
package.json
```

5. Ensuring you are in the same directory as foo.js, run

```
npm install
```

You should see that the underscore library is installed in a node_modules folder.

Using a package.json file to manage your Node.js modules is strongly encouraged, even if you are just installing one module.

Summary

In this hour, you learned how to install npm, the package manager for Node.js. In addition, you learned how to install modules with npm and use them in Node.js applications. You learned the difference between installing modules locally and globally and how to find documentation on modules. Finally, you learned how to use a package.json to declare dependencies in your application.

Q&A

Q. I am just getting started with Node.js. Should I use modules?

A. Yes. You can quickly add a lot of functionality to an application by using modules. Modules can often remove common difficulties for developers. For example, the Express module makes web development with Node.js much simpler.

Q. There is more than one module available for my problem. Which module is best?

A. You should use the most popular modules among the community. You can assess popularity by using the search tools located at http://blago.dachev.com/modules and http://eirikb. github.com/nipster/. The number of GitHub watchers is the best metric for popularity.

Q. Should I use third-party modules or should I write my own code?

A. Writing your own code is the best way to understand a problem, but for many scenarios it can be the case that someone has already solved the problem for you. In this case, you can consider using a third-party module in your application. Many developers eventually contribute bug fixes and new features back to the modules they are using.

Q. Do I have to pay to use Node.js modules?

A. No. Node.js modules are almost always published under an open-source license and are free to use. You can normally check the details of a license on a module's home page. If you are in any doubt, contact the module author.

Q. Should I install modules manually or use a package.json file?

A. You should use a package.json file to manage your Node.js modules wherever possible. This is so your application is easy to install for other developers and so you do not need to install modules one by one when your application becomes larger.

Workshop

This workshop contains quiz questions to help cement your learning in this hour.

Quiz

1. **What is a module?**

2. **What is the difference between installing a module locally and globally?**

3. **What are the advantages of using a package.json file for managing modules?**

Quiz Answers

1. A module is a reusable library of code. Examples include a module to interact with a database, a module to support web development, and a module to help communication via web sockets.

2. Installing a module locally means that it is installed to a folder called node_modules within your project. It is only available to that project. Installing a module globally means that it will be available wherever you are on your system. As a rule of thumb, install Node.js modules locally.

3. Using a package.json file means that you do not have to remember which modules your application depends on. Other developers will find it much easier to install your application and you can install all the modules that your application needs to run using `npm install`.

Exercises

1. Search for "template engine" using one of the tools described in this hour. Try to assess which is the most popular.

2. Search for and install the "coffee-script" module using one of the search tools described in this hour. Install the module locally in a new Node.js project.

3. Search for and install the "express" module using one of the tools described in this hour. Install the module globally on your system. Check that you can run the `express` command from anywhere on your system.

4. Create a new Node.js project with a package.json file and specify a module dependency that you want to install in the package.json file. Check that you can install the module by running `npm install`.

HOUR 3
What Node.js Is Used For

What You'll Learn in This Hour:

▶ What I/O means

▶ The problem that Node.js is trying to solve

▶ What concurrency means

▶ Different approaches to concurrency

What Node.js Is Designed to Do

Now that you have a brief understanding of how to run a Node.js program and how to use npm to install modules, this hour covers what Node.js is designed for. The Node.js website provides a short description of Node.js:

> Node.js is a platform built on Chrome's JavaScript runtime for easily building fast, scalable network applications. Node.js uses an event-driven, non-blocking I/O model that makes it lightweight and efficient, perfect for data-intensive real-time applications that run across distributed devices.

For a general web developer, there are a lot of confusing terms here! At the time of writing, Node.js is the most watched project on GitHub and has gained popularity with web developers and more recently business leaders. This attention has led to great deal of hype that is welcome, but often comes with misunderstandings about what Node.js is. You may have also heard things like "Node.js is the new Rails" or that "Node is Web 3.0." Both of these statements are not correct. Node.js is not an MVC framework like Rails or Django, and it will not make the bed for you in the morning. By the end of this hour, you will have a clearer understanding of what Node.js is and what it is designed to do.

Understanding I/O

You may have heard the term "I/O" associated with Node.js. *I/O* is shorthand for *input/output* and refers to communication between a computer and a human or data processing system. You can think of I/O as the movement of data between an input and an output. Some examples include the following:

▶ Entering text using a keyboard (input) and seeing the text appear on a screen (output)

▶ Moving your mouse (input) and seeing the mouse move on a screen (output)

▶ Passing data to a shell script (input) and seeing the output in a terminal

The idea of I/O can be illustrated by running a program in the terminal (see Figure 3.1):

```
echo 'Each peach pear plum'
```

On Mac OSX or Linux, the output will be

```
each peach pear plum
```

On Windows, the output will be

```
'each peach pear plum'
```

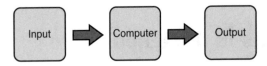

FIGURE 3.1
Data flowing through a computer

▼ TRY IT YOURSELF

Here, we are demonstrating input and output:

1. Open a terminal and type the following command:

   ```
   echo 'I must learn about Node.js'
   ```

2. You should see the line echoed back to you.

3. Note that your keyboard is the input here.

4. Note that your monitor is the output here.

Although this appears simple, there is a lot going on here. The program being used is echo, a simple utility for echoing whatever text it is given. What is happening in terms of the movement of data is as follows:

1. The text string is passed to the echo program (input).

2. The text string goes through the echo program's logic.

3. The echo program outputs it to the terminal (output).

Dealing with Input

In computer programs, input is often needed from users. This can be in the form of prompts from command-line scripts, forms, emails, or text messages. Much of computer programming is writing software that solves a problem and then deals with all of the possible unpredictability surrounding the problem. Consider a simple web form that requests the following information:

▶ First name

▶ Last name

▶ Email

When the user submits the form, the data will be saved to a database and displayed on a web page. But, many things can go wrong here:

▶ The user does not enter a first name.

▶ The user does not enter a last name.

▶ The user does not enter an email.

▶ The user enters an email that is not valid.

▶ The user enters text that is too long for the database field to hold.

▶ The user does not enter any data.

For developers, mapping these scenarios and defining responses for them is commonplace. This is important as it leads to stable software, and developers often choose to write automated tests for scenarios that they can run against their code base to ensure that their code is working as expected. The following is an example from a testing framework called Cucumber that allows developers to write tests in plain English:

```
Feature: Managing user
  In order to manage users
  As an administrator
  I want to be able to manage users on the system

Scenario: User does not enter a first name
  Given I am on the homepage
  When I press "Save"
  Then I should see "First name can't be blank"
```

This is a sound approach to software development as it is feasible to map the universe of the software and write the software against a predictable list of inputs and the order that they will be received. The way the program will respond can be carefully written to send the correct output based on the received input. In this example, the software has one input: a human entering data into a form. This makes it easy to map the scenarios, write code to respond correctly, and to write tests that validate it.

A computer program can receive more than one input, however. Consider a game console, like a Nintendo Wii or Xbox. It is possible to play games on your own, but it is more fun when you play against others! Let's assume that your friend has come over and you are playing Mario Kart on your Wii. In this game, you select characters and then race around a track in Go-Karts. Immediately, the number of possible scenarios of how data can be inputted becomes much more complicated. The input here can be considered as the two Wii controllers and the output as a television (see Figure 3.2). Instead of one user and one form, as in the previous example, there are now many more things to consider, such as

▶ Two players

▶ Two Wii remotes, each with eight digital buttons

Working through the number of scenarios that can occur becomes a vast job as players are able to move remotes in any direction at any time and press any one of the eight digital buttons, sometimes in combination. It is difficult to predict exactly how users will play the game and in what order things will happen.

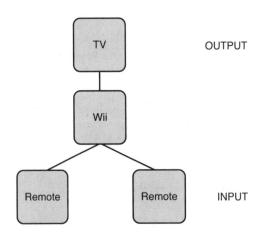

FIGURE 3.2
Two inputs complicate things.

Some games allow players to connect to the Internet and play against other players online. In a game like Battlefield for the Xbox, players are also able to communicate via voice and text over the Internet. The number of inputs into software quickly becomes astronomical:

▶ Potentially millions of players.

▶ Potentially millions of Xbox controllers.

▶ Potentially millions of headsets.

▶ Players move randomly through 3D virtual worlds.

Mapping each scenario of things that can happen and the order that they can occur becomes impossible, mainly because human beings are beautifully unpredictable. You may have also noticed that by connecting to the Internet, many more human inputs have been added to the software, but also that there are other inputs and outputs:

▶ Load balancers

▶ Database servers

▶ Voice servers

▶ Messaging servers

▶ Game servers

There are probably many more. The point to note is that it becomes extremely complicated to map scenarios and the order in which they will occur for this type of software, because there are a vast number of variables that include humans and networks (see Figure 3.3).

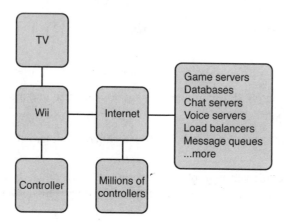

FIGURE 3.3
Inputs and outputs become complicated.

In developing software for the Web, developers have historically been able to predict inputs and outputs reliably, and programming styles have reflected that. The Web was original designed as a way to read HTML documents; these were stored on a server and made available to anyone with an Internet connection via a web server. The diagram for this is simple (see Figure 3.4).

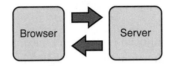

FIGURE 3.4
A web server serving an HTML page

As the Web became more sophisticated, it became common to add a database and a scripting language to web-based software (see Figure 3.5). This greatly increased the possibilities of what software developers could do without hugely increasing the complexity of inputs and outputs. It was relatively easy to predict how inputs would be used and map the number of possible scenarios to code.

FIGURE 3.5
Adding a database server

Today, the design of web applications is vastly more complex. I/O is fragmented, and I/O operations are more frequent:

▶ Heavy interactions with third-party Application Programming Interfaces (APIs).

▶ Data is sent and received from many different devices, including mobile devices, televisions, and billboards.

▶ Huge numbers of clients connecting at the same time and interacting in real-time.

Much like the earlier Battlefield example, the diagram of inputs and outputs now looks much more complex (see Figure 3.6). This is the problem that Node.js is interested in and provides one way of solving it.

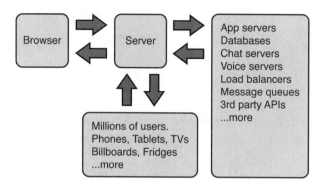

FIGURE 3.6
A complicated web application

Networked I/O Is Unpredictable

Now that you understand a little more about the idea of I/O and how modern applications are much more complex, it is important to understand that for web applications, I/O is unpredictable, particularly in relation to time. To demonstrate this, you will run a small Node.js program that fetches the home pages of different web servers (see Listing 3.1). Do not worry if you do not understand the code exactly, because Hour 5, "HTTP," covers this.

Listing 3.1   Demonstrating Network I/O

```
var http = require('http'),
    urls = ['shapeshed.com', 'www.bbc.co.uk', 'edition.cnn.com'];

function fetchPage(url) {
  var start = new Date();
  http.get({ host: url }, function(res) {
    console.log("Got response from: " + url);
    console.log('Request took:', new Date() - start, 'ms');
  });
}

for(var i = 0; i < urls.length; i++) {
  fetchPage(urls[i]);
}
```

In this example, you instruct Node.js to visit three URLs and report that a response was received and how long it took. When the program is run, the output is printed to the terminal:

```
Got response from: edition.cnn.com
Request took: 188 ms
Got response from: www.bbc.co.uk
Request took: 252 ms
Got response from: shapeshed.com
Request took: 293 ms
```

The inputs here are the responses from three different web servers, and Node.js sends the output to your terminal. If you run the same code again, you might expect the same results, but you see a different output:

```
Got response from: edition.cnn.com
Request took: 192 ms
Got response from: shapeshed.com
Request took: 294 ms
Got response from: www.bbc.co.uk
Request took: 404 ms
```

If you run this yourself, you may see that the order of the responses has changed or at the very least that the response times have changed. This is because response times are not regular in the way they behave. The time that a web server takes to respond can vary a great deal depending on some of the following:

▶ The time it took to resolve a DNS query

▶ How busy the server is

▶ How big the data response is

▶ The bandwidth available to the server and client

▶ The efficiency of the software serving the response

▶ How busy the network you are using is

▶ How far the data has to travel

▼ TRY IT YOURSELF

If you downloaded the code examples for this book, this code is hour03/example01.

Here, we are demonstrating network I/O:

1. Copy the code in Listing 3.1 into a file on your system called app.js.

2. Run it from the terminal:

```
node app.js
```

3. Watch the responses coming back from the servers.

4. Run it again from the terminal:

```
node app.js
```

5. Examine the output and compare the response times.

This simple example demonstrates that, in relation to time, network-based I/O is not predictable.

Humans Are Unpredictable

If you have developed any JavaScript for the browser, you understand that if you are writing code that humans are going to use to interact with a web page, you use a different style of programming. It is impossible to say the order or time that humans will perform certain actions. Here is some JavaScript code to show an alert to a user when she clicks a link with an id of "target":

```
var target = document.getElementById("target");
target.onclick = function(){
  alert('Hey you clicked me!');
}
```

You may be more familiar with jQuery, so here it is again, but this time in jQuery:

```
$('#target').click(function() {
  alert('Hey you clicked me!');
});
```

Both examples show an alert in the browser whenever a user clicks the link. These examples create a listener for the click event and bind it to an element in the Hypertext Markup Language (HTML) or Document Object Model (DOM). When a user clicks the link, the event is fired and the alert is shown. Instead of structuring code around a linear list of actions that a user might take, the code is instead structured around events. An event can occur at any time and can happen more than once. We describe this as event-driven programming because for something to happen in the program, an event must occur. Event-driven programming is an excellent way of dealing with unpredictability as you are able to map the events that will happen, even though you do not know the order in which they will happen.

JavaScript has used this model to great effect in browsers allowing developers to create rich browser-based applications that are based around events and how humans interact with the page.

▼ TRY IT YOURSELF

If you downloaded the code examples for this book, this code is hour03/example02.

Here, we are demonstrating JavaScript's code execution:

1. Create a new file called index.html and add the following content:

```html
<!DOCTYPE html>
<html lang="en">
  <head>
    <meta charset="utf-8" />
    <title>JavaScript Events</title>
    <style type="text/css">
      p { width: 200px; }
    </style>
    <!--[if lt IE 9]><script src="http://html5shiv.googlecode.com/svn/trunk/
➥html5.js"></script><![endif]-->
    <script type="text/javascript" src="http://ajax.googleapis.com/ajax/libs/
➥jquery/1.7.1/jquery.min.js"></script>
    <script type="text/javascript">
      $(document).ready(function() {
        $('#click-trigger').click(function() {
          alert('You triggered the click event');
          });
        $("p").mouseover(function () {
          alert('You triggered the mouseover event');
          });
        });
    </script>
  </head>
  <body>
    <h1>JavaScript Events</h1>
    <h2>Click events</h2>
    <button id="click-trigger">Click me</button>
    <h2>Mouseover events</h2>
    <p>Move your mouse over this paragraph</p>
  </body>
</html>
```

2. Open the file using a web browser.

3. Click the button. Note an alert is shown as the click event is fired.

4. Mouse over the paragraph. Note an alert is shown as the mouseover event is fired.

Dealing with Unpredictability

You have seen how web applications are now vastly more complex than just serving an HTML page to a browser. Some of the trends in modern web applications include

▶ Many different types of device can connect to a web application.

▶ Devices can act as inputs and outputs.

▶ Applications have different servers for different services within an application.

▶ Applications interact heavily with many third-party data sources.

▶ Real-time two-way data flow between clients and servers.

All these trends point to concurrency, which is a well-known and difficult problem in computing. *Concurrency* is a term to describe things that happen at the same time and can potentially interact with each other. A great example of a use case for Node.js is ql.io, a service created by eBay to provide developers with a single interface into multiple eBay data sources. This service makes it easy to request data from across the eBay organization. The service was created using Node.js and Subbu Allamaraju, Principal Member of Technical Staff, noted that the choice of using Node.js liberated them from some issues traditionally associated with concurrency.

> Node's evented I/O model freed us from worrying about locking and concurrency issues that are common with multithreaded async I/O.

To learn more about ql.io and why eBay chose to use Node.js, visit http://bit.ly/MywngG.

Node.js brings JavaScript's event-driven approach of dealing with unpredictability to the list of possible ways to solve Concurrency in programming. Event-driven programming is not a new idea. Python's Twisted and Ruby's Event Machine are both examples of server technologies that are similar to Node.js. There are also other approaches to solving concurrency including threads and using separate processes. What makes Node.js different is that the language it gives to developers to deal with concurrency is JavaScript. JavaScript is an event-driven language and is designed to be able to respond to events from the outset. You can absolutely write event-driven code in Ruby or Python, but if the suggestion is that using events is the best way to solve concurrency problems, it is worth at least considering a language that is designed around events.

BY THE WAY

Node.js Had Some Hostile Reactions

Initially, developers from other languages were scornful of the idea of using JavaScript as a way to solve concurrency. There were accusations that JavaScript is a toy language, that it was designed for the browser not for servers, and that attempting to solve concurrency with a single process is stupid. If you are interested in understanding a bit more of this debate, try Googling "Node.js is Cancer".

Summary

In this hour, you were introduced to more about what Node.js is and the problems that Node.js is designed to solve. You understood the idea that web applications have moved from serving single HTML pages to become much more complicated. You were introduced to the idea of I/O and how inputs and outputs have become more numerous in modern web applications. You learned that predicating the behavior of humans in relation to time and sequence in software development is difficult and saw how JavaScript offers an event-driven approach to respond to this idea. You then learned about the idea of concurrency, one of the main problems that Node.js is attempting to solve.

You were introduced to the idea that concurrency is a long-standing problem in software development and that Node.js is one response to that problem, particularly in the context of working with networks. In this hour, you learned more about what Node.js is trying to solve. In the next hour, you learn more about the approach it takes to concurrency.

Q&A

Q. I'm developing small content sites. Is Node.js a good fit?

A. You can absolutely create small content sites with Node.js, and a number of frameworks have been created to help you do that. It should be noted, though, that when Node.js was designed and created, it was not designed with this in mind.

Q. Concurrency seems difficult to understand. Should I worry if I don't fully understand it now?

A. Concurrency is a difficult concept, and you will be introduced to practical examples in future hours. For now, understand that concurrency means many people trying to do the same thing at once.

Q. Does I/O relate to the .io domain that I see appearing around the Web?

A. Yes. Developers working with real-time and Node.js applications realized that they were dealing heavily with I/O in their applications. The .io domain actually has nothing to do with computing; it is the domain for the Indian Ocean. You might have seen this domain used in relation to real-time software with sites like http://socket.io.

Workshop

This workshop contains quiz questions to help cement your learning in this hour.

Quiz

1. What are some of the ways that web applications have changed since the time when websites were just HTML documents?

2. What criteria do you consider are a good fit for using Node.js?

3. Why is JavaScript an event-driven language?

Quiz Answers

1. Some of the ways that web applications have become more complex include the addition of scripting languages and databases. Increasingly data is now distributed around the Web and glued together using APIs and networks.

2. Node.js is a good fit when your application needs to send and receive data over a network. This might be third-party APIs, networked devices, or real-time communication between a browser and server.

3. JavaScript is structured around events that initially were related to the Document Object Model (DOM). This allows developers to do things when events happen. Some examples of these events are a user clicking an element or the page finishing loading. Using events allows developers to write listeners for events that fire whenever the event happens.

Exercises

1. If you have developed any websites or software, pick one and try to draw an input and output diagram for it. Understand the devices or things that represent the inputs and outputs.

2. Pick your favorite computer game and try to understand the inputs and outputs involved in the game. How many inputs are there? Are there things that could happen at the same time or nearly the same time?

3. Take some time to read the following two articles: "Node.js is good for solving problems I don't have" (http://bit.ly/LyYFMx) and "Node.js is not a cancer, you are just a moron" (http://bit.ly/KB1HcW). Do not worry if you do not understand all the articles, but understand that the approach that Node.js is taking to solving concurrency is innovative, controversial, and provokes healthy debate.

HOUR 4
Callbacks

What You'll Learn in This Hour:

▶ What callbacks are and how they are used in JavaScript

▶ How callbacks are used in Node.js

▶ The difference between synchronous and asynchronous programming

▶ What an event loop is

What Is a Callback?

If you are familiar with using jQuery, you are probably using callbacks on a regular basis. A *callback* is a function that is passed as an argument to another function and is generally called when the first function is finished. In the following jQuery example, a paragraph tag is hidden using jQuery's `hide()` method. This method takes an optional argument of a callback function. If a callback function is given as an argument, it will be called when the hiding of the paragraph is complete. This makes it possible to do something when the hiding has finished—in this case, showing an alert.

```
$('p').hide('slow', function() {
  alert("The paragraph is now hidden");
});
```

A callback can be optional, however. If you do not want a callback, you could write this code:

```
$('p').hide('slow');
```

Comparing the two code examples, the first one adds an anonymous function as a second argument and is called once the first function has finished. In the second example, there is no callback. Because functions in JavaScript are first-class objects, they can be passed as arguments to other functions in this way. This allows you to write code that says, "Do this and when you are finished doing that, do this." To illustrate the difference between writing code with and without callbacks, you look at two jQuery examples in the browser.

```
<!doctype html>
<html lang="en">
```

```
<head>
  <meta charset="UTF-8">
  <title>Callback Example</title>
</head>
<body>
  <h1>Callback Example</h1>
  <p>Lorem ipsum dolor sit amet, consectetur adipiscing elit. Integer ut augue
et orcialiquam aliquam. Lorem ipsum dolor sit amet, consectetur adipiscing elit.
Pellentesquehabitant morbi tristique senectus et netus et malesuada fames ac turpis
egestas. Etiamfermentum dictum convallis. In at diam et orci sodales sollicitudin.
Sed viverra, orcisit amet faucibus condimentum, nibh augue consectetur ipsum, eu
tristique dolor diaminterdum tellus. Donec in diam nunc. Nulla sollicitudin elit
sit amet neque elementum accursus nibh lobortis.</p>
  <script src="https://ajax.googleapis.com/ajax/libs/jquery/1.7.1/jquery.min.
➥js"></script>
  <script>
    $(function () {
      $('p').hide('slow');
      alert("The paragraph is now hidden");
    });
  </script>
</body>
</html>
```

In this example, the alert is shown before the paragraph is hidden. This is because JavaScript
executes the alert straight after the `hide()` method is executed, even though the paragraph has
not finished hiding.

▼ TRY IT YOURSELF

If you have downloaded the code examples for this book, this code is hour04/example01.

The following steps help you to understand code execution in JavaScript:

1. Create a file called index.html and copy the following code into it:

```
<!doctype html>
<html lang="en">
  <head>
    <meta charset="UTF-8">
    <title>Callback Example</title>
  </head>
  <body>
    <h1>Callback Example</h1>
```

```
    <p>Lorem ipsum dolor sit amet, consectetur adipiscing elit. Integer
ut augue et orcialiquam aliquam. Lorem ipsum dolor sit amet, consectetur
adipiscing elit. Pellentesquehabitant morbi tristique senectus et netus et
malesuada fames ac turpis egestas. Etiamfermentum dictum convallis. In at diam
et orci sodales sollicitudin. Sed viverra, orcisit amet faucibus condimentum,
nibh augue consectetur ipsum, eu tristique dolor diaminterdum tellus. Donec
in diam nunc. Nulla sollicitudin elit sit amet neque elementum accursus nibh
lobortis.</p>
    <script src="https://ajax.googleapis.com/ajax/libs/jquery/1.7.1/jquery.
min.js"></script>
    <script>
      $(function () {
        $('p').hide('slow');
        alert("The paragraph is now hidden");
      });
    </script>
  </body>
</html>
```

2. Open the file in a web browser.

3. You should see an alert displayed and, after a short pause, the paragraph will be hidden (see Figure 4.1).

FIGURE 4.1
An alert being shown before the `hide()` method has finished

In the previous example, you saw that the alert message was shown before the paragraph was hidden. This is because the alert is executed before the paragraph has finished hiding. This is a great example of where callbacks can be used to ensure that something is executed after something else has finished. Here is the same example using a callback:

```
<!doctype html>
<html lang="en">
  <head>
    <meta charset="UTF-8">
    <title>Callback Example</title>
  </head>
  <body>
    <h1>Callback Example</h1>
      <p>Lorem ipsum dolor sit amet, consectetur adipiscing elit. Integer ut augue
et orcialiquam aliquam. Lorem ipsum dolor sit amet, consectetur adipiscing elit.
Pellentesquehabitant morbi tristique senectus et netus et malesuada fames ac turpis
egestas. Etiamfermentum dictum convallis. In at diam et orci sodales sollicitudin.
Sed viverra, orcisit amet faucibus condimentum, nibh augue consectetur ipsum, eu
tristique dolor diaminterdum tellus. Donec in diam nunc. Nulla sollicitudin elit
sit amet neque elementum accursus nibh lobortis.</p>
      <script src="https://ajax.googleapis.com/ajax/libs/jquery/1.7.1/jquery.min.
➥js"></script>
    <script>
      $(function () {
        $('p').hide('slow', function() {
          alert("The paragraph is now hidden");
        });
      });
    </script>
  </body>
</html>
```

The example now shows the alert after the paragraph has been hidden, and the alert now appears correctly after the event rather than before it.

▼ TRY IT YOURSELF

If you have downloaded the code examples for this book, this code is hour04/example02.

Follow these steps to use callbacks with jQuery:

1. Create a file called index.html and copy the following code into it:

```
<!doctype html>
<html lang="en">
  <head>
    <meta charset="UTF-8">
    <title>Callback Example</title>
  </head>
  <body>
    <h1>Callback Example</h1>
```

```
      <p>Lorem ipsum dolor sit amet, consectetur adipiscing elit. Integer
ut augue et orcialiquam aliquam. Lorem ipsum dolor sit amet, consectetur
adipiscing elit. Pellentesquehabitant morbi tristique senectus et netus et
malesuada fames ac turpis egestas. Etiamfermentum dictum convallis. In at diam
et orci sodales sollicitudin. Sed viverra, orcisit amet faucibus condimentum,
nibh augue consectetur ipsum, eu tristique dolor diaminterdum tellus. Donec
in diam nunc. Nulla sollicitudin elit sit amet neque elementum accursus nibh
lobortis.</p>
      <script src="https://ajax.googleapis.com/ajax/libs/jquery/1.7.1/jquery.
➥min.js"></script>
      <script>
        $(function () {
          $('p').hide('slow', function() {
            alert("The paragraph is now hidden");
          });
        });
      </script>
   </body>
</html>
```

2. Open the file in a web browser.

3. After a short pause, you should see the paragraph is hidden, and after that an alert is displayed (see Figure 4.2).

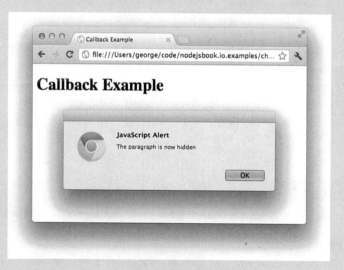

FIGURE 4.2
An alert being shown after the `hide()` method has finished

The Anatomy of a Callback

You have seen how callbacks work in jQuery, but how does a callback work internally in JavaScript? The key concept to grasp is that functions can be passed into other functions as arguments and then called. In the following example, a haveBreakfast function is created that takes two arguments of "food" and "drink". The third argument is "callback," and this is expected to be a function. The function haveBreakfast logs what is being eaten to the console and then calls the callback function that has been passed in as an argument.

```
function haveBreakfast(food, drink, callback) {
  console.log('Having breakfast of ' + food + ', ' + drink);
  if (callback && typeof(callback) === "function") {
    callback();
  }
}
```

To use the haveBreakfast function, we pass in what is being eaten as the food and drink variables (in this case, toast and coffee) and then a third argument of a function. This is the callback function and will be executed within the haveBreakfast() function.

```
haveBreakfast('toast', 'coffee', function() {
  console.log('Finished breakfast. Time to go to work!');
});
```

This callback pattern is used everywhere in Node.js, so take some time to understand what is happening here. In this example, the callback does something after the haveBreakfast() function has finished. Exactly what to do is defined by the function that is passed in as a callback. In this case, it is going to work! Running the script shows the following output:

```
Having breakfast of toast, coffee
Finished breakfast. Time to go to work!
```

▼ TRY IT YOURSELF

If you have downloaded the code examples for this book, this code is hour04/example03.

The following steps illustrate callbacks:

1. Create a file called app.js and copy the following code into it:

```
function haveBreakfast(food, drink, callback) {
  console.log('Having breakfast of ' + food + ', ' + drink);
  if (callback && typeof(callback) === "function") {
    callback();
  }
}
```

```
haveBreakfast('toast', 'coffee', function() {
  console.log('Finished breakfast. Time to go to work!');
});
```

2. Run the file.

```
node app.js
```

3. You should first see "Having breakfast of toast, coffee" and then the callback being fired that prints "Finished breakfast. Time to go to work!".

How Node.js Uses Callbacks

Node.js uses callbacks everywhere and especially where any I/O (input/output) operation is happening. Consider the following example where Node.js is used to read the contents of a file from disc using the filesystem module:

```
var fs = require('fs');

fs.readFile('somefile.txt', 'utf8', function (err, data) {
  if (err) throw err;
  console.log(data);
});
```

Here's what's happening:

1. The `fs` (filesystem) module is required so it can be used in the script.
2. The `fs.readFile` method is given a path to a file on a filesystem as a first argument.
3. A second argument of `utf8` is given to indicate the encoding of the file.
4. A third argument of a callback function is given to the `fs.readFile` method.
5. The callback function takes a first argument of `err` that will hold any errors returned from reading the file.
6. The callback function takes a second argument of `data` that will hold the data returned from reading the file.
7. Once the file has been read, the callback will be called.
8. If `err` is true, an error will be thrown.
9. If `err` is false, the data from the file is available and can be used.
10. In this case, the data is logged to the console.

You will see callbacks being used in this way over and over again in Node.js. Another example of this is the `http` module. The `http` module allows developers to create http clients and servers. You have already seen the `http` module in use with the Hello World server. The `http.get()` method from the `http` module allows requests to be made to a web server and for the response data to be used somehow.

```
var http = require('http');

http.get({ host: 'shapeshed.com' }, function(res) {
  console.log("Got response: " + res.statusCode);
}).on('error', function(e) {
  console.log("Got error: " + e.message);
});
```

An explanation of this code is as follows:

1. The `http` module is required, so it can be used in the script.

2. The `http.get()` method is given two arguments.

3. The first is an object of the options. In this example, it is instructed to fetch the home page of shapeshed.com.

4. The second argument is the callback that takes the response as an argument.

5. When the response is returned from the remote server, the callback function is fired.

6. Within the callback function, the response status code is logged or, in the case of an error, this is logged.

The callback function is called when the response comes back from the remote server and not before. This example demonstrates much of what Node.js is trying to achieve. As this piece of code has to go out to a network (the Internet) to fetch data, it is not possible to know exactly when or even if the data will return. Particularly when you are fetching data from multiple sources and multiple networks, writing code that responds to the unpredictable nature of when data will return can be difficult. Node.js is a response to this problem and aims to provide a platform for creating networked applications. Callbacks are one of the key ways that Node.js approaches network programming as they allow code to be run when another event happens (in this case, data being returned from shapeshed.com). Callbacks are said to be "fired" when events happen that cause the callback function be called.

In Listing 4.1, four separate I/O operations are happening, and all of them use callbacks.

Listing 4.1 Demonstrating Network I/O and Callbacks

```
var fs = require('fs'),
    http = require('http');

http.get({ host: 'shapeshed.com' }, function(res) {
  console.log("Got a response from shapeshed.com");
}).on('error', function(e) {
  console.log("There was an error from shapeshed.com");
});

fs.readFile('file1.txt', 'utf8', function (err, data) {
  if (err) throw err;
  console.log('File 1 read!');
});

http.get({ host: 'www.bbc.co.uk' }, function(res) {
  console.log("Got a response from bbc.co.uk");
}).on('error', function(e) {
  console.log("There was an error from bbc.co.uk");
});

fs.readFile('file2.txt', 'utf8', function (err, data) {
  if (err) throw err;
  console.log('File 2 read!');
});
```

When the code runs, it does the following:

1. Fetch the home page of shapeshed.com.

2. Read the contents of file1.txt.

3. Fetch the home page of bbc.co.uk.

4. Read the contents of file2.txt.

Looking at the example, can you tell which one will return first? A good guess would be that the two files that are being read from disk are likely to return first as they do not have to go out to the network. After that, though, it is difficult to say which of the files being read will return first as you do not know how big the files are. As for fetching the two home pages, the script goes out to the network, and the response time depends on a number of things that are difficult to predict. The Node.js process will also not exit while it has registered callbacks that have not yet fired. Callbacks are first a way to account for unpredictability, but also an efficient way to deal with concurrency (or doing more than one thing at once).

If you have downloaded the code examples for this book, this code is hour04/example04.

The following steps demonstrate callbacks:

1. Copy the code in Listing 4.1 into a file on your system called app.js.

2. Create two files called file1.txt and file2.txt and add some text to them. You might want to use some Latin text from http://www.lipsum.com/.

3. Run the script.

   ```
   node app.js
   ```

4. You should see that the callbacks from reading the file are fired first and then the two `http.get` operations.

5. Run the script a few more times. Think about how these events are happening asynchronously and how callbacks are used to do other things when operations have finished.

Synchronous and Asynchronous Code

Node.js runs on a single process and dictates that developers use an asynchronous style of coding. In the last example, you saw how four operations were performed asynchronously through the callback pattern. Coding in an asynchronous way is not specific to Node.js or JavaScript, though. It is a style of programming.

Synchronous code means that operations are performed one at a time and that until one operation is over, the code execution is blocked from moving onto the next operation. Listing 4.2 is a demonstration of blocking code and demonstrates two operations that you may do with Node.js: fetching a web page and fetching data from a third-party API. The example simulates these operations taking a long time and the effect that this has on the execution of code. Note that, in this example, the `sleep()` function is just a way of simulating the time spent completing these operations.

Listing 4.2 Synchronous (or Blocking) Code

```
function sleep(milliseconds) {
  var start = new Date().getTime();
  while ((new Date().getTime() - start) < milliseconds){
  }
}

function fetchPage() {
  console.log('fetching page');
  sleep(2000); // simulate time to fetch a web page
  console.log('data returned from requesting page');
```

```
}

function fetchApi() {
  console.log('fetching api');
  sleep(2000); // simulate time to fetch from an api
  console.log('data returned from the api');
}

fetchPage();
fetchApi();
```

In this example, the `fetchPage()` function simulates fetching a page from the Internet and the `fetchApi()` function simulates fetching data from a third-party API. They are not fetching actual data but rather demonstrating what happens in a synchronous style of programming when the amount of time it takes to respond is unknown.

If you run this example, you see the following output:

```
fetching page
page fetched
fetching api
data returned from the api
```

When the script runs, the `fetchPage()` function is called, and until this returns the script's execution is blocked. Until the `fetchPage()` function returns, it cannot move onto the `fetchApi()` function. This is known as a blocking operation as this style of coding blocks the processing until a function returns. Effectively one thing happens after the other.

TRY IT YOURSELF ▼

If you have downloaded the code examples for this book, this code is hour04/example05.

The following steps demonstrate synchronous or blocking code:

1. Copy the code in Listing 4.2 into a file on your system called app.js.

2. Run the script:

   ```
   node app.js
   ```

3. You should see the simulation of a page being fetched from the Internet, and when it is finished a simulation of fetching data from an API is made. The point to understand here is that they happen one after the other and that until one function has finished the execution is blocked.

Node.js almost never uses this style of coding. Instead callbacks are called asynchronously. Listing 4.3 demonstrates the same operations but using Node's asynchronous style. Note that instead of using a simulated `sleep()` function, this example makes a request over the network to a web service that simulates slow responses.

Listing 4.3   Asynchronous (or Non-Blocking) Code

```
var http = require('http')

function fetchPage() {
  console.log('fetching page');
  http.get({ host: 'trafficjamapp.herokuapp.com', path: '/?delay=2000' },
    function(res) {
      console.log('data returned from requesting page');
    }).on('error', function(e) {
      console.log("There was an error" + e);
    }
  );
}

function fetchApi() {
  console.log('fetching api');
  http.get({ host: 'trafficjamapp.herokuapp.com', path: '/?delay=2000' },
    function(res) {
      console.log('data returned from the api');
    }).on('error', function(e) {
      console.log("There was an error" + e);
    }
  );
}

fetchPage();
fetchApi();
```

When this code is run instead of waiting for the `fetchPage()` function to return, the `fetchApi()` function is called immediately afterwards. This is possible because the code is non-blocking through the use of callbacks. Once called, both functions then listen for a response to be returned by the remote server and this fires the callback functions. Note that there is no guarantee as to which order these functions might return in. This depends on the network. If you run this script, you see the following output:

```
fetching page
fetching api
page fetched
data returned from the api
```

If you have downloaded the code examples for this book, this code is hour04/example06.

The following steps demonstrate asynchronous code:

1. Copy the code in Listing 4.3 into a file on your system called app.js.

2. Run the script:

```
node app.js
```

3. You should see the simulation of a database query being made and data being fetched from an API asynchronously. The point to understand here is that now an asynchronous style is used so these operations can be performed at the same time and when the data comes back a callback is fired.

By running these two examples in your terminal, it should become clear how these two styles of coding affect what is run and when. Node.js is opinionated on how best to handle concurrency (or doing more than one thing at once), within the context of networks and I/O operations, advocating the asynchronous style.

If you are new to Node.js and JavaScript the terms asynchronous, synchronous, blocking, and non-blocking may be confusing. These are used liberally throughout the Node.js community and within documentation, so it is important to understand them.

The terms *synchronous* and *blocking* can be used interchangeably and refer to the example that you saw where execution of code stops until a function returns. A script is not able to continue if an operation blocks, and for the end user, this means that they simply have to wait.

The terms *asynchronous* and *non-blocking* can also be used interchangeably and refer to the callback-based approach of allowing a script to perform operations in parallel. A script does not need to wait for the outcome of an operation before proceeding as this will be handled by callback when the event happens. Using the asynchronous approach, operations no longer have to happen one after another.

The Event Loop

At this point, you might be wondering how does all of this magic happen? Node.js uses JavaScript's event loop to support the asynchronous programming style that it advocates. This can be another tricky concept to come to grips with, but it basically allows callback functions to be saved and then run at a point in the future when an event happens. This might be data being returned from a database, or an HTTP request returning data. Because the execution of the callback function is deferred until the event happens, there is no need to halt the execution, and control can be returned to the Node runtime environment so that other things can happen.

The event loop is not specific to JavaScript, but the language excels at it. JavaScript was designed around the event loop as a way to respond to different events happening in the browser as someone interacts with a web page. This includes events like clicking a mouse or rolling over a part of the page. An event loop is a good choice for browser-based interaction as it is difficult to predict when these events will happen. Node.js applies this approach to server-side programming, particularly within the context of networks and I/O operations. Node.js is often referred to as a network programming framework because it is designed to deal with the unpredictability of data flowing around networks. It is JavaScript's event loop and using callbacks that facilitates this, allowing programmers to write asynchronous code that responds to network or I/O events.

As you have seen with the blocking and non-blocking examples in this hour, using an event loop is a different way of programming. Some developers refer to it as writing programs inside out, but the key idea is that you structure your code around events rather than an expected order of inputs. Because the event loop is based on a single process, there are some rules that you should follow to ensure high performance:

▶ Functions must return quickly.

▶ Functions must not block.

▶ Long-running operations must be moved to separate process.

In this context, some programs are not suitable for event loops. If a program or function needs a long time to run to complete processing, an event loop is not a good choice. Examples of where Node.js is not a good fit include crunching large amounts of data or long-running computations. Node.js is designed to push data around networks and to do it fast!

Summary

You covered a lot in this hour! You learned about callbacks and how these work in JavaScript. You then saw how Node.js uses callbacks and saw some examples of Node.js using callbacks when reading a file from disc and fetching a home page from the Web. You explored the difference between synchronous and asynchronous programming and were introduced to the difference between blocking and non-blocking code. Finally, you learned about the event loop that allows callbacks to be registered and run at a later time when an event happens.

This hour has been heavy on theory, but you will see in future hours that learning how Node.js uses callbacks and the general philosophy of asynchronous programming is central to Node.js as a technology.

Q&A

Q. What about if I want to control the order of things when using callbacks?

A. You can nest a function with a callback within another so that when the first callback is fired, it calls the next function. A good example of this would be getting some data from a database and then doing something with the data with another function that involves a callback.

Q. Aren't threads the best way of doing this?

A. Many programmers coming to Node.js will have experience of using threads to address the same problems that Node.js is trying to solve. Node.js is opinionated about the way it approaches network programming, using callbacks, the event loop, and a single process. Some third-party modules have been created to make using threads and fibers possible, but the core philosophy of Node is to try and program within the context of an event loop and a single process.

Q. Can I program synchronously in Node.js?

A. Many developers coming to Node.js are used to programming in other languages and find switching to using asynchronous programming a mind shift. If you are feeling this way, give it some time and explore what using an event loop and programming in an asynchronous style gives to you. Node.js is opinionated that you should use the asynchronous style of programming, so if you insist on using a synchronous style, you are using it in a way it was not designed for.

Q. Isn't this a lot more complicated and more code?

A. It's true that using the asynchronous style of programming will lead to more code and more complexity than coding synchronously. Node.js is trying to solve a complex problem, though!

Workshop

This workshop contains quiz questions to help cement your learning in this hour.

Quiz

1. What are the synonyms for blocking and non-blocking code that are often used in Node.js?

2. Why is asynchronous code a good approach for working with networks?

3. What are some of the problems that you might run into when using callbacks?

Quiz Answers

1. The synonyms for blocking and non-blocking code are synchronous and asynchronous.

2. Networks are often beyond the control of a developer. You may be fetching code from a remote server that you do not own and dealing with many elements that are beyond your control. By using an asynchronous style, you can allow your script to respond when a network event returns.

3. You may run into issues around control flow when using callbacks. This is where you need to specify the execution order of callbacks. You may also find that you have nested callbacks that become four or five levels deep. This goal of this hour is to understand callbacks, but as your experience with Node.js grows, you will come across deeply nested callbacks and control flow issues.

Exercises

1. Return to the jQuery example in this hour and ensure that you understand how callbacks work. Next, look at the Node.js Hello World web server on the Node.js home page (http:// nodejs.org). Point out to yourself where and how a callback is being used.

2. Think about the world of teaching and how this can be synchronous and asynchronous. Think about how class of students attending a physical class with a teacher is a synchronous event. Next think about how distance learning is asynchronous. Remote students can watch videos and use online resources to learn whenever they want to and individuals are able to learn asynchronously. Try to think of some other examples outside programming that are synchronous and asynchronous.

3. To gain a deeper understanding of event loops within the context of JavaScript, watch Douglas Crockford's lecture on Loopage. It is available to watch for free at http:// www.yuiblog.com/blog/2010/08/30/yui-theater-douglas-crockford-crockford-on-javascript-scene-6-loopage-52-min/.

PART II

Basic Websites With Node.js

HOUR 5
HTTP

What You'll Learn in This Hour:

▶ Understanding HTTP

▶ Creating HTTP servers with Node.js

▶ Creating HTTP clients with Node.js

What Is HTTP?

Hypertext Transfer Protocol (HTTP) is long-standing protocol for communicating on the Internet. Essentially, it defines how a server and client should send and receive data while communicating. You use HTTP every day when your web browser loads up web pages where your browser is the client connecting to the server of the website you are browsing.

Node.js allows you to create both servers and clients using a low-level application programming interface (API) with the HTTP module.

In this hour, you explore how this module works and how to write HTTP servers and clients with Node.js.

HTTP Servers with Node.js

Node.js excels at HTTP. It allows developers to create servers and clients with few lines of code. Understanding the fundamentals of Node's HTTP module takes you a long way to understanding what Node.js can offer.

A Basic Server

In Hour 1, "Introducing Node.js," you learned how to create a simple Node.js server to output "Hello World" to a web browser (see Listing 5.1).

Listing 5.1   Hello World Server Revisited

```
var http = require('http');
http.createServer(function (req, res) {
  res.end('Hello world\n');
}).listen(3000, "127.0.0.1");
console.log('Server running at http://127.0.0.1:3000/');
```

This example contains a lot of information about the HTTP module. Here is what's happening:

1. The HTTP module is required from the Node.js core and assigned to a variable so it can be used later in the script. This allows the script to access methods that enable using the HTTP protocol via Node.js.

2. A new web server object is created using `http.createServer`.

3. The script passes the web server an anonymous function telling the web server object what should happen every time it receives a request. In this case, when a request comes in, it should respond with the string 'Hello World' and then close the connection.

4. On line 4 of the script, the port and host for the web server are defined. This means the server can be accessed at http://127.0.0.1:3000.

5. The script logs a message to console of where the server can be accessed.

▼ TRY IT YOURSELF

If you have downloaded the code examples for this book, this code is hour05/example01.

The following steps demonstrate a basic HTTP server:

1. Copy the code in Listing 5.1 into a file on your system called server.js.

2. Start the server by running

   ```
   node server.js
   ```

3. Open your browser and visit http://127.0.0.1:3000.

Adding Headers

With every HTTP request and response, HTTP headers are sent. HTTP headers send additional information including the type of content, the date that the server sent the response, and HTTP status codes.

In the simple Hello World server, Node.js already sends some basic information:

```
HTTP/1.1 200 OK
Connection: keep-alive
```

This shows any client requesting a page from this server that

▶ The version of HTTP in use is 1.1.

▶ The response code is 200 indicating a successful response.

▶ The connection is persistent in line with HTTP 1.1 protocol. Persistent connections are available from HTTP 1.1 and enable many real-time capabilities.

BY THE WAY

HTTP Headers Have Lots of Information!

You can gather a lot of information from HTTP headers. Here are the HTTP headers from the BBC website:

```
HTTP/1.1 200 OK
Date: Sat, 12 Nov 2011 14:27:37 GMT
Server: Apache
Set-Cookie: BBC
-UID=b47e9b3e289245d93524ac809080b1af9b1380f9b010a01c72c993ff1992dc4f0curl%2f
7%2e21%2e4%20%28universal%2dapple%2ddarwin11%2e0%29%20libcurl%2f7%2e21%2e4%20
OpenSSL%2f0%2e9%2e8r%20zlib%2f1%2e2%2e5; expires=Wed, 11-Nov-15 14:27:37 GMT;
path=/; domain=bbc.co.uk;
Vary: X-Ip-is-advertise-combined
Etag: "1321108048"
X-Lb-Nocache: true
Cache-Control: private, max-age=60
Age: 9
Content-Length: 136556
Content-Type: text/html
```

From the headers, it is possible to see that the web server is Apache, the content being sent is HTML, the date it was sent, and more.

In the Hello World example that you created, it is easy to send a header to say that the content is plain text (see Listing 5.2).

Listing 5.2   Adding Headers to the Server

```
var http = require('http');
http.createServer(function (req, res) {
  res.writeHead(200, {
    'Content-Type': 'text/plain'
  });
```

```
  res.end('Hello world\n');
}).listen(3000, "127.0.0.1");
console.log('Server running at http://127.0.0.1:3000/');
```

If you have downloaded the code examples for this book, this code is hour04/example02. The `writeHead` method adds a response code and headers to the response that the server sends to the client. Now, whenever a request is made to the server, the server tells the client that the content type is plain text.

```
HTTP/1.1 200 OK
```
Content-Type: text/plain
```
Connection: keep-alive
```

WATCH OUT
_____

Restart Your Server!

Be sure to restart your server each time you make modifications to the code. If you do not restart the server, you will not see the changes that you have made. You can restart the server by killing the server process from your terminal using Ctrl+C and then starting the process again.

_____

Checking Response Headers

It is often useful to check response headers for pages when developing with Node.js. A number of tools can help you do this.

HTTP Headers Extension for Chrome

If you are Chrome user, the HTTP Headers extension works very well. You can install the extension here: http://bit.ly/MoIcMd.

▼ TRY IT YOURSELF

Follow these steps to use the HTTP Headers extension for Chrome:

1. Install the HTTP Headers extension for Chrome.

2. Ensure your Node.js server is running:

   ```
   node server.js:
   ```

3. Open your browser and visit http://127.0.0.1:3000.

4. Click the HTTP Headers extension icon.

5. You will the HTTP headers for your Node.js server (see Figure 5.1).

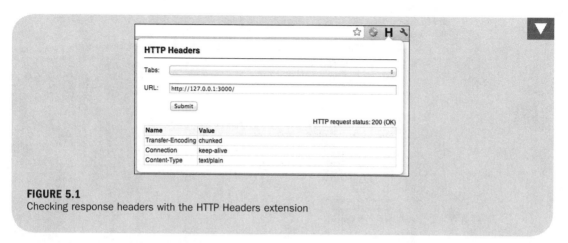

FIGURE 5.1
Checking response headers with the HTTP Headers extension

Live HTTP Headers Firefox Add-On

If you are a Firefox user the Live HTTP Headers Add-On for the Firefox web browser is useful. You can install the add-on here: http://bit.ly/LdJBSW.

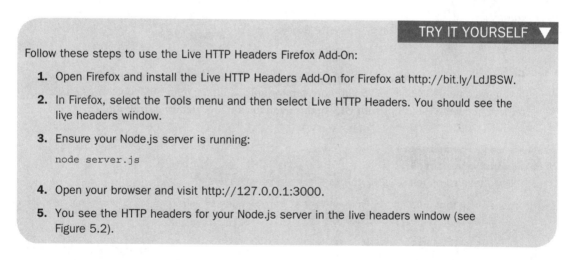

TRY IT YOURSELF ▼

Follow these steps to use the Live HTTP Headers Firefox Add-On:

1. Open Firefox and install the Live HTTP Headers Add-On for Firefox at http://bit.ly/LdJBSW.

2. In Firefox, select the Tools menu and then select Live HTTP Headers. You should see the live headers window.

3. Ensure your Node.js server is running:

   ```
   node server.js
   ```

4. Open your browser and visit http://127.0.0.1:3000.

5. You see the HTTP headers for your Node.js server in the live headers window (see Figure 5.2).

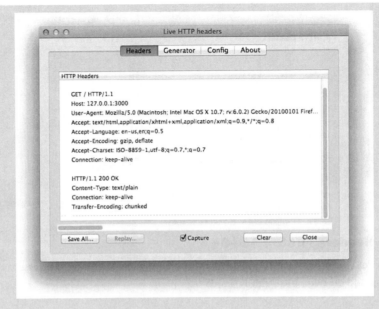

FIGURE 5.2
Checking response headers with the Live HTTP Headers Add-On

cURL

If you are on a UNIX type system and are comfortable using the terminal, you can use cURL to retrieve headers. cURL ships with OSX and is available on most Linux distrubutions.

▼ TRY IT YOURSELF

Follow these steps to use cURL to examine response headers:

1. Ensure that cURL is available on your system by opening your terminal and typing `curl`. If it is installed, you should see

   ```
   curl: try 'curl --help' for more information
   ```

2. Ensure your Node.js server is running:

   ```
   node server.js
   ```

3. In your terminal, run the following command:

   ```
   curl -I 127.0.0.1:3000
   ```

4. You should see the following response (see Figure 5.3).

```
HTTP/1.1 200 OK
Content-Type: text/plain
Connection: keep-alive
```

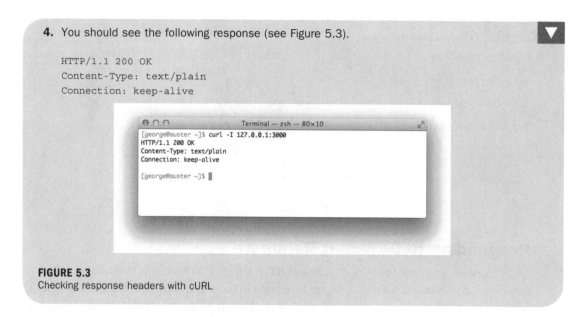

FIGURE 5.3
Checking response headers with cURL

A Redirect in Node.js

Using the techniques learned in this hour, it is easy to create a simple server that redirects visitors to another web page.

The criteria for a redirect are as follows:

▶ Send the client a 301 response code, telling the client that the resource has moved to another location.

▶ Send a Location Header to tell the client where to redirect to. In this case, we direct visitors to Strong Bad's home page (see Listing 5.3).

Listing 5.3   A Redirect with Node.js

```
var http = require('http');
http.createServer(function (req, res) {
  res.writeHead(301, {
    'Location': 'http://www.homestarrunner.com/sbsite/'
  });
  res.end();
}).listen(3000, "127.0.0.1");
console.log('Server running at http://127.0.0.1:3000/');
```

This example uses the `writeHead` method again, but this time, a 301 response code is sent. A location header is also set to tell the client where to redirect to.

▼ TRY IT YOURSELF

If you have downloaded the code examples for this book, this code is hour05/example03.

Follow these steps to create a 301 redirect:

1. Copy the code in Listing 5.3 into a file on your system called server.js.

2. Start the server by running:

```
node server.js
```

3. Open your browser and visit http://127.0.0.1:3000.

4. You are redirected to Strong Bad's website.

Responding to Different Requests

Until this point, you have been creating simple HTTP servers with Node.js that return a single response. But what if you want your server to respond to more than one type of request? In this scenario, you need to add routes to your application. Node.js makes this straightforward with the URL module. The URL module makes it possible to read a URL, parse it, and then do something with the output.

BY THE WAY

Routes Define Responses

Routing refers to the requests that your application will respond to. So for example, if you want to show an About Us page at /about-us, you need to set up a route to respond to that request in your application.

▼ TRY IT YOURSELF

Here's how to use the URL module:

1. Open your terminal and start a Node.js process:

```
node
```

2. Type the following to require the URL module and assign it to a variable:

```
var url = require('url')
```

3. Type the following that you will use to simulate an example request URL:

```
var requestURL = 'http://example.com:1234/pathname?query=string#hash'
```

4. Now, you can start to parse the request URL and extract pieces of it. To get the hostname, type

```
url.parse(requestURL).hostname
```

It should return "example.com."

5. Retrieve the port number. Type the following:

```
url.parse(requestURL).port
```

It should return "1234."

6. Retrieve the pathname. Type the following:

```
url.parse(requestURL).pathname
```

It should return "/pathname."

It is possible to parse all aspects of a URL with the URL module. Consult the Node.js documentation for a full list.

Using your new knowledge of the URL module, you can modify the simple server that you created earlier to respond to different requests with different responses by parsing the URL requested (see Listing 5.4).

Listing 5.4   Adding Routes to Your Server

```
var http = require('http'),
    url = require('url');

http.createServer(function (req, res) {
  var pathname = url.parse(req.url).pathname;

  if (pathname === '/') {
     res.writeHead(200, {
     'Content-Type': 'text/plain'
   });
   res.end('Home Page\n')
  } else if (pathname === '/about') {
     res.writeHead(200, {
     'Content-Type': 'text/plain'
   });
   res.end('About Us\n')
  } else if (pathname === '/redirect') {
     res.writeHead(301, {
     'Location': '/'
   });
   res.end();
```

```
  } else {
     res.writeHead(404, {
     'Content-Type': 'text/plain'
   });
     res.end('Page not found\n')
  }
}).listen(3000, "127.0.0.1");
console.log('Server running at http://127.0.0.1:3000/');
```

In Listing 5.4, the server examines the pathname of the request on line 5 using the URL module. On line 6, an if statement is used to respond to the requested pathname with a relevant response. The application can now respond to multiple requests depending on what the URL pathname is. If the pathname is not found, a default response of a 404 page is sent.

Using this technique, it is possible to create servers responding to many different requests. Node.js developers quickly recognized though that this can become complicated, difficult to read, and difficult to maintain. As such, a number of libraries exist to help abstract some of the complexities of creating servers with Node.js. You are introduced to Express in Hour 6, "Introducing Express," but nevertheless, it is useful to understand how a Node.js server works at the base level.

▼ TRY IT YOURSELF

If you have downloaded the code examples for this book, this code is hour05/example04.

Follow these steps to respond to multiple requests:

1. Copy the code in Listing 5.4 into a file on your system called server.js.

2. Start the server by running

   ```
   node server.js
   ```

3. Open your browser and visit http://127.0.0.1:3000.

4. You should see "Home Page".

5. Using either the HTTP Headers extension for Chrome, the Live HTTP Headers Add-On for Firefox, or cURL, examine the HTTP headers.

6. You should see

   ```
   HTTP/1.1 200 OK
   Content-Type: text/plain
   Connection: keep-alive
   ```

7. Back in your browser, navigate to http://127.0.0.1:3000/unknown-page.

8. You should see "Page not found".

9. Using either the HTTP Headers extension for Chrome, the Live HTTP Headers Add-On for Firefox, or cURL, examine the HTTP headers.

10. You should see

```
HTTP/1.1 404 Not Found
Content-Type: text/plain
Connection: keep-alive
```

HTTP Clients with Node.js

Although you can create HTTP servers with Node.js, it is also possible to create HTTP clients.

BY THE WAY
___

An HTML Client Is Not Always a Browser

HTML clients are anything that requests a response from a server. Examples of an HTML client include a web browser, a search engine robot, an email client, and a web scraper.
___

Some scenarios where you might want to use an HTML client include

▶ Monitoring the uptime of a server

▶ Scraping web content that isn't available by an API

▶ Creating a mashup that combines two or more sources of information from the Web

▶ Making an API call to a popular web service like Twitter or Flickr

To create an HTML client with Node.js, you require the HTTP module just as you do when creating a server. The HTTP module has a convenience method `http.get` for making GET requests to the server. To use it, specify an option's object that contains details of the page that you want to fetch. This includes details like the host, port number, and path. Then, use the `http.get` method to make the request. In Listing 5.5, you create a client to fetch the HTTP status code of a page and check the response code. If the response code is 200, you can assume the website is up. If it is anything else, you can infer that there is a problem with the site. Note that some websites can redirect home pages to other locations with a 302 response, so watch out for this if you choose to use another URL.

Listing 5.5   An HTML Client in Node.js

```
var http = require('http');

var options = {
  host: 'shapeshed.com',
  port: 80,
  path: '/'
};

http.get(options, function(res) {
  if (res.statusCode  == 200) {
    console.log("The site is up!");
  }
  else {
    console.log("The site is down!");
  }
}).on('error', function(e) {
  console.log("There was an error: " + e.message);
});
```

▼ TRY IT YOURSELF

If you have downloaded the code examples for this book, this code is hour05/example05.

Follow these steps to create an HTTP client:

1. Copy the code in Listing 5.5 into a file on your system called client.js.

2. Start the server by running

    ```
    node server.js
    ```

3. You should see The site is up!, indicating the site returned a 200 response. If you see anything else, there may be a problem with the site.

Summary

In this hour, you learned about the HTTP protocol and how to interact with it using Node.js. You learned how to create a simple web server and how to send headers back to the client. You then extended your simple web server to create a redirect and then made it respond to more than one type of request. Finally, you created an HTTP client to check the status of web server.

This hour showcased the low-level features of Node.js for using the HTTP protocol. In the next hour, you are introduced to Express, a web framework for Node.js that makes creating HTTP servers more user friendly.

Q&A

Q. **HTTP looks complicated. Do I need to understand HTTP to use Node.js?**

A. You can get by in Node.js without completely understanding the HTTP protocol. In essence, HTTP just defines how a server and client interact to send and receive information, so the more you create HTTP clients or servers, the more you will understand HTTP. Especially if you are creating web applications, understanding the HTTP protocol will help you a great deal in your development.

Q. **I've heard of the Express framework in Node.js. Do I really want to write servers using the HTTP module?**

A. If you are getting started, Express lowers the barriers to creating a web server with Node.js. It takes care of many common scenarios like routing and templates and is recommended for creating most web applications. Understanding how the HTTP module works is useful, though. There may be scenarios where you want to create a small web server that does not need a framework like Express. Understanding what is going on under the hood is always a good idea, too.

Q. **How does Apache or Nginx fit with Node.js?**

A. Apache and Nginx are popular, mature web servers. It is entirely possible to proxy web traffic from Apache or Nginx to a Node.js server. Equally you can serve traffic directly from a Node.js server.

Q. **I created a Node.js server that I want to deploy already! How do I do that?**

A. Don't worry! You learn about deployment in Hour 11, "Deploying Node.js Applications"!

Workshop   .

This workshop contains quiz questions to help cement your learning in this hour.

Quiz

1. **What does a 200 HTTP response mean?**

2. **What information can be sent in HTTP headers?**

3. **Why is the** `Connection: Keep-Alive` **header important?**

Quiz Answers

1. A 200 response code means that the request has succeeded. A detailed specification of possible response codes can be found at http://bit.ly/KD3qC8.

2. You can send a large amount of information in HTTP headers including acceptable character sets, authorization credentials, the date, and the user agent. For a full list, see http://bit.ly/KWge56.

3. The `Connection: Keep-Alive` header allows a client and a server to keep a persistent connection open. This enables real-time communication between the client and the server introducing all kinds of possibilities.

Exercises

1. Using Listing 5.1, change the response code to 501. Use one of the tools discussed in this hour to check that the HTTP response code is 501.

2. Using Listing 5.4, extend the web server to include more routes. Experiment with sending different response codes and content for different routes.

3. Using Listing 5.5, change the options object to check the status of different websites or servers.

Introducing Express

What You'll Learn in This Hour:

▶ What Express is and how you can use it

▶ Creating a basic site with Express

▶ Using Jade as a template engine within Express

What Is Express?

Express is a web framework for Node.js. Web applications share common patterns, so using a framework is often a good idea. You will find that you can develop faster and write applications on top of stable, tested code.

Some other web frameworks that you may be familiar with are

▶ Ruby on Rails (Ruby)

▶ Sinatra (Ruby)

▶ Django (Python)

▶ Zend (PHP)

▶ CodeIgniter (PHP)

Why Use Express?

Express is a lightweight framework, which means that it does not make too many assumptions but gives you enough to avoid reinventing the wheel.

Some of the things you can do with Express include

▶ JSON-based APIs

▶ Single-page web applications

▶ Real-time web applications

Some reasons for using a framework like Express include

▶ It takes less time to create applications using a framework.

▶ Common patterns like routing and view layers are accounted for in a framework like Express, meaning you do not have to write code for this.

▶ A framework like Express is actively used, maintained, and tested. The stability of the code can be expected.

Frameworks like Express are not appropriate for everything, though. If you are creating a command-line script, you would certainly not want to use something like Express.

BY THE WAY

Express Was Inspired by Sinatra

Sinatra is a popular lightweight web framework for Ruby. Express supports template engines, routing, and passing data to views in much the same way that Sinatra does in Ruby. If you have used Sinatra, you will feel right at home in Express. If you have not used Sinatra, most developers like the simplicity of its design.

Installing Express

You can install express via npm:

```
npm install -g express
```

WATCH OUT

Make Sure You Use the -g Flag

In the example, notice the -g flag. This means that Express will be installed globally and will be available anywhere you run the command on your system. If you forget the -g flag, you will not be able to run the generator without providing the full path to the executable. Note that you may need to use sudo for this command depending on your operating system.

Creating a Basic Express Site

Now that you have installed Express, you are ready to get a basic site up and running.

If you have downloaded the code examples for this book, this code is hour06/example01.

Follow these steps to install a basic Express site:

1. Open your terminal and generate a skeleton Express site by running the following command (see Figure 6.1):

```
express express_example
```

```
● ○ ○                    Terminal — zsh — 80×24
[george@auster ~]$ express express_example

   create : express_example
   create : express_example/package.json
   create : express_example/app.js
   create : express_example/public
   create : express_example/routes
   create : express_example/routes/index.js
   create : express_example/views
   create : express_example/views/layout.jade
   create : express_example/views/index.jade
   create : express_example/public/javascripts
   create : express_example/public/stylesheets
   create : express_example/public/stylesheets/style.css
   create : express_example/public/images

   dont forget to install dependencies:
   $ cd express_example && npm install

[george@auster ~]$ ▌
```

FIGURE 6.1
Installing a basic site with Express

2. Express politely reminds you to install the dependencies needed to run Express. So, make sure you install the dependencies:

```
cd express_example && npm install
```

3. Start the application by running

```
node app.js
```

4. Open up your web browser of choice and browse to http://127.0.0.1:3000. You see a basic website served from Express (see Figure 6.2).

FIGURE 6.2
Installing a basic site with Express

Exploring Express

If you look in the folder for the example Express site that you just created, you see the following structure:

▶ app.js

▶ node_modules

▶ package.json

▶ public

▶ routes

▶ views

app.js

app.js is the application file used to start the application. It contains configuration information for the application.

node_modules

node_modules holds any node modules that are defined in package.json and have been installed.

package.json

package.json gives information on the application including the dependencies that should be installed for it to run.

public

The public folder that serves the application to the Web. You will find stylesheets, javascripts, and images in this folder. You will not find any application logic in this folder; this is a common pattern to ensure web application security.

routes

In simple terms, a *route* defines the pages that an application should respond to. For example, if you want to have an About page in your application, you need to set up an `about` route. The routes folder holds these declarations. Routing is covered in more depth in Hour 7, "More on Express."

views

The views folder defines the layouts for the application.

BY THE WAY

Folder Structure Is Optional

The Express generator creates a suggested layout for an Express project. This is just a suggestion, so if your application has specific requirements or your personal preference is different, you can structure Express projects however you want. If you are getting started with Express, it is recommended that you use the structure from the generator.

Introducing Jade

Looking inside the views folder for the example project, you see a number of files with the .jade extension. Express makes use of template engines to compile views to HTML. By default, Express uses Jade as the template engine.

Template Engines Generate HTML

Template engines are used in most web frameworks to generate HTML and are typically used within a views folder. They allow developers to output data from an application to HTML. Typical features include variables and loops. Template engines can also be known as template processors or filters. Two popular template engines are Smarty (PHP) and ERB (Ruby).

Jade is an indentation-based template engine. To understand this, compare HTML and how it is represented in Jade (see Listing 6.1).

Listing 6.1   HTML and Jade Comparison

```
<div class="wrapper">
  <h1>My holiday in Prague</h1>
  <p>I had a great holiday in Prague where I met some great people.</p>
  <img src="images/photo.jpg" alt="Me on holiday!" />
</div>


.wrapper
  h1 My holiday in Prague
  p I had a great holiday in Prague where I met some great people
  img(src='images/photo.jpg', alt='Me on holiday')
```

Notice several things:

▶ Jade is much more terse than HTML.

▶ Jade uses indentation to declare the hierarchy of an HTML document.

▶ You do not have to use tags in Jade. The <> characters are automatically added when the template is compiled.

▶ You do not have to close HTML tags in Jade. When Jade generates the HTML, it will close the tags for you.

Indentation Is Important

How code is indented in Jade is important because it defines the hierarchy of a document. At some point, when developing with Jade, you see an error generated from your views. It is likely that this will be because of incorrect indentation, so check this carefully!

When the page is generated, Jade compiles the template to HTML. In Listing 6.1, the output is exactly the same as vanilla HTML. So why bother with a template engine? The answer is that it allows applications to output data dynamically to HTML. Examples of where you may use a template engine include

▶ To display a list of blog posts stored in a database

▶ To create a single template for displaying many different blog posts

▶ To change the `<title></title>` element of a page based on a variable

▶ To create header and footer includes that can be reused across templates

BY THE WAY

Jade Takes Its Inspiration from Haml

Jade takes much of its inspiration from Haml (HTML Abstraction Markup Layer). Haml is a popular template engine used in the Ruby Community.

Defining Page Structure with Jade

Jade defines page structure by indentation. If a line is indented under another one, it is assumed to be a child of the previous line. If you are new to template languages, this can take a little getting used to. This should become clear with examples, however.

```
html
```

compiles to

```
<html></html>
```

You can use any HTML tag here (body, `section`, p, and so on).

To add an id to a tag, append a # symbol and then the name of your id. Note that spaces are not allowed.

```
section#wrapper
```

compiles to

```
<section id="wrapper"></section>
```

You can add a class by appending a dot followed by the name of your class.

```
p.highlight
```

compiles to

```
<p class="highlight"></p>
```

If you need a class and an id, Jade supports chaining.

```
section#wrapper.class-name
```

compiles to

```
<section id="wrapper" class="class-name"></section>
```

Jade also supports more than one class on a tag.

```
p.first.section.third.fourth
```

compiles to

```
<p class="first second third fourth">
```

To create HTML structure, indentation is used:

```
p
  span
```

compiles to

```
<p><span></span></p>
```

To add text within a tag, simply add it after the tag declaration.

```
h1 Very important heading
```

compiles to

```
<h1>Very important heading<h1>
```

Jade also supports large bodies of text by using the pipe delineator:

```
p
  | Text can be over
  | many lines
  | after a pipe symbol
```

compiles to

```
<p>Text can be over many lines after a pipe symbol<p>
```

If you have downloaded the code examples for this book, this code is hour06/example02.

Follow these steps to create a page structure in Jade:

1. Open your terminal and generate a skeleton Express site by running the following command:

```
express jade_structure
```

2. Enter the directory that you created and install the required dependencies:

```
cd jade_structure && npm install
```

3. Start the application, change into the jade_structure folder, and then run

```
node app.js
```

4. Open up your web browser of choice and browse to http://127.0.0.1:3000. You see a basic website served from Express.

5. Edit the file index.jade file found at views/index.jade. You see a bare bones structure for the page:

```
h1= title
p Welcome to #{title}
```

6. Add the following code to the page:

```
section#wrapper
  h2 Basic Structure
  section
    p
      span This is a span within a p within a div!
```

7. Reload the page and check the HTML on the page by viewing the source. Although the HTML will be compressed, you should see the following HTML:

```
<section id="wrapper">
  <section>
    <p>
      <span>This is a span within a p within a div!</span>
    </p>
  </section>
</section>
```

The Section Tag Is New in HTML5

HTML5 is the fifth revision of the Hypertext Markup Language (HTML). There are a number of new elements in HTML5, including `article`, `header`, `nav`, and `section`. These are intended to enhance the semantic meaning of web pages, something good for both humans and technology. If you are interested in learning more about the new elements in HTML 5, you may want to consider reading *Introducing HTML5*, Second Edition, by Remy Sharp and Bruce Lawson (published by New Riders, 0321784421).

Outputting Data with Jade

While building page structure with Jade is good, the real power of a template language comes from manipulating data and outputting it to HTML.

Jade uses two special characters to decide how it should interpret code. The first, the minus sign (-), is used to tell Jade that the code that follows should be executed.

The second is the equals sign (=). This tells the interpreter that the code should be evaluated, escaped, and then outputted.

This can be a little confusing at first, but examples will make it clear.

Variables

In this example, the code is executed and no output is to be returned. Jade just sets the variable of `foo` to be `bar`:

```
- var foo = bar;
```

With the variable set, it can be used later on:

```
p I want to learn to use variables. Foo is #{foo}!
```

The special syntax of `#{variable}` tells Jade to replace the variable with the string value. This compiles to

```
<p>I want to learn how to use variables. Foo is bar!<p>
```

If you have downloaded the code examples for this book, this code is hour06/example03.

Follow these steps to use variables with Jade:

1. Open your terminal and generate a skeleton Express site by running the following command:

```
express jade_variables
```

2. Enter the directory that you created and install the required dependencies:

```
cd jade_variables && npm install
```

3. Start the application, change into the jade_variables folder, and then run:

```
node app.js
```

4. Open up your web browser of choice and browse to http://127.0.0.1:3000. You see a basic website served from Express.

5. Edit the file index.jade file found at views/index.jade and add the following code:

```
- var name = "Your Name"
h1 Hello #{name}!
```

6. Reload the page in your browser. Check the HTML on the page by viewing the source. You should see the following HTML:

```
<h1>Hello Your Name</h1>
```

Loops

Loops allow you to iterate over arrays and objects. If you are creating anything other than a basic brochure site, you will find yourself using loops a lot. This is commonly known as iteration, meaning that you iterate over an array or object and do the same thing over and over again.

Perhaps because this is such a common pattern, Jade makes using the minus sign optional. Admittedly, it is confusing that you use a minus sign to specify a variable but not a loop. In these examples, the minus sign is included before each loop for clarity, although it is optional.

```
- users = ['Sally', 'Joseph ', 'Michael', 'Sanjay']
- each user in users
  p= user
```

compiles to

```
<p>Sally</p>
<p>Joseph</p>
<p>Michael</p>
<p>Sanjay</p>
```

If you prefer to use the `for` keyword, this can also be written as

```
- for user in users
  p= user
```

It is also possible to iterate over objects:

```
- obj = { first_name: 'George', surname: 'Ornbo'}
- each val, key in obj
  li #{key}: #{val}
```

compiles to

```
<li>first_name: George</li>
<li>surname: Ornbo</li>
```

▼ TRY IT YOURSELF

If you have downloaded the code examples for this book, this code is hour06/example04.

Follow these steps to use loops with Jade:

1. Open your terminal and generate a skeleton Express site by running the following command:

```
express jade_loops
```

2. Enter the directory that you created and install the required dependencies:

```
cd jade_loops && npm install
```

3. Start the application, change into the jade_loops folder, and then run:

```
node app.js
```

4. Open up your web browser of choice and browse to http://127.0.0.1:3000. You see a basic website served from Express.

5. Edit the file index.jade file found at views/index.jade and add the following code:

```
- beatles = ['John', 'Paul', 'Ringo', 'George']
ul
  each beatle in beatles
    li #{beatle}
```

6. Reload the page in your browser. Check the HTML on the page by viewing the source. You should see the following HTML:

```
<ul>
  <li>John</li>
```

```
    <li>Paul</li>
    <li>Ringo</li>
    <li>George</li>
  </ul>
```

Conditions

If you have had exposure to any programming language, you will be familiar with conditions. In plain English, we can describe conditional flow as "If something is true, do something; otherwise, do something else." In Jade, conditions look like this:

```
- awake = false
- if (awake)
 p You are awake! Make coffee!
- else
 p You are sleeping
```

Note again that the minus sign (-) in front of the `if` and `else` keywords is optional.

TRY IT YOURSELF

If you have downloaded the code examples for this book, this code is hour06/example05.

Follow these steps to use conditions in Jade:

1. Open your terminal and generate a skeleton Express site by running the following command:

   ```
   express jade_conditions
   ```

2. Enter the directory that you created and install the required dependencies:

   ```
   cd jade_conditions && npm install
   ```

3. Start the application, change into the jade_conditions folder, and then run

   ```
   node app.js
   ```

4. Open up your web browser of choice and browse to http://127.0.0.1:3000. You see a basic website served from Express.

5. Edit the file index.jade file found at views/index.jade and add the following code:

   ```
   - raining = true
   - if (raining)
    p It is raining. Take an umbrella!
   - else
    p No rain. Take the bike!
   ```

6. Reload the page in your browser. Check the HTML on the page by viewing the source. You should see the following HTML:

```
<p>It is raining. Take an umbrella!</p>
```

7. Change the value of raining in views/index.jade to false:

```
- raining = false
```

8. Reload the page in your browser. Check the HTML on the page by viewing the source. You should see the following HTML:

```
<p>No rain. Take the bike!</p>
```

Inline JavaScript

It is possible to execute inline JavaScript in Jade templates. To do this, declare a script block and then add your JavaScript within it:

```
script
  alert('You can execute inline JavaScript through Jade')
```

▼ TRY IT YOURSELF

If you have downloaded the code examples for this book, this code is hour06/example06.

Follow these steps to execute inline JavaScript in Jade:

1. Open your terminal and generate a skeleton Express site by running the following command:

```
express jade_inline_javascript
```

2. Enter the directory that you created and install the required dependencies:

```
cd jade_inline_javascript && npm install
```

3. Start the application, change into the jade_inline_javascript folder, and then run:

```
node app.js
```

4. Open up your web browser of choice and browse to http://127.0.0.1:3000. You see a basic website served from Express.

5. Edit the file index.jade file found at views/index.jade and add the following code:

```
script
  alert('Inline JavaScript in Jade')
```

6. Reload the page in your browser. You should see a JavaScript alert.

Includes

Most websites have parts of the page that appear on every page of the site. Example of these include

- ▶ Headers
- ▶ Footers
- ▶ Sidebars

Includes Make It Easier to Maintain a Website

Includes move common parts of a website into single files. This means that when a client asks for an extra item to be added to a header, you only have to change a single file.

Jade supports includes with the `include` keyword and then name of the template that you want to include.

```
html
  body
    include includes/header
```

This includes code from the views/includes/header.jade file.

TRY IT YOURSELF ▼

If you have downloaded the code examples for this book, this code is hour06/example07.

Follow these steps to use includes in Jade:

1. Open your terminal and generate a skeleton Express site by running the following command:

    ```
    express jade_includes
    ```

2. Enter the directory that you created and install the required dependencies:.

    ```
    cd jade_includes && npm install
    ```

3. Start the application, change into the jade_includes folder, and then run

    ```
    node app.js
    ```

4. Open up your web browser of choice and browse to http://127.0.0.1:3000. You see a basic website served from Express.

5. Create a new folder at views/includes.

6. Within views/includes, add a file called footer.jade.

7. Add some content into the footer.jade file:

```
p This is my footer. Get me. I have a footer on my website.
```

8. Include your footer file in views/index.jade:

```
h1 Jade Includes Example
include includes/footer
```

9. Reload the page in your browser. You should see your footer included on the page.

Mixins

Mixins are a feature of Jade that not many other template engines have. If you find yourself repeating the same blocks of code over and over again, using mixins is a good way to keep your code maintainable and clean. Think of mixins as includes for your code. An example of where you may want to use a mixin is outputting data in a loop. To define a mixin, use the `mixin` keyword:

```
mixin users(users)
  ul
    each user in users
      li= user
```

Once the mixin is defined, you can use it and reuse it in your templates:

```
- users = ['Krist', 'Kurt', 'Dave']
mixin users(users)
```

▼ TRY IT YOURSELF

If you have downloaded the code examples for this book, this code is hour06/example08.

Follow these steps to use mixins in Jade:

1. Open your terminal and generate a skeleton Express site by running the following command:

```
express_jade_mixins
```

2. Start the application, change into the jade_mixins folder, and then run:

```
node app.js
```

3. Open up your web browser of choice and browse to http://127.0.0.1:3000. You see a basic website served from Express.

4. Edit the file index.jade file found at views/index.jade and add the following code:

```
mixin users(users)
  ul
    each user in users
      li= user
- users = ['Tanya', 'Jose', 'Kim']
mixin users(users)
- more_users = ['Mark', 'Elena', 'Dave', 'Pete', 'Keiron']
mixin users(more_users)
```

5. Reload the page in your browser. You should see two lists of users, generated from a single mixin.

Summary

In this hour, you learned about Express, a web framework for Node.js. You learned about when you might choose to use a web framework and what it can offer you.

You learned about Jade, a template engine for Node.js, and how to use it to output variables, loops, conditional statements, inline JavaScript, includes, and mixins.

After this hour, you are able to create basic sites with Node.js and Express and begin to display data within your applications.

Q&A

Q. Should I always use Express with Node.js or just sometimes?

A. Express is a web framework for Node.js, so there are times when it is not appropriate. If your requirements are to work with views and showing data within a web browser Express is a good fit. If you are building a command-line script with Node.js or a tiny web service, Express is probably not the right fit. In all cases, pick the best tool for the job.

Q. I'm not keen on indentation-based template engines. Are there any others?

A. Although Express uses Jade as the default template engine, it is agnostic to the template engine that is used. Another popular choice for Express is the EJS (Embedded JavaScript Templates) Template Engine. This is not indentation based and is close to how ERB works in Ruby. You may also use jQuery templates with Jade. New template engines are appearing all the time, many with support for Express. Check the Node.js wiki for a comprehensive list: https://github.com/joyent/node/wiki/modules#wiki-templating.

Q. **What about performance?**

A. Jeremy Ashkenas created a test to show the performance of different JavaScript template languages. If you are interested in the performance of template languages, the post gives a benchmark and performance comparisons (http://bit.ly/KKa3nw).

Q. **What are the pros and cons of using a template engine like Jade?**

A. Using a template engine allows you to develop more quickly and take advantage of built-in checks for your code. With indentation, Jade is easy to read and hence maintain. In terms of cons, Jade adds a layer of complexity by abstracting plain HTML that for very simple projects may be overkill.

Workshop

This workshop contains quiz questions to help cement your learning in this hour.

Quiz

1. Why might you want to use a framework over Express instead of writing your own code?

2. Where do you place any dependencies for an Express project?

3. Does Express have a set folder structure?

Quiz Answers

1. For many web applications, there are common patterns such as templates and routes. You can write your own code for this, but many developers avoid this work by using and contributing to frameworks like Express.

2. You place dependencies for an Express project in the package.json file just as you would any other Node.js project.

3. No. Although the Express generator produces a folder structure for you, there is no requirement to follow the suggested structure.

Exercises

1. Create an Express site using the command-line generator. Explore each of the folders and understand what they do. Refer to the notes in this hour on folder structure.

2. From the terminal, run `express --help`. Note how it is possible to change how the generator works by passing in arguments when generating new Express sites. Try switching the template engine used when you generate an Express site.

3. Generate a new Express site and practice your understanding of using Jade by assigning a variable and then outputting it. Create an array of data and then use a loop to show the data. Finally, create a header include file and use it in your template.

More on Express

What You'll Learn in This Hour:

▶ How routing works in Express

▶ Adding routes in Express

▶ Using parameters in routes

▶ Passing data to the view layer

▶ Displaying data in the view layer

Routing in Web Applications

Routing describes whether and how an application should respond to certain Hypertext Transfer Protocol (HTTP) requests. Your browser makes these requests when you are interacting with an application or website.

Routing is just a term for defining the end points for HTTP requests in an application. So if you want your application to be able to do something, you need to set up a route for it!

How Routing Works in Express

Express uses HTTP verbs to define routes. HTTP verbs describe the type of request that is made to a server. The most common ones that you are likely to use are:

▶ **GET**— This retrieves data from a server.

▶ **POST**— This sends data to a server.

Other HTTP verbs include PUT, DELETE, HEAD, OPTIONS, and TRACE.

When you generate a basic Express site, the generator expects you to define routes for your application. To understand this, you generate a basic Express application and examine the routes available.

▼ TRY IT YOURSELF

If you have downloaded the code examples for this book, this code is hour07/example01.

To generate a basic Express application and examine the available routes, follow these steps:

1. Create a basic Express site:

```
express express_routing
cd express_routing
npm install
```

2. Now start the server:

```
node app.js
```

3. Open up your web browser of choice and browse to http://127.0.0.1:3000. You should see a basic website served from Express.

4. Change the address in your browser to http://127.0.0.1:3000/about/.

5. A Page Not Found 404 header will be returned, and you should see this:

```
Cannot GET / about
```

In the example, there is no route available for /about, so a Page Not Found (404) response is returned.

BY THE WAY

You Make GET and POST Requests All the Time!

When you load a web page, your browser is making GET requests to retrieve HTML, CSS, JavaScript, and image files. When you submit a form, your browser is most likely making a POST request. HTTP verbs are actually quite simple, and if you are browsing the Web, you are making GET and POST requests all the time.

Adding a GET Route

In the simple Express application that you just created, there was no route for a GET request at /about. As a result, a 404 Page Not Found response was served by Express. So how do we add the GET /about route?

To specify a GET request, the GET HTTP verb is used.

```
app.get('/about', function(req, res){
  res.send('Hello from the about route!');
});
```

Technically, the code calls an anonymous function that takes the request and response as arguments. Express then returns the response using the `res.send` method. The `res.send` is a method provided by Express to send a response. In this example, a string of text is returned as the response.

If you have downloaded the code examples for this book, this code is hour07/example02.

To add a GET route, follow these steps:

1. Return to the basic Express site that you created.

2. Edit the main app.js file and add a definition for GET request to /about after the `app.get('/', routes.index);` line:

```
app.get('/about', function(req, res){
  res.send('Hello from the about route!');
});
```

3. Now start the server:

```
node app.js
```

4. Open your browser at http://127.0.0.1:3000/.

5. You should see a basic Express site.

6. Change the address in your browser to http://127.0.0.1:3000/about/.

7. There should no longer be a 404 page, and you should see this:

```
Hello from the about route!
```

DID YOU KNOW?

Express Takes Care of Some Routes for You

Because some routes are assumed to be needed by all applications, Express provides some Middleware that will serve anything you add to the /public folder. This is included if you use the site generator. Imagine how tedious it would be to add a route for every single image that you want to show! So, you can safely assume that anything you put into the public folder will be served and does not need a route declaring for it.

Adding a POST Route

You learned how to create a GET request in Express, but what about if you want to allow users to submit data to your application?

The process is the same, but instead of using the GET verb, the POST verb is specified.

```
app.post('/', function(req, res){
  res.send(req.body);
});
```

In this example, the application receives a POST request to the index page and outputs the data to the browser.

▼ TRY IT YOURSELF

If you have downloaded the code examples for this book, this code is hour07/example03.

To add a POST request, follow these steps:

1. Create a basic Express site:

   ```
   express express_post
   cd express_post
   npm install
   ```

2. Add a form to the index view by opening index.jade and adding the following code:

   ```
   h2 Form example
   form(method='post', action='/')
     fieldset
       legend Add a user
       p
         label First name
         input(name='user[first_name]')
       p
         label Last name
         input(name='user[surname]')
       p
         input(type='submit', value='Save')
   ```

3. Add a route to receive the POST request in app.js. In this example, it outputs the data posted to the browser.

   ```
   app.post('/', function(req, res){
     res.send(req.body);
   });
   ```

4. Now start the server:

```
node app.js
```

5. Open your browser at http://127.0.0.1:3000/.

6. Fill in the form with your name and click Submit.

7. You should see your name in the data posted.

Of course, this example is very basic. In reality, you would want to perform some validation on the data and save it to a database. Don't worry; you learn how to do that shortly!

Using Parameters in Routes

A common pattern in web applications is to reuse templates and change content based on a parameter passed in via a route.

You may be familiar with URLs like

```
/users/12
/projects/2345
```

Here, the application uses an integer (or number) to set which user or project should be displayed. In the first example, a user with an id of 12 will be shown. In the second example, a project with an id of 2345 will be shown.

This is a useful pattern for a number of reasons:

▶ The application can use a single template to display user records.

▶ The application creates a unique URL or link for each user.

▶ It is easier to add create, update, and delete methods using this approach.

Thankfully, this approach is fully supported in Express. To declare a route that captures a parameter looks like this:

```
app.get('/users/:id', function(req, res){
  res.send('show content for user id' + req.params.id);
});
```

Anything that comes after the forward slash following user in the request will be captured and made available to the application through the `req` object. So if you do a GET request to `/user/24`, Express extracts that number and makes it available for the application to use within `req.params.id`. The symbol that you specify in the route becomes the `params` key, so if you were to use `'/users/:name'`, it would be accessible by `req.params.name`.

At this point, a web application normally fetches the data for the user with the id and returns it.

▼ TRY IT YOURSELF

If you have downloaded the code examples for this book, this code is hour07/example04.

Follow these steps to use parameters in routes:

1. Create a basic Express site:

```
express express_parameters
cd express_parameters
npm install
```

2. Add the following to the app.js file within the routes section:

```
app.get('/users/:id', function(req, res){
  res.send('show content for user id ' + req.params.id);
});
```

3. Now start the server:

```
node app.js
```

4. Open up your web browser of choice and browse to http://127.0.0.1:3000/users/12.

5. You should see

```
show content for user id 12
```

6. Change the address in your browser to http://127.0.0.1:3000/users/99999.

7. You should see

```
show content for user id 99999
```

Keeping Routes Maintainable

You have seen how to create POST and GET requests by adding declarations to the app.js file. But with this approach, the app.js can quickly become full of route declarations leading to a maintenance problem. As you add more routes, you may find that

▶ It becomes difficult to have a clear picture of all of your routes.

▶ It takes a long time to find a route.

▶ Everything is in one really, really big file!

If you have been using the Express generator, you may have seen that the suggestion is to move routes to a separate file or files. These routes are then required in the main app.js file.

```
var routes = require('./routes')
```

If you used the Express generator, look inside the routes folder; you see a single file index.js that contains the route declarations.

```
/*
 * GET home page.
 */

exports.index = function(req, res){
  res.render('index', { title: 'Express' })
};
```

Just like the GET and POST requests we have already seen, this defines how the application should respond to a request. The difference is that the function is assigned to a variable that can be used elsewhere. By using the `require` statement and assigning it to a variable, it becomes available to the main application file as `routes.index`.

Having required the routes file in the main application file app.js, it then becomes possible to declare the route to the home page using `routes.index`.

```
app.get('/', routes.index);
```

How you organize your routes files is not enforced, but you see a typical pattern of dividing up routes by resources in Hour 8, "Persisting Data."

Separating routes into their own files is a good idea because

- ▶ It makes code more maintainable and readable.
- ▶ You can use version control to quickly view the history of a single file.
- ▶ It supports future growth of the application while keeping it maintainable.

View Rendering

You will have noticed that you have been using `res.render` and `res.send` to specify what is sent as the response. View rendering describes how and what the application should render in response to an HTTP request.

Examples of responses that you might use for view rendering include

▶ Sending HTML

▶ Sending JSON (JavaScript Object Notation) data

▶ Sending XML (Extensible Markup Language) data

All these are specified within the response section of a route.

Most of the time, you will use `res.render`. It is powerful and allows you to

▶ Render templates, including different template engines.

▶ Pass local variables to templates.

▶ Use a layout file.

▶ Set the HTTP response code.

A common pattern is to use `res.render` within a route to render a template and to pass local variables to it.

```
app.get('/', function(req, res){
  res.render('index.jade', { title: 'My Site' });
});
```

This defines a number of things:

▶ The index.jade template found at views/index.jade should be used to render the page.

▶ A local variable of 'title' should be passed to the views/index.jade template.

▶ A layout file should be used. This isn't explicitly declared but is assumed by Express unless you disable it. The default file that is used for the layout is views/layout.jade.

If you want to use a different layout file, you can specify it like this:

```
res.render('page.jade', { layout: 'custom_layout.jade' });
```

This would use the layout file found at views/custom_layout.jade.

If you do not want to use a layout file, you can specify it like this:

```
res.render('page.jade', { layout: false });
```

Using Local Variables

Within a `res.render` function, a key thing to grasp is using local variables. Using local variables allows you to

▶ Set data to be shown in the view layer.

▶ Pass that data through to the view layer.

You first saw this in the example that used parameters to show different users. When you understand how to pass data around using local variables, you are ready to create more complex applications.

Before an application sends a response, it typically sets or gets the data from somewhere.

This could mean:

▶ Fetching it from a database

▶ Fetching some data from an API

▶ Some simple mathematics to calculate a number

▶ Combining one string with another

Whatever you do, this needs to be set before the `res.render` function and stored in a variable. In the following example, we set some data for a user and store it in a variable. When it has been set, we pass it to the view as a local variable of user.

```
app.get('/', function(req, res){
  // You would probably get this data from a data store
  var user = {
    first_name: 'Lord',
    surname: 'Lucan',
    address: 'I'm not telling!',
    facebook_friends: '1356200'
  };
  // Note how the user object is passed as local variable to the view
  res.render('index.jade', { title: 'User', user: user  });
});
```

The data is now available to view, so it can be accessed within the views/index.jade template.

```
h1 Accessing data

h3 First Name
p= user.first_name

h3 Surname
p= user.surname
```

When the page renders, it will show `'Lord'` under the `h3` heading `'First Name'` and `'Lucan'` under the `h3` heading `'Surname'`. This data has been passed through to the view layer from the local variable user.

If you have downloaded the code examples for this book, this code is hour07/example05.

To pass data to the View layer, follow these steps:

1. Create a new Express site:

   ```
   express express_locals
   cd express_locals
   npm install
   ```

2. Open the app.js file and remove the line that reads

   ```
   app.get('/', routes.index);
   ```

3. After the // Routes comment in the app.js file, add the following code:

   ```
   app.get('/', function(req, res){
     var user = {
       first_name: 'Barak',
       surname: 'Obama',
       address: 'The White House',
       facebook_friends: '10000000000000'
     };
     res.render('index.jade', { title: 'User', user: user  });
   });
   ```

4. Open the views/index.jade file and replace the contents with the following code:

   ```
   h1 Passing data through to the view layer

   h3 First Name
   p= user.first_name

   h3 Surname
   p= user.surname

   h3 Address
   p= user.address

   h3 Facebook Friends
   p= user.facebook_friends
   ```

5. Now start the server:

```
node app.js
```

6. Open your browser at http://127.0.0.1:3000/.

7. You should see the data being passed through to the view.

8. You should see your name in the data posted.

Summary

In this hour, you learned more about Express. In particular, you learned about routing and how it works in Express. You learned how to add GET and POST requests to your Express applications and how to use parameters to show content dynamically. Finally, you learned how to pass data through to the view layer.

Now you have a great foundation to build Node.js applications using Express!

Q&A

Q. **Where can I learn more about HTTP verbs?**

A. If you want to read the specification on HTTP verbs, you may do so here: http://bit.ly/0px29E.

Q. **Should I use the Express generator?**

A. While you are getting started, using the Express generator is a great way to start developing. Over time you may have more opinions about how to structure your application. Express offers you a suggested structure, but you do not have to stick to it!

Q. **Are other frameworks available for Node.js?**

A. A number of frameworks are available for Node.js. These include Geddy (http://geddyjs.org/), Tako (https://github.com/mikeal/tako), and Flatiron (http://flatironjs.org/).

Workshop

This workshop contains quiz questions to help cement your learning in this hour.

Quiz

1. **If you create a POST route to receive a form, will it save to a database?**

2. **What are the advantages of using parameters to set the data shown in routes?**

3. **When should you move routes to a separate file?**

Quiz Answers

1. No. Creating a route for a POST request does nothing more than make sure the application can receive a POST request. You need to set what you want to do with the data received. Typically this would be to validate the data and then save it somewhere. Data submitted by a form will not be saved anywhere by creating the route.

2. Using parameters allows you to reuse templates and change content based on one or more parameter. This makes your code maintainable and makes it simple to display thousands of different records. Using this approach, a relatively small code base can power many, many different pages.

3. There is no right answer to this, but maintenance is the key thing to consider here. If your application is three or four routes, you are unlikely to need a separate file for your routes. Once you get above that, it makes sense for your routes to be moved into separate files. It is up to you, but always think of how readable and maintainable your code is for another developer.

Exercises

1. Create an Express site that includes GET requests for /about, /contact, and /products.

2. Create an Express site with a single / route that does not use a layout file.

3. Create an Express site that uses parameters to show different content depending on a GET request parameter. Using the following example data, your application should display Keyser Soze's details at /users/1 and Roger Kint's details at /users/2. One way of solving this can be found in hour07/example06 of the code examples.

```
var users = {
  1 : {
    first_name: 'Keyser',
    surname: 'Soze',
    address: 'Next door',
    facebook_friends: '4'
  },
  2 : {
    first_name: 'Roger',
    surname: 'Kint',
    address: 'London, England',
    facebook_friends: '10000000000000'
  }
}
```

Persisting Data

What You'll Learn in This Hour:

▶ Read data from a file

▶ Write data to a file

▶ Read environment variables

▶ Store data with MongoDB

▶ Create a CRUD (Create, Read, Update, Delete) application with Express and MongoDB

What Is Persistent Data?

In web applications, the term *persistent data* refers to data that is saved somewhere and can be used by the application at a point in the future.

Examples of persistent data include

▶ Items in a shopping cart

▶ A user's account details

▶ Order history

▶ Credit card details

There are many ways that this data can be stored:

▶ On a hard disk or flash drive

▶ In the memory of a computer

▶ In a database

▶ In a cookie or session

As you develop Node.js applications, you will quickly come up against a requirement to persist data in some form. This hour shows you how to do that.

Writing Data to a File

If your application needs to store small pieces of information that seldom need to be read or written, using text files is a quick, lightweight option. Node.js has a rich File System module that allows you to interact with the filesystem however you need to. Writing data to a file looks like Listing 8.1.

Listing 8.1   Writing Data to a File

```
var fs = require('fs'),
    data = "Some data I want to write to a file";
fs.writeFile('file.txt', data, function (err) {
  if (!err) {
    console.log('Wrote data to file.txt');
  } else {
    throw err;
  }
});
```

The File System module is required on the first line and then a variable is set to hold the data that should be written to the file. The `writeFile` method is then used to write the data to a file.

Points to note here are

▶ The `writeFile` method also creates the file for you if it does not exist. There is no need for you create it.

▶ The file will be written to a location relative to where the script is run. If you need to control exactly where the file is written, you may specify the full path (e.g., /full/path/to/file.txt).

▶ Errors can include the file not existing or not having permissions to read the file.

Some scenarios where you may want to write to a file to store data include

▶ To back up data to a file

▶ To store timestamps so other scripts can use them

▶ To track the Process Identifier (PID) of a process

▶ To log information about a script or application

If you have downloaded the code examples for this book, this code is hour08/example01.

Follow these steps to write data to a file:

1. Copy the code in Listing 8.1 into a file on your system called app.js.

2. Run the script:

```
node app.js
```

3. In the same folder as your app.js file, you should see a new file ('file.txt') has been created.

4. Open the file.

5. It should contain "Some data I want to write to a file".

Reading Data from a File

If you are writing data to a file, it is highly likely that your application will need to read the file at some point. The File System module also provides a way to do that. Assuming there is a text file named file.txt containing "Hello Node.js!," it can be read like this (see Listing 8.2).

Listing 8.2   Reading Data from a File

```
var fs = require('fs');
fs.readFile('file.txt', 'utf8', function (err, data) {
  if (!err) {
    console.log(data);
  } else {
    throw err;
  }
});
```

If you run the script, it reads the contents of the file and outputs it to the console.

```
node app.js
Hello Node.js!
```

As in the example where you wrote to a file, the File System module is required on the first line, but this time the `readFile` method is used. This takes a file and a character encoding as arguments.

Points to note here are

▶ The location of file.txt is relative to where the script was run. You may also specify the full path—for example, /full/path/to/file.txt.

▶ If you do not provide a character encoding, the raw buffer will be returned.

▶ Possible errors include not having permission to read the file or the file not existing.

WATCH OUT

Encoding Is Important!

Data on computers is stored and transmitted as bits. A bit is a unit of information on a computer that it is not human readable. When a computer outputs text, it converts bits to characters using character encoding to make it human readable. Character encoding defines how a computer should map bits to certain character sets. The de facto character set for encoding on the Web is UTF-8, so if in any doubt always use that.

▼ TRY IT YOURSELF

If you have downloaded the code examples for this book, this code is hour08/example02.

Follow these steps to read data from a file:

1. Copy the code in Listing 8.2 into a file on your system called app.js

2. In the same directory, create a file called file.txt.

3. Add some text into the file.

4. Run the script:

```
node app.js
```

5. The script reads the file and outputs the text you wrote in file.txt.

Reading Environment Variables

If all you need to do is store an item of data once and then retrieve it later, environment variables are an excellent choice. Environment variables store pieces of data relating to the operating system, such as where your HOME folder is or your username on the system. It is possible to use environment variables to store small bits of data that can be used by Node.js applications.

Examples of when you might want to use environment variables include

▶ Storing connection string details for databases

▶ Storing secrets and keys for services like Amazon S3

▶ Storing usernames for different services

Environment variables are useful for data specific to where your application is running. You might have a development version of your site that uses a different database than your production site. Setting the database settings as environment variables and then reading them into your Node.js application is one way to solve this, although you should always consider security with this approach.

BY THE WAY

Environment Variables Are Important!

Environment variables set many things for the environment that your Node.js scripts run in. This includes where to look for the Node.js binary, and where to find globally installed Node.js modules. Environment variables are generally set automatically for you but play an important part in any operating system that you use. To see a full list of environment variables, open your terminal and run the command `env` on UNIX systems or `SET` on Windows.

Setting environment variables differs slightly depending on whether you are using Windows or a UNIX type system.

On Windows, run the following from the terminal:

```
SET SOMETHING='12345678'
```

On UNIX, run the following from the terminal:

```
export SOMETHING='12345678'
```

Once an environment variable is set, Node.js can read it with just one line of code:

```
var something = process.env.SOMETHING
```

TRY IT YOURSELF ▼

If you have downloaded the code examples for this book, this code is hour08/example03.

Follow these steps to read environment variables:

1. Create a file called app.js and copy the following code into it:

   ```
   console.log(process.env.SECRET_KEY)
   ```

2. Set an environment variable of SECRET_KEY. If you are on a UNIX type system, run

   ```
   export SECRET_KEY='c6YFPvdT7Yh3JAFW62EBa5LDe4X'
   ```

   If you are on a Windows type system, run

   ```
   SET SECRET_KEY='c6YFPvdT7Yh3JAFW62EBa5LDe4X'
   ```

3. Run the script:

```
node app.js
```

4. You should see c6YFPvdT7Yh3JAFW62EBa5LDe4X printed to the terminal.

Using Databases

The examples in this hour have shown how to set and retrieve small amounts of data using files or environment variables. If you are creating web applications with Node.js, you will definitely want to use a database or data store at some point. Some of the scenarios that you need a database for include

▶ Allowing users to save information

▶ Allowing users to create, read, update, and delete records

▶ Creating a web service, or API, from your data

Node.js has good support for most major databases, so which one should you use?

Relational Databases

You may have had exposure to some of the following relational databases:

▶ MySQL

▶ PostgresSQL

▶ Oracle

▶ Microsoft SQL Server

▶ SQLite

Relational databases store data in separate tables and create relationships between tables using primary and foreign keys. Let's say you have a blogging application with a database including tables for blog posts and comments. Using primary and foreign keys within the tables, it is easy to write queries for things like

▶ The last 10 blog posts in date order

▶ All of the comments for a blog post

▶ All blog posts between two moments in time

A common approach with relational databases is to join tables together to create views onto data. This can be very powerful as it keeps data separate so it can be queried in any way, but also provides complex views into the data. If you are building a web application that creates relationships between data that fits neatly into a table structure, then relational databases are a great option.

DID YOU KNOW?

Search npm for Database Libraries

You can search npm to find libraries for connecting to your database of choice. These libraries are written and maintained by developers around the world. Most major databases are fully supported.

NoSQL Databases

NoSQL is a term that has emerged in recent years to cover a broad range of databases that do not conform to the Relational Database model. Some databases that are grouped into the NoSQL bracket are

- ▶ Cassandra

- ▶ Redis

- ▶ Memcached

- ▶ MongoDB

- ▶ Hadoop

The feature sets for these databases can vary wildly but generally do not require fixed table schemas, avoid using joins, and are designed to scale horizontally. Because Node.js is a disruptive technology, many use cases match using NoSQL databases very well.

The database you choose is very much down to personal choice and the type of application you will be creating. If you are just creating basic applications, you should probably pick a database that you are familiar with.

Using MongoDB with Node.js

A popular choice in the Node.js community is MongoDB. MongoDB is a document-oriented database that does not follow the relational model of joining relational data together. It can perform most of the features of a relational database and is designed to be highly available and scalable.

To learn how to use MongoDB with Node.js, you will be creating a todo application with Express that allows a user to create, read, update, and delete todo items.

The final application looks like what's shown in Figure 8.1.

FIGURE 8.1
The completed todo application

Installing MongoDB

MongoDB is available for Mac OSX, UNIX, and Windows. Instructions for installing MongoDB on all three platforms are available at http://www.mongodb.org/display/DOCS/Quickstart.

Unless you are familiar with using the MongoDB command-line interface, using a GUI (Graphical User Interface) to develop is a good idea. A number of GUIs are available for MongoDB. If you are on OSX, there is MongoHub (http://mongohub.todayclose.com/), which supports connecting to different MongoDB instances, querying, importing, and exporting data, and importing and exporting to MySQL (see Figure 8.2). MongoHub is free software.

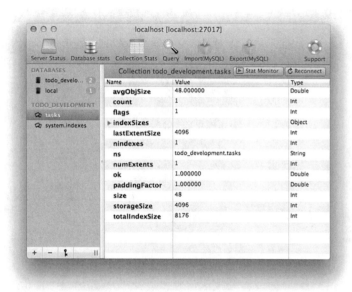

FIGURE 8.2
MongoHub, a MongoDB client for OSX

For Windows, there is MongoVUE (http://mongovue.com). MongoVUE has a limited free version or is $35 for a single user. MongoVUE depends on the .NET framework, so you need to install that if you do not have it on your system (see Figure 8.3).

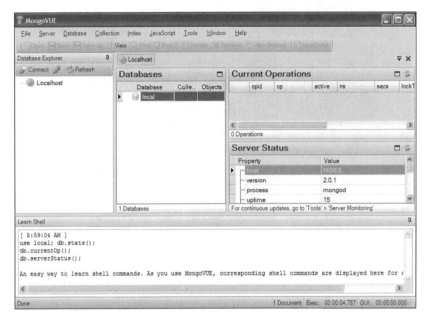

FIGURE 8.3
MongoVUE, a MongoDB client for Windows

For Linux, there is JMongoBrowser, which is a Java-based client, so you need a Java Runtime (see Figure 8.4).

FIGURE 8.4
JMongoBrowser, a MongoDB client for Linux

Connecting to MongoDB

Mongoose (http://mongoosejs.com/) is a fully featured third-party module for working with MongoDB in Node.js. You use Mongoose to interact with MongoDB in the example todo application to save todo items.

To add the Mongoose module to a project, include it as a dependency in the project's package.json file:

```
{
  "name": "your-application",
  "version": "0.0.1",
  "dependencies": {
    "mongoose": ">= 2.3.1"
  }
}
```

Do not forget to run `npm install` after you have added it to install it into your project!

After you install Mongoose, it must be required in the application file.

```
var mongoose = require('mongoose');
```

Then, the application can connect and work with MongoDB.

```
mongoose.connect('mongodb://localhost/your_database');
```

TRY IT YOURSELF ▼

If you have downloaded the code examples for this book, this code is hour08/example04.

Follow these steps to connect to MongoDB:

1. Create a basic Express site:

```
express connect_to_mongo
cd connect_to_mongo
npm install
```

2. Open the package.json file and add Mongoose as a dependency. The file should look like this:

```
{
  "name":"application-name",
  "version":"0.0.1",
  "private":true,
  "dependencies":{
```

```
    "express":"2.5.1",
    "jade":">= 0.0.1",
    "mongoose":">= 2.3.1"
  }
}
```

3. Run npm install to install the dependencies to your application.

4. Open the app.js file and require mongoose in the application in the section at the top of the file.

```
var express = require('express'),
    routes = require('./routes'),
    mongoose = require('mongoose');
```

5. Immediately after the preceding section, add a line to connect to MongoDB. Note you are specifying the database as 'todo_development'. There is no need to create the database.

```
mongoose.connect('mongodb://localhost/todo_development', function(err) {
  if (!err) {
    console.log('connected to MongoDB');
  } else {
    throw err;
  }
});
```

6. Make sure that MongoDB is running on your machine and then start the server by running:

```
node app.js
```

7. In the console, you should see

```
Express server listening on port 3000 in development mode
connected to MongoDB
```

Defining Documents

In MongoDB, there is no concept of tables as in relational database. Instead, MongoDB structures data around the idea of documents. This is a little disjointing at first but will soon become familiar. A document in MongoDB has attributes. For example, if you had a dog document, it might have the following attributes:

▶ Name

▶ Breed

▶ Color

▶ Age

For your todo application, you define a task document. This is simple: It just has a single attribute of `'task'`.

To define a document in MongoDB with the Mongoose module, the process is to go through the Schema interface provided by Mongoose and then declare the attributes. When using Mongoose, you may be confused between MongoDB's documents and Mongoose's models. Mongoose provides some additional functionality, such as validators, getters, and setters, which is wrapped up in the concept of a model. Ultimately, however, a model maps to a MongoDB document.

Depending on the type of data you want to use in your attributes, Mongoose allows you to declare the following types:

▶ String

▶ Number

▶ Date

▶ Boolean

▶ Buffer

▶ ObjectID

▶ Mixed

▶ Array

For the tasks model, a single attribute is needed and looks like this:

```
var Schema = mongoose.Schema,
    ObjectId = Schema.ObjectId;

var Task = new Schema({
  task      : String
});

var Task = mongoose.model('Task', Task);
```

Notice that there are two declarations of the variable `'Task'`. The first is to define the schema for the model; the second is so that the variable can be used to create new tasks. Admittedly this pattern does not seem elegant, and you may choose to have separate names for the variables.

In the model declaration, the task is declared as a `String`. This tells MongoDB what type of data to expect. A string is a sequence of characters, exactly the right fit for a task like `'Feed the dog'` or `'Eat Lunch'`.

You do not need to run any database migrations or create Structured Query Language (SQL) scripts to set up the database. This is the only thing you need to do; so with just a few lines of code, you have defined your data structure and are ready to start building the views in your application!

▼ TRY IT YOURSELF

If you have downloaded the code examples for this book, this code is hour08/example05.

Follow these steps to define a Mongoose model:

1. Return to the example Express application that you created to connect to MongoDB.

2. Open app.js and declare your todo model. Replace the block starting with `'mongo.con-nect'` with the following code:

```
mongoose.connect('mongodb://localhost/todo_development')
var Schema = mongoose.Schema;
var ObjectId = Schema.ObjectId;

var Task = new Schema({
  task: String
});

var Task = mongoose.model('Task', Task);
```

3. That's it! You are now ready to start building the views.

DID YOU KNOW?

Twitter Bootstrap Is Great for Prototyping

The Engineering team at Twitter open sourced a framework called Bootstrap for bootstrapping the layouts of web applications. It includes base HTML and CSS that covers typography, forms, buttons, and more. If you are looking for a quick way to add styling to your application, Bootstrap is a great choice. You use Bootstrap to create the todo application.

Including Twitter Bootstrap

You use Twitter Bootstrap to style the views of the example application. To include it, update your views/layout.jade file to have the following content:

```
!!
html
  head
    title= title
    link(rel='stylesheet', href='http://twitter.github.com/bootstrap/1.4.0/
```

```
➥bootstrap.min.css')
  body
    section.container!= body
```

The Index View

Now that you have a structure for your data, it is time to start creating views. Follow the same pattern as Hour 7, "More on Express": First create the route and then add the view template.

The tasks index view contains a list of all tasks. To create this, a new route is added to app.js:

```
app.get('/tasks', function(req, res){
  res.render('tasks/index', {
    title: 'Todos index view'  });
});
```

Next, a view file is added by creating a new file at /views/tasks/index.jade and adding the following content:

```
h1 Your Tasks
```

Hopefully, this pattern is familiar to you from Hour 7! The next step is to fetch the todo items from MongoDB so that you can display them. Through the Mongoose module, there is an easy way to fetch all records stored in a model.

```
YourModel.find({}, function (err, docs) {
  // do something with the data here
});
```

The tasks index route can now be updated to query MongoDB and pass the results through to the view layer.

```
app.get('/tasks', function(req, res){
  Task.find({}, function (err, docs) {
    res.render('tasks/index', {
      title: 'Todos index view',
      docs: docs
    });
  });
});
```

Note that docs is passed through to the view layer and contains any records that have been returned from MongoDB. The view file at /views/tasks/index.jade can now be updated to show these results if there are any.

```
h1 Your tasks

- if(docs.length)
```

```
table
  tr
    th Task
      each task in docs
        tr
          td #{task.task}
- else
  p You don't have any tasks!
```

The Jade template checks to see whether there are any tasks by calling length on docs. If there are no tasks, this is returned as false and the template tells the user that they do not have any tasks. If there are documents, then a loop outputs each one.

▼ TRY IT YOURSELF

If you have downloaded the code examples for this book, this code is hour08/example06.

Follow these steps to display data from MongoDB:

1. Return to the example Express todo application that you have been working on.

2. Open app.js and add the tasks route. This fetches all tasks from MongoDB.

```
app.get('/tasks', function(req, res){
  Task.find({}, function (err, docs) {
    res.render('tasks/index', {
      title: 'Todos index view',
      docs: docs
    });
  });
});
```

3. Create a new file at views/tasks/index.jade and add the following content:

```
h1 Your tasks

- if(docs.length)
  table
    tr
      th Task
        each task in docs
          tr
            td #{task.task}
  - else
    p You don't have any tasks!
```

4. Start the server using

```
node app.js
```

5. Browse to http://0.0.0.0:3000/tasks.

6. You should see a page saying you have no tasks (see Figure 8.5). You need to add a way of adding tasks!

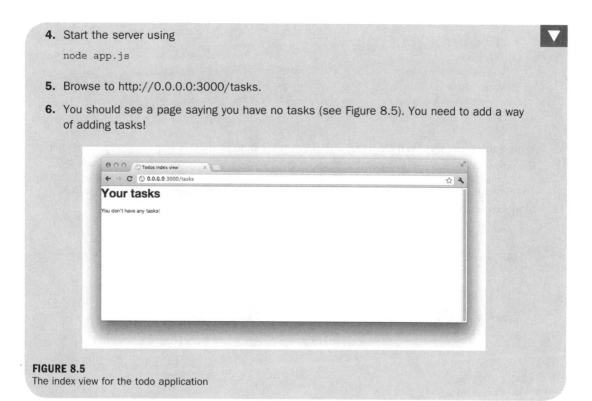

FIGURE 8.5
The index view for the todo application

The Create View

So far, you have a page that tells you that you have no tasks but no way to add a task. To allow the app to create records, two new routes are created. First, a new route to allow users to enter a task:

```
app.get('/tasks/new', function(req, res){
  res.render('tasks/new.jade', {
    title: 'New Task'
  });
});
```

The corresponding view files show a form to allow the user to submit a task. As forms are being styled with Twitter Bootstrap, the elements have class names to apply the correct styling.

```
h1 New task view

form(method='post', action='/tasks')
  fieldset
    legend Add a task
```

```
div.clearfix
  label Task
  div.input
    input(name='task[task]', class='xlarge')
div.actions
  input(type='submit', value='Save', class='btn primary')
  button(type='reset', class='btn') Cancel
```

Within this form, there is a single field that sends the data as a POST request to /tasks, where the post will be received and saved to MongoDB.

To receive the data, a new route is created that receives the POST request and creates a task. Mongoose makes it easy to do this:

```
app.post('/tasks', function(req, res){
  var task = new Task(req.body.task);
  task.save(function (err) {
    if (!err) {
      res.redirect('/tasks');
    }
    else {
      res.redirect('/tasks/new');
    }
  });
});
```

On line 2 of the code example, a new Task model is instantiated and the POST data passed to it. On line 3, save is called on the task. This saves the task to MongoDB if there are no errors. Once the task has saved, the user is redirected to the index view.

Now that users can add tasks, a link can be added on the index view to the new view so that tasks can be created.

```
p
  a(href='/tasks/new', class='btn primary') Add a Task
```

▼ TRY IT YOURSELF

If you have downloaded the code examples for this book, this code is hour08/example07.

Follow these steps to allow tasks to be created:

1. Return to the example Express todo application that you have been working on.

2. Open app.js and add the new tasks route.

```
app.get('/tasks/new', function(req, res){
  res.render('tasks/new.jade', {
    title: 'New Task'
  });
});
```

3. Create a new file at views/tasks/new.jade and add the following content:

```
h1 New task view

form(method='post', action='/tasks')
  fieldset
    legend Add a task
    div.clearfix
      label Task
      div.input
        input(name='task[task]', class='xlarge')
    div.actions
      input(type='submit', value='Save', class='btn primary')
      button(type='reset', class='btn') Cancel
```

4. Add a second new route to the app.js file to receive the POST request and create a task:

```
app.post('/tasks', function(req, res){
  var task = new Task(req.body.task);
  task.save(function (err) {
    if (!err) {
      res.redirect('/tasks');
    }
    else {
      res.redirect('/tasks/new');
    }
  });
});
```

5. Add a link to views/tasks/index.jade to allow users to create tasks:

```
p
  a(href='/tasks/new', class='btn primary') Add a Task
```

6. Start the server using

```
node app.js
```

7. Browse to http://0.0.0.0:3000/tasks.

8. You should see a link to add tasks and be able to create new tasks (see Figure 8.6).

FIGURE 8.6
The create view for the todo application

The Edit View

The todo application currently allows users to add new tasks and view a list of tasks. But what if they want to edit an existing task? To add editing, two routes are required: one to show a form to allow the task to be edited and another one to receive the post and update the record.

First, though, a way to retrieve the task that should be edited is needed so that it can be displayed in the form. Because each MongoDB record has a unique ID, this can be used to fetch the record. Mongoose provides a simple way to do that:

```
YourModel.findById( someId, function (err, doc) {
  // do something with the data here
});
```

Using findById, the record can be found and a route can be created for the edit form. This route captures the id request parameter so the record can be retrieved from MongoDB. Note how the route also passes the task through to the view layer so that the existing data can be shown to the user.

```
app.get('/tasks/:id/edit', function(req, res){
  Task.findById(req.params.id, function (err, doc){
    res.render('tasks/edit', {
      title: 'Edit Task View',
      task: doc
    });
  });
});
```

The corresponding view shows the data to the user and allows the user to edit it. Because the form is an update, a PUT request is used. Express has a helper that converts standard post requests into other methods by specifying the name as '_method'. The form uses this feature in a hidden input field to make sure that Express converts the POST into a PUT. Express does this as most HTML forms only support GET and POST.

```
h1 Edit task view
form(method='post', action='/tasks/' + task.id)
  input(name='_method', value='PUT', type='hidden')
  fieldset
    legend Editing task
    div.clearfix
      label Task
      div.input
        input(name='task[task]', class='xlarge', value="#{task.task}")
    div.actions
      input(type='submit', value='Save', class='btn primary')
      button(type='reset', class='btn') Cancel
```

To receive the data, another route is added to receive the PUT request and update the record. If the update is a success, the user is redirected to the index view.

```
app.put('/tasks/:id', function(req, res){
  Task.findById(req.params.id, function (err, doc){
    doc.task = req.body.task.task;
    doc.save(function(err) {
      if (!err){
        res.redirect('/tasks');
      }
      else {
        // error handling
      }
    });
  });
});
```

Finally, now that the application supports editing, a link can be added to the home page to allow users to edit records.

```
- if(docs.length)
  table
    tr
      th Task
      th
    each task in docs
      tr
        td #{task.task}
        td
```

```
        a.btn(href="/tasks/#{task.id}/edit") Edit
- else
  p You don't have any tasks!
```

▼ TRY IT YOURSELF

If you have downloaded the code examples for this book, this code is hour08/example08.

Follow these steps to allow tasks to be edited:

1. Return to the example Express todo application that you have been working on.

2. Open app.js and add the edit tasks route:

```
app.get('/tasks/:id/edit', function(req, res){
  Task.findById(req.params.id, function (err, doc){
    res.render('tasks/edit', {
      title: 'Edit Task View',
      task: doc
    });
  });
});
```

3. Create a new file at views/tasks/edit.jade and add the following content:

```
h1 Edit task view

form(method='post', action='/tasks/' + task.id)
  input(name='_method', value='PUT', type='hidden')
  fieldset
    legend Editing task
    div.clearfix
      label Task
      div.input
        input(name='task[task]', class='xlarge', value="#{task.task}")
    div.actions
      input(type='submit', value='Save', class='btn primary')
      button(type='reset', class='btn') Cancel
```

4. Add a second new route to the app.js file to receive the PUT request and update the task:

```
app.put('/tasks/:id', function(req, res){
  Task.findById(req.params.id, function (err, doc){
    doc.task = req.body.task.task;
    doc.save(function(err) {
      if (!err){
        res.redirect('/tasks');
      }
      else {
```

```
                // error handling
            }
        });
    });
});
```

5. Update the tasks/index.jade view to include a link to the edit view:

```
- if(docs.length)
  table
    tr
      th Task
      th
    each task in docs
      tr
        td #{task.task}
        td
          a.btn(href="/tasks/#{task.id}/edit") Edit
- else
  p You don't have any tasks!
```

6. Start the server using

```
node app.js
```

7. Browse to http://0.0.0.0:3000/tasks.

8. You should see a link to add tasks and be able to edit tasks (see Figure 8.7).

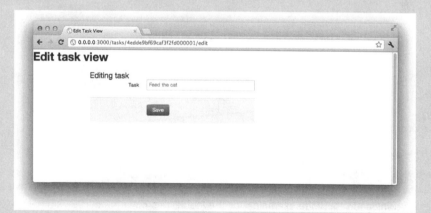

FIGURE 8.7
The edit view for the todo application

Deleting Tasks

The todo application can now create, read, and edit records. The final piece of functionality is to add the capability to delete records. First, a route is created to receive a DELETE request that uses the id from the request to find which task to delete. The same `findById` method provided by Mongoose is used to find the task to be deleted. If no task is found for the id that is passed in, an error is returned.

```
app.del('/tasks/:id', function(req, res){
  Task.findById(req.params.id, function (err, doc){
    if (!doc) return next(new NotFound('Document not found'));
    doc.remove(function() {
      res.redirect('/tasks');
    });
  });
});
```

To send the DELETE request, a form is needed. This is added to the output of each task record to allow users to delete it. As with the PUT request for the edit action, a hidden field with the name of '_method' is used so that Express will convert the POST request into a DELETE.

```
- if(docs.length)
  table
    tr
      th Task
      th
    each task in docs
      tr
        td #{task.task}
        td
          a.btn(href="/tasks/#{task.id}/edit") Edit
        td
          form(method='post', action='/tasks/' + task.id)
            input(name='_method', value='DELETE', type='hidden')
            button.btn(type='submit') Delete
- else
  p You don't have any tasks!
```

▼ TRY IT YOURSELF

If you have downloaded the code examples for this book, this code is hour08/example09.

Follow these steps to allow tasks to be deleted:

1. Return to the example Express todo application that you have been working on.

2. Open app.js and add the delete tasks route:

```
app.del('/tasks/:id', function(req, res){
  Task.findById(req.params.id, function (err, doc){
    if (!doc) return next(new NotFound('Document not found'));
    doc.remove(function() {
      res.redirect('/tasks');
    });
  });
});
```

3. Update the tasks/index.jade view to include a link to the edit view.

```
- if(docs.length)
  table
    tr
      th Task
      th
      each task in docs
        tr
          td #{task.task}
          td
            a.btn(href="/tasks/#{task.id}/edit") Edit
          . td
            form(method='post', action='/tasks/' + task.id)
              input(name='_method', value='DELETE', type='hidden')
              button.btn(type='submit') Delete
- else
  p You don't have any tasks!
```

4. Start the server using

```
node app.js
```

5. Browse to http://0.0.0.0:3000/tasks.

6. You should see a link to delete tasks and be able to delete tasks.

Adding Flash Messages

The todo application can create, read, edit, and delete! It would be great if the application could tell users that their actions have been successful, though. Through the Express framework, this can be added to the application by first enabling session support.

To enable sessions within Express, the following two lines are added within the app.configure section of the app.js file:

```
app.use(express.cookieParser());
app.use(express.session({ secret: "OZhCLfxlGp9TtzSXmJtq" }));
```

The first line tells Express to enable the `cookieParser`. This allows Express to save sessions. The second line sets a secret for Express to use to secure the session. This can be any string you want. A useful tool is available at random.org for generating random strings: http://www.random.org/strings/.

The common term for describing messages that notify the user of what has happened is *flash messages*. Figure 8.8 shows an example of a message shown to a user after he has created a task.

FIGURE 8.8
An example of a flash message

Once session support is enabled in the application, it is possible to set flash messages within routes:

```
req.flash('info', 'It worked!');
req.flash('error', 'Something went wrong!');
```

This adds the message to the user's session so it will be available between views. An example of where this can be used is to redirect the user from the create view to the index view and show the user a flash message.

To add the flash message to the session, it is included in the route before the redirect.

```
app.post('/tasks', function(req, res){
  var task = new Task(req.body.task);
  task.save(function (err) {
    if (!err) {
      req.flash('info', 'Task created');
      res.redirect('/tasks');
    }
    else {
      // Error handling
```

```
      }
   });
});
```

To show a flash message, a Jade template can check for the existence of a message and show it if present. The example uses the styling available via Twitter Bootstrap to style the alert messages.

```
-if(typeof flash != 'undefined')
  - if(flash.warning)
    div.alert-message.warning
      p= flash.warning
  - if(flash.info)
    div(data-alert='alert').alert-message.success
      p= flash.info
```

As flash messages are something that are reused across templates, this is a good example where the code can be abstracted into a mixin. You were introduced to mixins in Hour 6, "Introducing Express," and they allow snippets of code to be reused across different views.

The flash message can be abstracted into a mixin file and saved to views/mixins/flash-messages.jade:

```
mixin flash-messages(flash)
  - if(flash.warning)
    div.alert-message.warning
      p= flash.warning
  - if(flash.info)
    div(data-alert='alert').alert-message.success
      p= flash.info
```

This can then be reused across views. To add flash messages to the tasks/index.jade view, the following lines are added. Now if there is a flash message, it will be shown to the user.

```
-if(typeof flash != 'undefined')
  include ../mixins/flash-messages
  mixin flash-messages(flash)
```

Finally, routes need to be updated to set the flash depending on the outcome of manipulating the data. This is done through req.flash.

```
app.post('/tasks', function(req, res){
  var task = new Task(req.body.task);
  task.save(function (err) {
    if (!err) {
      req.flash('info', 'Task created');
      res.redirect('/tasks');
    }
    else {
```

```
      req.flash('warning', err);
      res.redirect('/tasks/new');
    }
  });
});
```

For a full example, refer to hour08/example10 in the book's code examples.

Validating Input Data

Validating data that is inputted by a user is an important part of any web application. In the example you have been working through, there is currently no validation. A task can be created without any text being entered!

Mongoose allows validations to be set within the model on attributes that you defined at the start of the example. It is possible to create custom functions to validate the data in any way that you want. To validate the presence of a string, a simple JavaScript function can be created.

```
function validatePresenceOf(value) {
  return value && value.length;
}
```

The model can now be updated to validate that a string is present:

```
var Task = new Schema({
  task : { type: String, validate: [validatePresenceOf, 'a task is required'] }
});
```

Now if no string is present when a user submits a form, validation will fail, the record will not save, and the application can tell the user via a flash message.

The post route is updated to catch the error and set a warning flash message (see Figure 8.9). Note that if the data fails to pass validation, then `err` is true and the user will be redirected back to the form with a warning.

```
app.post('/tasks', function(req, res){
  var task = new Task(req.body.task);
  task.save(function (err) {
    if (!err) {
      req.flash('info', 'Task created');
      res.redirect('/tasks');
    }
    else {
      req.flash('warning', err);
      res.redirect('/tasks/new');
    }
  });
});
```

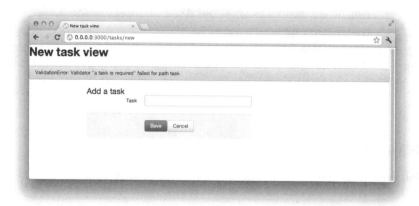

FIGURE 8.9
A validation flash message

For a full example, refer to hour08/example11 in the book's code examples.

Summary

In this hour, you learned about persisting data and some ways to persist data with Node.js. You learned about reading and writing from a file and how to use environment variables to set data values in an application. Finally you worked through a full example of a CRUD (Create, Read, Update, Delete) application and learned about flash messages and validation.

Q&A

Q. When should I save data to a file and when should I use a database?

A. If you are saving small bits of data infrequently, performing backups, or logging data from an application, a file is a good option. If the data is being accessed frequently by the users of the web application, this is generally a sign that it is time to move it to a database. Reading data from a disk on file is much slower than reading it from a database.

Q. Which database should I choose?

A. There are many databases to choose from, and each has different strengths. For general purposes, many in the Node.js community favor MongoDB, and many libraries support interacting with MongoDB. If, however, you are more familiar with another database, Node.js has good support for other databases via third-party libraries. Basically, it is down to personal choice!

Q. Why is validating data important before saving it?

A. To create stable software, an application needs to know what types of data to expect. If you put a form on the Web, you will be amazed by what humans fill in. You should expect the unexpected in data input forms and validate the data accordingly. Good validations lead to a better user experience too as the application can help users recover from errors with helpful messages.

Workshop

This workshop contains quiz questions to help cement your learning in this hour.

Quiz

1. Should you store sensitive data like passwords in a text file?

2. Which HTML verb should be used to update records?

3. When security considerations are there in the example in this hour?

Quiz Answers

1. No. Storing data in text files is a good option for data that is not sensitive. Examples of this might be a PID (Process Identifier) or logging.

2. The PUT verb should be used to update records. Because HTML forms do not natively support PUT requests, Express provides a convenience method to add this.

3. In the example in this hour, the security could be improved. You should consider any data that comes from outside your application as tainted. This means you should clean the data when it is received to prevent things like SQL injection and XSS attacks. Similarly when you are displaying data, you should also sanity check the data. A security mantra worth repeating when you are working with data is "Filter input, escape output".

Exercises

1. Create a simple Node.js application that writes your name into a text file.

2. Create a second application that reads the text file created in exercise 1 and prints "Hello [Your Name]!" to the console.

3. In the example application that you created, add a new attribute to the Task model called `'Details'` so that users can add details about the task. Update the forms and views to include this attribute.

PART III

Debugging, Testing, and Deploying

Debugging Node.js Applications

What You'll Learn in This Hour:

▶ What debugging is

▶ Debugging using the STDIO module

▶ Debugging with Node.js's debugger

▶ Debugging with Node Inspector

Debugging

Before too long in software development, you will hit something developers learn to deal with every day: bugs. A bug in software is an error or issue that causes unexpected behavior in an application. Some examples of bugs include

▶ An error caused by a syntax error in source code

▶ A feature that does not behave as expected

▶ A poorly performing piece of code that makes an application run slowly

▶ A security vulnerability

Bugs can be found by developers or reported by the users of an application. Either way, the responsibility for investigating a bug (or debugging) lies with the developer. Many developers use bug or issue trackers to keep track of bug reports, and once software is released, a large part of a developer's job is dealing with bug reports. If you find a bug or have a bug reported by a user, you need to go through a debugging process. Debugging simply describes investigating what went wrong and fixing it. Once bugs are resolved, they are described as fixed or sometimes squashed. In this hour, you learn about some of the tools and techniques available to you for debugging Node.js applications.

The STDIO Module

The Node.js core ships with the STDIO module, which is a lightweight way of debugging your applications that, for many purposes, is a great fit. The module has no other dependencies, meaning that you can use it without any setup. It follows the conventions of debugging JavaScript in the browser by using the console object, so if you have done any debugging of JavaScript in the browser, it will feel familiar to you. Not all the features found in the browser's console object are supported, but many are.

In the STDIO module, information is logged to the terminal and using it is straightforward. You simply add lines to your script where you want to log something to the terminal. When the script hits that line, it will be logged to the terminal:

```
console.log("Look! I'm in your terminal!")
```

▼ TRY IT YOURSELF

If you have downloaded the code examples for this book, this code is hour09/example01.

Follow these steps to debug with the STDIO module:

1. Create a file called app.js and copy the following code into it:

   ```
   console.log('Debugging message')
   ```

2. Run the script:

   ```
   node app.js
   ```

3. You should see "Debugging Message!" in your terminal.

Using `console.log()` is often a quick-and-dirty solution for debugging the following scenarios:

▶ Checking the value of a variable or string

▶ Logging that a script has called a function

▶ Logging responses from third-party services

If you want to log errors, you can use `console.warn()`, which is also aliased to `console.error()`, and both of these methods print to the standard error stream.

Programs Write to Different Streams

On UNIX-type systems data streams are often joined together or piped. This allows small, distinct programs to be combined to create more complicated functionality. To help glue programs together, programs write to standard input, output, and error interfaces. These are known as Standard Input (stin), Standard Output (stout), and Standard Error (sterr). One example of using these standard streams in use is a test runner. When a set of automated tests pass, the output is sent to Standard Output. When tests fail, a message is sent to Standard Error. This allows other software to understand the results of running the tests and act accordingly. Node.js's STDIO module follows this convention, so make sure that you write to the correct stream!

An example of how you might use console.error() is to log why an error was caused. For example, if you are not checking that a function is defined, or if a function is deleted after you have written some code that calls the function, an error will be thrown. To make the problem explicit, you can use console.error() within a try catch statement to log why the error has occurred.

Listing 9.1   Using console.error()

```
function notDefined(){
  try {
    someFunction(); // undefined
  } catch (e) {
    console.error(e);
  }
}
notDefined();
```

If you run this code, you see the following error in the terminal:

```
[ReferenceError: someFunction is not defined]
```

TRY IT YOURSELF ▼

If you have downloaded the code examples for this book, this code is hour09/example02.

Follow these steps to write errors to sterr with the STDIO module:

1. Copy the code in Listing 9.1 into a file on your system called app.js.

2. Run the script:

   ```
   node app.js
   ```

3. You should see [ReferenceError: someFunction is not defined] in your terminal, which indicates that the someFunction is undefined.

Using `console.error()` is useful as it provides information about the type of error that was thrown and precisely what the problem is. In the example, it is possible that, at a later date, the function `someFunction()` will be defined, but that there will be an error within that function. This might look like Listing 9.2.

Listing 9.2   Catching Errors with console.error()

```
function someFunction(){
  return undefinedVar; // undefined
}
function notDefined(){
  try {
    someFunction(); // now defined
  } catch (e) {
    console.error(e);
  }
}
notDefined();
```

If you run this code again, you will see that the error message has changed and that it is immediately clear where the problem lies:

```
[ReferenceError: undefinedVar is not defined]
```

▼ TRY IT YOURSELF

If you have downloaded the code examples for this book, this code is hour09/example03.

Here's an example to show you how to understand errors with the STDIO module:

1. Copy the code in Listing 9.2 into a file on your system called app.js.

2. Run the script:

   ```
   node app.js
   ```

3. You should see `[ReferenceError: undefinedVar is not defined]` in your terminal, which indicates that the `undefinedVar` is undefined.

Using `console.error()` is a lightweight way of finding out why an error has been thrown. For discovering where bottlenecks are in code or quick benchmarking of parts of your code, the STDIO module has `console.time()` and `console.timeEnd()`. Both of these methods take an argument of a label that effectively ties the two methods together. To start a timer, use `console.time()`; to end it, use `console.timeEnd()`. These methods are useful for benchmarking small bits of code or anything time related. Using these methods, you can easily find out where your code is slow or compare two ways of executing the same code for optimum performance.

Listing 9.3 A Simple Benchmark

```
var sum = 0;
var arr = new Array(1000000);

for (var i = 0; i < arr.length; i++) {
  arr[i] = Math.random();
}

console.time('for-loop-1');
for (var i in arr) {
  sum += arr[i];
}
console.timeEnd('for-loop-1');

console.time('for-loop-2');
for (var i = 0; i < arr.length; i++) {
  sum += arr[i];
}
console.timeEnd('for-loop-2');
```

In this example, the exercise is to discover the most efficient way of performing a simple operation on an array of a million random numbers. Using the methods provided by the STDIO module, it is easy to discover which way is faster by timing both loops. This can be useful when debugging performance issues. Running the script shows that the second option is much faster.

```
for-loop-1: 431ms
for-loop-2: 27ms
```

TRY IT YOURSELF ▼

If you have downloaded the code examples for this book, this code is hour09/example04.

The following steps show performance testing with the STDIO module:

1. Copy the code in Listing 9.3 into a file on your system called app.js.

2. Run the script:

   ```
   node app.js
   ```

3. You should see the execution times for the two loops outputted to the terminal:

   ```
   for-loop-1: 431ms
   for-loop-2: 27ms
   ```

If you want to see a stack trace of where you are at any point during the execution of a script, do this with the `console.trace()` method (see Listing 9.4).

Listing 9.4   Viewing a Stack Trace

```
function notDefined(){
  console.trace();
  try {
    someFunction();
  } catch (e) {
    console.error(e);
  }
}
notDefined();
```

This prints a stack trace from the point of the code at which it was inserted:

```
Trace:
    at notDefined (/Users/george/code/nodejsbook.io.examples/hour09/example05/app.
➥js:2:11)
    at Object.<anonymous> (/Users/george/code/nodejsbook.io.examples/hour09/
➥example05/app.js:10:1)
    at Module._compile (module.js:432:26)
    at Object..js (module.js:450:10)
    at Module.load (module.js:351:31)
    at Function._load (module.js:310:12)
    at Array.0 (module.js:470:10)
    at EventEmitter._tickCallback (node.js:192:40)
```

▼ TRY IT YOURSELF

If you have downloaded the code examples for this book, this code is hour09/example05.

Here's how to print a stack trace with the STDIO module:

1. Copy the code in Listing 9.4 into a file on your system called app.js.

2. Run the script:

   ```
   node app.js
   ```

3. You should see the stack trace shown in your terminal.

BY THE WAY

Stack Traces Help Debugging

A stack trace is a list of function or method calls at a point in the application. Often, an error or bug may be in code that has been included from another file or module. A stack trace allows a developer to read through how the script has reached a point in execution and track down where a problem has occurred.

The Node.js Debugger

Node.js provides access to the V8 debugger, and by including it in your scripts, you can walk through your code by setting breakpoints. A breakpoint allows a developer to halt the execution of a script and inspect what is happening. Breakpoints are an extremely powerful debugging technique as they allow you to inspect the state of an application at a particular point in the execution. To set breakpoints using the Node.js debugger, add the following line where you want a breakpoint to occur:

```
debugger
```

Now, you can run your program with debugging by running Node.js with the additional debug argument:

```
node debug app.js
```

The Node.js debugger allows you to do the following:

- ▶ Step through the code

- ▶ Set breakpoints

- ▶ Get information at a breakpoint in a script including a stack trace and the scripts loaded

- ▶ Drop into a REPL (Read, Evaluate, Print, Loop) for debugging in detail at a breakpoint

- ▶ Run, restart, and stop a script

A common pattern when using Node's debugger is to insert breakpoints and then use the REPL to examine the state of objects and variables. This is useful for debugging scoping issues in JavaScript. The following example is taken from Douglas Crockford's *JavaScript: The Good Parts* and is a great example of how scope can easily become confusing in JavaScript. At different points in the following script, the values of a, b, and c are different or not set at all (see Listing 9.5).

Listing 9.5   A JavaScript Scope Example

```
var foo = function(){
  var a = 3, b = 5;
  var bar = function() {
    var b = 7, c = 11;
    a += b + c;
  }
  bar ();
};
foo();
```

If the result of a function like this is not returning the expected values, a sound debugging approach is to put debugger breakpoints into the script so that the debugger can step through the script. The debugger REPL can then be used to check the values of variables.

Listing 9.6   The JavaScript Scope Example with Breakpoints

```
var foo = function(){
  var a = 3, b = 5;
  debugger;
  var bar = function() {
    var b = 7, c = 11;
    a += b + c;
    debugger;
  }
  bar ();
  debugger;
};
foo();
```

This script can now be run with the debug argument and the debugger will break at line 1. This freezes the execution of the script and the state of the script at that point.

```
node debug app.js
< debugger listening on port 5858
connecting... ok
break in app.js:1
  1 var foo = function(){
  2   var a = 3, b = 5;
  3   debugger;
debug>
```

To advance to the first breakpoint, type **cont**. This moves the debugger forward to line 3 of the script. It is now possible to enter the REPL and query the values of a, b, and c:

```
debug> repl
Press Ctrl + C to leave debug repl
> a
3
> b
5
> c
ReferenceError: c is not defined
```

To exit the REPL, press Ctrl+C and type **cont** to jump to the next breakpoint in your code. In this example, this moves to line 7 of the code. Once again it is possible to query the values of a, b, and c by entering the REPL by typing **repl**.

```
debug> repl
```

```
Press Ctrl + C to leave debug repl
> a
21
> b
7
> c
11
```

To jump to the final breakpoint, press Ctrl+C again and type **cont**. This is the last breakpoint in the code, and entering **repl**, you will be able to check the values of a, b, and c again.

```
debug> repl
Press Ctrl + C to leave debug repl
> a
21
> b
5
> c
ReferenceError: c is not defined
```

TRY IT YOURSELF ▼

If you have downloaded the code examples for this book, this code is hour09/example06.

The following steps show you how to debug with the V8 debugger:

1. Copy the code in Listing 9.6 into a file on your system called app.js.

2. Run the script with the debugger enabled:

   ```
   node debug app.js
   ```

3. You should see the debugger start and then halt the execution of the script.

4. Type **cont** to continue to the first breakpoint.

5. Type **repl** and query the values of a, b, and c.

6. Press Ctrl+C and then type **cont** to skip to the next breakpoint.

7. Type **repl** and query the values of a, b, and c.

8. Press Ctrl+C and then type **cont** to skip to the next breakpoint.

9. Type **repl** and query the values of a, b, and c.

10. Press Ctrl+C and then type **cont**.

11. You should see "program terminated" to indicate that the program has finished.

12. Press Ctrl+D to exit the debugger.

Node Inspector

Perhaps the most useful tool for debugging Node.js applications is Node Inspector. This third-party tool was created by dannycoates (Danny Coates). To use Node Inspector, you must have a WebKit browser on your machine, so this means installing either Chrome or Safari. Node Inspector allows you to use the Webkit JavaScript debugger to step through your code and supports the following features:

▶ Browsing source code files for your application

▶ Using a console to interact with your application

▶ Adding and removing breakpoints

▶ Stepping through the function calls in your code

▶ Stepping in and out of functions

▶ Setting watch expressions

▶ Viewing the stack trace at different points in your code

▶ Viewing scope variables

Providing you have a WebKit browser on your machine, you can install Node Inspector from npm:

```
npm install -g node-inspector
```

The process for starting Node Inspector is twofold. First, start your application with the `--debug` or `--debug-brk` flags to enable the JavaScript debugger. If you use `--debug-brk`, then Node Inspector places a breakpoint on the first line of your application. Note that to begin debugging, you need to press Play to jump to your first breakpoint.

```
node --debug-brk app.js
```

Once your application is running in debug mode, you must start a separate process for Node Inspector. In a separate terminal tab, run the following command:

```
node-inspector
```

This outputs a message if it's successful:

```
visit http://0.0.0.0:8080/debug?port=5858 to start debugging
```

You can now begin debugging your application by opening a WebKit browser at http://
0.0.0.0:8080/debug?port=5858. You then have a comprehensive view into your application in
front of you!

You can add breakpoints to your code by clicking on the line numbers in the left column. If you
started Node with --debug-brk, the execution of your script will be paused there. You can then
step through the code by clicking the Play icon at the top of the right column and the script will
halt at the next breakpoint. If you do not set any breakpoints, the code will just run, so make
sure you set some breakpoints!

Node Inspector is similar to the debugger that comes with Node but is much more interactive.
Using the same example that you looked at when using the Node.js debugger, the debugger
statements can now be removed from the code. It is generally a good idea not to leave debugger
statements in your code, and using Node Inspector you do not need to worry about that.

Listing 9.7   The JavaScript Scope Example with Breakpoints Removed

```
var foo = function(){
  var a = 3, b = 5;
var bar = function() {
    var b = 7, c = 11;
    a += b + c;
}
  bar ();
};
foo();
```

The script can be started with debugging and breaking at the first line with the following command:

```
node --debug-brk app.js
```

Node Inspector can then be started with the following command:

```
node-inspector
```

Finally, opening a browser at http://0.0.0.0:8080/debug?port=5858 shows the WebKit JavaScript
debugger (see Figure 9.1). By clicking the line numbers, you can add and remove breakpoints.
For this example, add breakpoints at lines 4, 7, 9, and 11.

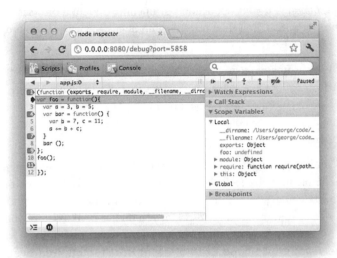

FIGURE 9.1
Launching Node Inspector

You can step through the breakpoints by hitting the Play button at the top right-hand column. Note how the information in the right-hand column changes as you step through and allows you to inspect the current state of your application (see Figure 9.2).

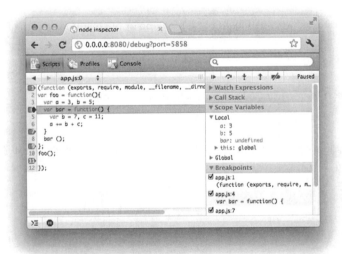

FIGURE 9.2
Stepping through breakpoints

TRY IT YOURSELF ▼

If you have downloaded the code examples for this book, this code is hour09/example07.

Here's how to debug with Node Inspector:

1. Copy the code in Listing 9.7 into a file on your system called app.js.

2. Run the script, enabling the JavaScript debugger and breaking on the first line:

```
node --debug-brk app.js
```

3. You should see "debugger listening on port 5858."

4. In a separate terminal tab or window, start Node Inspector:

```
node-inpsector
```

5. You should see "visit http://0.0.0.0:8080/debug?port=5858 to start debugging."

6. Open a Webkit browser (Chrome or Safari) at http://0.0.0.0:8080/debug?port=5858.

7. You should see your script.

8. Add breakpoints by clicking the line numbers 4, 7, 9, and 11.

9. Click the Play button to step through your breakpoints.

10. Note how the variable values change under Scope Variables in the right-hand column.

DID YOU KNOW?

Node Inspector Is a Great Way to Learn

Another use of Node Inspector is learning about how code works in Node.js. Node Inspector allows you to step through the execution of code and see the files and modules that it is referencing. By using Node Inspector, reading code can become interactive rather than just reading the code in a text editor.

A Note on Testing

How you use a debugger depends on your style of development. Some developers like to build an application organically. This means they write code and continue to refresh the page or repeat expected inputs until they are satisfied that it works. For this style of development, Node Inspector is useful, because it gives you a view right into the heart of your application. Most professional developers, however, follow a test-driven development process. This involves writing automated tests that can be run over and over again to ensure that an application is working as expected. In this case, the debugger will be used to troubleshoot tricky bugs and edge cases.

You are encouraged to write tests for your applications rather than use a debugger to help write new code. You learn about testing and how this can help development in Hour 10, "Testing Node.js Applications." There are times, though, when you are writing code that you need to examine data or what a function has returned, and it is often quicker to use a debugger to view this than write a test and make it pass. Use your judgment about when to write tests and when to use a debugger, but always test if you can.

Summary

In this hour, you learned about debugging and some of the tools you can use to debug applications in Node.js. You learned about the STDIO module, a quick and easy way to add debugging to your scripts. You then saw how you can gain access to the V8 debugger and use breakpoints to stop the execution of your code and check the value of variables. Finally, you were introduced to Node Inspector, a third-party module that provides access to the WebKit JavaScript debugger.

Q&A

Q. **Which debugger should I use and when?**

A. Generally if your problem seems small and easy to investigate, using the STDIO module is the quickest way to resolve issues. Many developers love Node Inspector for the interactive view that it gives into code as it is executing and only use Node Inspector. Debugging is a personal thing for developers, so try all of the tools and try to understand their strengths and weaknesses. Debugging is something you will do a lot so it is worth investing some time in understanding your options.

Q. **When should I rely on the debugger and when should I write tests?**

A. There is no right or wrong way to develop Node.js applications, but building up a test suite for your application will make it more stable in the long term. If you are creating new software, you are encouraged to write tests and then make them pass. You learn more about this in Hour 10. Debugging tools should be used to investigate issues, and if possible a test should be written to validate that the bug has been squashed.

Q. **How should I track bugs?**

A. Many bug trackers are available. GitHub Issues is a popular choice for many developers as it integrates with source control if you use Git and provides an easy web-based interface for managing bugs and issues.

Workshop

This workshop contains quiz questions and exercises to help cement your learning in this hour.

Quiz

1. Why is a bug called a bug in software development?

2. How do you refer to a bug that is no longer a problem?

3. What is the best type of bug?

Quiz Answers

1. Many people think that the term "bug" was invented by Grace Hopper, a pioneer of computer science. While investigating a problem on a computer prototype, she is said to have discovered a moth trapped in a relay, coining the term bug.

2. A bug that is no longer a problem is said to be "fixed," "closed," or "squashed." Many issue trackers provide support for marking the status of bugs and calculating how many open bugs there are.

3. There is only one good type of bug in computing: A dead bug!

Exercises

1. If you have developed any Node.js applications, try using all three of the debugging tools described in this hour to examine your application. Think about the strengths and weaknesses of each debugging tool. Which tool do you prefer and why?

2. Using the Hello World server on the Node.js home page, start the server with `–debug-brk` and then start Node Inspector. Explore the JavaScript debugger and set some breakpoints. Explore the files list and see which files are included. Set some breakpoints and try to understand a little of how the script works and how Node Inspector gives you access to many details on how the script is working.

3. Explore the Github Issues page on the Node.js repository at https://github.com/joyent/node/issues. Examine how bug and issue reports are sent in. Try to understand that some reports are good with examples while others may be light on information and difficult for developers to investigate. It may help you file better bug reports in the future!

Testing Node.js Applications

What You'll Learn in This Hour:

▶ Why testing is important

▶ Testing with the assert module

▶ Testing with the Nodeunit module

▶ Testing with the Vows module

▶ Testing with the Mocha module

Why Test?

In the last hour, you learned about how to debug Node.js applications, and you may be asking why you need to write tests for your application with such powerful debugging tools. Writing tests for applications is something that many developers do not do. This can work if the codebase is small and there is only one developer on the project. But as applications change and become more complex, it is increasingly difficult to ensure of the stability of code. Tests are repeatable pieces of code that assert that your application is functioning in the way that you expect it to. Examples of tests that you might write include the following:

▶ Does an HTTP response return a 200 code?

▶ Does a method return a particular value?

▶ Does a method return a string?

▶ Does a method take two numbers, perform a calculation, and then return the correct number?

Having repeatable tests allows developers to be sure that when they make a change to code, they are not introducing new bugs or errors into the application. Many developers also use tests to drive the creation of applications in a process called Test Driven Development (TDD). In this process, developers first write tests describing how they want their application to work and then write code to make their tests pass. The test suite helps to drive development but also helps with the long-term stability of the application as at any time a developer can run the tests and check everything is still working. Writing tests is strongly encouraged and has many advantages:

▶ It is a simple layer of quality assurance.

▶ It allows developers to be sure that an application behaves as expected.

▶ It supports developers in creating new functionality without breaking existing features.

▶ It can be integrated with third-party code quality and testing tools.

▶ It allows teams of developers to maintain a consistent understanding of how an application should work.

▶ It greatly enhances the stability of code.

▶ It allows developers to refactor the codebase and ensure it is still working as expected.

The Assert Module

Node.js ships with a simple testing framework in the assert module. This provides a list of assertion methods that allow developers to create low-level tests for Node.js applications. The following assertions are available in Node.js's assert module:

▶ Assert that a value is true

▶ Assert that two values are equal using JavaScript's == equality operator

▶ Assert that two values are not equal using JavaScript's != equality operator

▶ Assert that two values are deeply equal

▶ Assert that two values are deeply not equal

▶ Assert that two values are strictly equal using JavaScript's === equality operator

▶ Assert that two values are strictly not equal using JavaScript's !== equality operator

▶ Assert that an error is thrown

▶ Assert that an error is not thrown

▶ Assert errors that are thrown in callbacks

For the deeply equal assertion, this is defined in the CommonJS specification as

▶ All identical values are equivalent, as determined by ===.

▶ If the expected value is a Date object, the actual value is equivalent if it is also a Date object that refers to the same time.

▶ For other pairs that do not both pass typeof value == "object", equivalence is determined by ==.

▶ For all other Object pairs, including Array objects, equivalence is determined by having the same number of owned properties (as verified with Object.prototype. hasOwnProperty.call), the same set of keys (although not necessarily the same order), equivalent values for every corresponding key, and an identical "prototype" property. Note: This accounts for both named and indexed properties on Arrays.

It is important to understand that in JavaScript, there are two ways that you can compare equality. This first is with the == operator. This is not strict in making comparisons, so you can compare strings with numbers and expect a true result. This leads to some scenarios that may produce unexpected results if you are unfamiliar with JavaScript:

```
"8" == 8 // true
'' == '0' // false
0 == '' // true
```

The second comparison operator is ===. This checks that the values are the same value and the same type. So if you try to compare a string with a number, it will return false. Many experienced JavaScript developers recommend only using this comparison operator.

```
"8" === 8 // false
'' === '0' // false
0 === '' // false
```

To use Node.js's assert module, you must require it in your script.

```
var assert = require('assert');
```

You can then use the module to compare values using the assertion methods that the assert module provides. The assert.strictEqual() method allows you to compare two values using JavaScripts === comparison operator, and it is recommended that you use this.

```
assert.strictEqual("hello", "hello");
```

To run the test, you run the file as you would run any normal node program. So if you saved your file as test.js, you can run the test as follows:

```
node test.js
```

If the test passes, you see no output in the terminal. The assert module is deliberately silent unless there is a failure.

If you have downloaded the code examples for this book, this code is hour10/example01.

Follow these steps to compare values using the assert module:

1. Create a file called test.js and copy the following code into it:

```
var assert = require('assert');
assert.strictEqual("hello", "hello");
```

2. Run the script:

```
node test.js
```

3. You should not see any output in your terminal, indicating that the test passed.

If you have a test that fails, though, you see that an exception is thrown. In the following example, the two values are not the same:

```
assert.strictEqual("hello", "there");
```

If you run this test, you see that an exception is thrown:

```
node.js:201
        throw e; // process.nextTick error, or 'error' event on first tick
              ^
AssertionError: "hello" == "there"
```

By default, `AssertionError` shows the comparison that failed, but you can also pass a third argument that is shown if an exception is thrown:

```
assert.equal("hello", "there", "Message to show if an exception is thrown");
```

Now if the test is run, it displays the custom message:

```
node.js:201
        throw e; // process.nextTick error, or 'error' event on first tick
              ^
AssertionError: Message to show if an exception is thrown
```

You might use this to log other values in your script that affect the assertion values.

If you have downloaded the code examples for this book, this code is hour10/example02.

Follow these steps to demonstrate an error being thrown:

1. Create a file called test.js and copy the following code into it:

```
var assert = require('assert');
assert.strictEqual("hello", "there");
```

2. Run the script:

```
node test.js
```

3. You should not see that an exception is thrown in your terminal.

To avoid any danger of being tripped up by JavaScript's comparison idiosyncrasies, here are the earlier examples within Node's assert module using assert.equal() and assert.strictEqual(). It is recommend that to avoid problems, you should use assert.strictEqual() by default.

```
assert.equal("8", 8) // true
assert.equal('', '0') // false
assert.equal(0, '') // true
assert.strictEqual("8", 8) // false
assert.strictEqual('', '0') // false
assert.strictEqual(0, '') // false
```

Third-Party Testing Tools

Node's assert module will get you surprisingly far in your testing, but it is low level and has a number of limitations. A number of testing frameworks have been created by third-party developers to add features on top of the assert module. These include the following:

▶ Test runners to handle running tests and reporting on the results

▶ Grouping tests together so they can be run independently

▶ Set up and tear down for tests so developers can write code to prepare an application state for a test and clean up afterwards

▶ The ability to run tests in a browser

▶ Adding test reporters so the results of tests can outputted as HTML, XML, and other formats

▶ Better support for asynchronous testing

Nodeunit

Nodeunit builds on top of Node's assert module and adds the ability to set up and tear down tests, asynchronous testing, and mocks and stubs. Nodeunit can be installed globally on your machine using the global flag with npm.

```
npm install -g nodeunit
```

You can also install Nodeunit using the package.json file. For testing modules, these are usually declared within devDependencies (see Listing 10.1).

Listing 10.1   A package.json File with Nodeunit

```
{
  "name": "nodeunit_example",
  "version": "0.0.0",
  "private": true,
  "devDependencies": {
    "nodeunit": "0.7.4"
  }
}
```

Assertions in Nodeunit map closely to the native assert module and tests are declared as shown in Listing 10.2.

Listing 10.2   Assertions with Nodeunit

```
exports.firstTest = function(test){
  test.expect(1);
  test.strictEqual("hello", "hello");
  test.done();
};
exports.secondTest = function(test){
  test.expect(1);
  test.strictEqual("hello", "there");
  test.done();
};
```

Each test is declared as exports.testName, where testName is a description of the test. At the beginning of the test, test.expect(n) is declared where n is the number of assertions you are expecting. This is used to avoid false test passes. After you have finished your test, be sure to call test.done() to indicate that the test has finished.

If you have called your file test.js and installed Nodeunit globally, tests can be run with the following command:

```
nodeunit test.js
```

If you choose to install Nodeunit using a package.json file, you need to reference the binary directly from your project folder.

```
./node_modules/nodeunit/bin/nodeunit test.js
```

For the preceding example, you see the following output (see Figure 10.1):

```
test.js
✓ firstTest
✗ secondTest

AssertionError: 'hello' === 'there'
..stacktrace here..
```

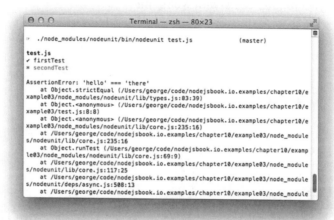

FIGURE 10.1
Running tests with Nodeunit

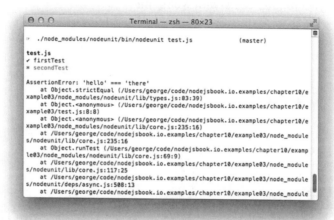

TRY IT YOURSELF ▼

If you have downloaded the code examples for this book, this code is hour10/example03.

Here's how to test with Nodeunit:

1. Copy the code in Listing 10.1 into a file on your system called package.json.

2. Copy the code in Listing 10.2 into a file on your system called test.js.

3. Install dependencies by running

```
npm install
```

4. Run the tests:

```
./node_modules/nodeunit/bin/nodeunit test.js
```

5. You should see one test pass and the other fail along with a stack trace of the failure.

Nodeunit also supports testing asynchronous code. In the following example, Node's fs module is used to read a file from the file system and assumes that there is a file called test.txt with some text in the same folder as the test. When the callback is invoked, two tests are run to test whether an error has been thrown and whether the file size is not 0. Note that the tests are within the callback function.

Listing 10.3   Asynchronous Tests with Nodeunit

```
var fs = require('fs');
exports.asyncTest = function(test){
  fs.stat('test.txt', function(err, stats) {
    test.expect(2);
    test.strictEqual(err, null);
    test.notStrictEqual(stats.size, 0);
    test.done();
  })
};
```

▼ TRY IT YOURSELF

If you have downloaded the code examples for this book, this code is hour10/example04.

Follow these steps to test callbacks with Nodeunit:

1. Copy the code in Listing 10.1 into a file on your system called package.json.

2. Copy the code in Listing 10.3 into a file on your system called test.js.

3. Install dependencies by running

```
npm install
```

4. Create a test file to be used in the test called `test.txt` and add the following contents:

```
This is a test file
```

5. Run the test:

```
./node_modules/nodeunit/bin/nodeunit test.js
```

6. You should see the test pass.

Behavior Driven Development

Many developers favor using Behavior Driven Development. Instead of testing how a program works from the inside, Behavior Driven Development thinks of an application from the outside in. Compare these two descriptions:

> When a user registers, the application should receive the POST request, check fields are valid, and increment the number of users in the database by one.

> As a user, when I successfully register, I should see 'Thanks for registering.'

The first example is more closely aligned to Test Driven Development where developers write tests for application code from the point of view of how the application is expected to function. The second example describes how a user interacts with the application and what they should expect to see. Currently, the trend in the Node.js community is to use BDD (Behavior Driven Development) over Test Driven Development (TDD). Both are equally valid approaches, but using BDD it is perhaps easier to involve stakeholders with testing. In BDD, testing is based on interactions with an application from the outside in rather than needing to understand the internals of an application. Typically when writing a BDD style test, you will use more plain English and describe what you are testing and then declare how it should work. There are a number of popular libraries within the Node.js community for testing using BDD.

Vows

Vows is a third-party module for testing Node.js applications using the BDD style. You can install Vows globally using npm:

```
npm install -g vows
```

You can also install it by adding it to the devDependencies section of the package.json file for your project (see Listing 10.4).

Listing 10.4   A package.json File with Vows

```
{
  "name": "vows_example",
  "version": "0.0.0",
  "devDependencies": {
    "vows": "0.6.2"
  }
}
```

Vows is also created on top of the assert module and adds BDD style testing. The synchronous testing example we have been using in this hour looks like this in Vows (see Listing 10.5).

Listing 10.5   Assertions with Vows

```
var vows = require('vows'),
    assert = require('assert');

vows.describe('Comparing strings').addBatch({
  'when comparing the same strings': {
    topic: "hello",
    'they should be equal': function (topic) {
      assert.strictEqual (topic, "hello");
    }
  },
  'when comparing different strings': {
    topic: "hello",
    'they should not be equal': function (topic) {
      assert.notStrictEqual (topic, "there");
    }
  }
}).run();
```

Note the way that Vows encourages you to include a lot of plain English in your tests. This is not only to help you to think about your application from the outside in, but also to help with test reporting and failures. Vows describes these plain English features as follows:

▶ **Description**—A description for your test suite

▶ **Context**— The context that you are running your test in

▶ **Topic**— What you are testing

▶ **Vow**— What you expect to happen in the test

Here is the same test annotated with these terms (see Listing 10.6).

Listing 10.6   Annotated Assertions Using Vows

```
var vows = require('vows'),
    assert = require('assert');

vows.describe('Comparing strings').addBatch({ // Description
  'when comparing the same strings': { // Context
    topic: "hello", // Topic
    'they should be equal': function (topic) { // Vow
      assert.strictEqual (topic, "hello");
    }
  },
  'when comparing different strings': { // Context
    topic: "hello", // Topic
```

```
  'they should not be equal': function (topic) { // Vow
    assert.notStrictEqual (topic, "there");
  }
 }
}).run();
```

If you have installed Vows and these example tests are saved in a file called test.js, you can run these tests with node command from the terminal:

```
node test.js
```

If tests pass, the output lists the number of vows that were honored. This is equivalent to tests passing.

```
·· ✓ OK » 2 honored
```

If a test fails, the report includes the context, vow, and the first line of an exception (see Figure 10.2). This can be useful when debugging.

```
✗·

  when comparing the same strings
    ✗ they should be equal
      » expected 'hello',
  got   'goodbye' (===) // test.js:8
✗ Broken » 1 honored · 1 broken
```

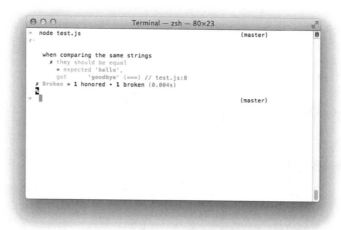

FIGURE 10.2
Running tests with Vows

▼ **TRY IT YOURSELF**

If you have downloaded the code examples for this book, this code is hour10/example05.

Follow these steps to test with Vows:

1. Copy the code in Listing 10.4 into a file on your system called package.json.

2. Copy the code in Listing 10.5 into a file on your system called test.js.

3. Install dependencies by running

   ```
   npm install
   ```

4. Run the test:

   ```
   node test.js
   ```

5. You should see the tests pass:

   ```
   · · ✓ OK » 2 honored
   ```

For testing asynchronous code, the topic in Vows becomes the asynchronous function that tests are to be performed on.

Listing 10.7   Asynchronous Tests with Vows

```
var vows = require('vows'),
    assert = require('assert'),
    fs = require('fs');

vows.describe('Async testing').addBatch({
  'When using fs.stat on a file': {
    topic: function () {
      fs.stat('test.txt', this.callback);
    },
    'it should be present': function (err, stat) {
      assert.strictEqual(err, null);
    },
    'it should not be empty': function (err, stat) {
      assert. notStrictEqual(stat.size, 0);
    }
  },
}).run();
```

The key thing to note here is that the callback is the special `this.callback` function. This is available inside all Vows topics, and this allows the results of the callback to be passed to the test functions.

If you have downloaded the code examples for this book, this code is hour10/example06.

Follow these steps to test asynchronous code with Vows:

1. Copy the code in Listing 10.4 into a file on your system called package.json.

2. Copy the code in Listing 10.7 into a file on your system called test.js.

3. Create a test file to be used in the test called test.txt and add the following contents:

   ```
   This is a test file
   ```

4. Install dependencies by running

   ```
   npm install
   ```

5. Run the test:

   ```
   node test.js
   ```

6. You should see the tests pass:

   ```
   · · ✓ OK » 2 honored
   ```

Mocha

Mocha is another third-party module for testing Node.js applications with a modular approach to testing. You can use a range of assertion libraries including Node's assert and a number of third-party modules. A large range of reporting formats are also supported, and Mocha is designed to give as much choice to developers as possible.

You can install Mocha by adding it to the `devDependencies` section of the package.json file for your project and then installing with `npm install`.

```
"devDependencies": {
  "mocha": "0.10.1"
}
```

To run Mocha tests, you must update the package.json file (see Listing 10.8) and let npm know how to run tests. By default, this runs anything in a `test/` folder. For this example, tests are in a single file called test.js.

Listing 10.8   A package.json File with Mocha

```
{
  "name": "mocha_example",
  "version": "0.0.0",
  "devDependencies": {
    "mocha": "0.10.1"
  },
  "scripts" : {
    "test" : "./node_modules/.bin/mocha test.js"
  }
}
```

When the package.json file has been updated, tests can be run from the terminal with the following command:

```
npm test
```

For the synchronous test example, it looks like this in Mocha (see Listing 10.9).

Listing 10.9   Assertions with Mocha

```
var assert = require('assert');
describe('Comparing strings', function(){
  describe('when comparing the same strings', function(){
    it('should return true', function(){
      assert.strictEqual ("hello", "hello");
    })
  })
  describe('when comparing different strings', function(){
    it('should return false', function(){
      assert.notStrictEqual ("hello", "there");
    })
  })
})
```

Note that just like the Vows module, Mocha encourages you to use plain English to describe your application in a BDD style. In the example, Mocha acts as a simple wrapper to Node's assert module to provide BDD style syntax. When run, Mocha offers a number of reporting formats with dots as the default (see Figure 10.3).

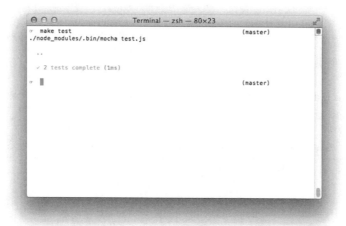

FIGURE 10.3
Running tests with Mocha

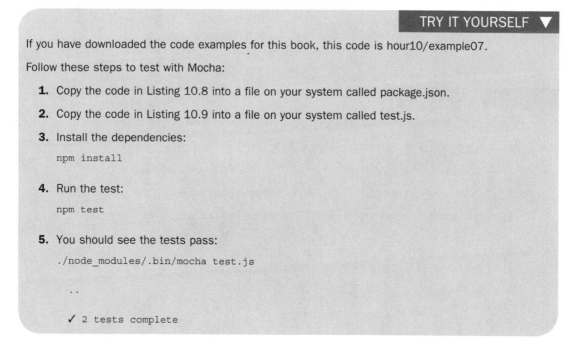

TRY IT YOURSELF ▼

If you have downloaded the code examples for this book, this code is hour10/example07.

Follow these steps to test with Mocha:

1. Copy the code in Listing 10.8 into a file on your system called package.json.

2. Copy the code in Listing 10.9 into a file on your system called test.js.

3. Install the dependencies:

   ```
   npm install
   ```

4. Run the test:

   ```
   npm test
   ```

5. You should see the tests pass:

   ```
   ./node_modules/.bin/mocha test.js

     ..

   ✓ 2 tests complete
   ```

The plain English descriptions are also used in the output from Mocha if a test fails. This can be useful when debugging to quickly see the context that the test failed in.

```
✗ 1 of 2 tests failed:

0) Comparing strings when comparing the same strings should return true:

AssertionError: "hello" === "goodbye"
```

For asynchronous testing, Mocha uses the same approach of using a done() callback as Vows to indicate that a test has completed.

Listing 10.10   Asynchronous Testing with Mocha

```
var assert = require('assert'),
    fs = require('fs');

describe('Async testing', function(){
  describe('When using fs.stat on a file', function(){
    it('should not be empty', function(done){
      fs.stat('test.txt', function (err, stat){
        assert.notEqual(stat.size, 0);
        done();
      });
    })
  })
})
```

▼ TRY IT YOURSELF

If you have downloaded the code examples for this book, this code is hour10/example08.

Follow these steps to test asynchronously with Mocha:

1. Copy the code in Listing 10.8 into a file on your system called package.json.

2. Copy the code in Listing 10.10 into a file on your system called test.js.

3. Create a test file to be used in the test called test.txt and add the following content:

   ```
   This is a test file
   ```

4. Install dependencies by running

   ```
   npm install
   ```

5. Run the test:

   ```
   npm test
   ```

6. You should see the tests pass:

   ```
   ./node_modules/.bin/mocha test.js
   ```

✓ 1 tests complete

Summary

In this hour, you were introduced to testing in Node.js. You saw how to use the assert module to run simple tests against your code. You were then introduced to some third-party testing tools that support both Test Driven Development and Behavior Driven Development. You were introduced to Nodeunit, Vows, and Mocha. For each of these modules, you also learned how to run asynchronous code. You now have a good introduction to test, so there are no excuses!

Q&A

Q. Do I really need to test my code?

A. Yes! Testing has a huge number of benefits. It improves the stability of the code, makes it easier for other developers to become involved in your project, and allows you to confidently refactor and add to your codebase. Do it!

Q. What should I test?

A. You should test code that you write that isn't related to Node's core or third-party modules. As these are generally already covered by their own tests, there is little point in retesting this code. As you develop more, you should constantly be thinking "Do I need to test this?" If there is any doubt in your mind, write a test for it.

Q. Which of the testing modules should I use?

A. There are many testing libraries in the Node.js ecosystem so it can be confusing to know which one to choose. You should certainly gain a good understanding of Node's assert module. It may be that you will feel this can fulfill many of your requirements, and many third-party testing tools rely on it. Beyond that, which library you choose will be down to the one that you like the most and which one matches your coding style.

Q. Can I use these libraries to test client-side code?

A. Yes. Using the browserify module (https://github.com/substack/node-browserify), you can use the assert module in the browser. At the time of writing, Nodeunit and Mocha can both be used in the browser.

Q. I'd like to learn more about testing. Where should I start?

A. Simply writing tests for your application and understand testing libraries is a great place to start. A good book on the topic is *Test-Driven JavaScript Development* by Christian Johansen. Although it is not Node.js specific, it contains relevant information for developing Node.js applications. For more information on that book, visit http://tddjs.com/.

Workshop

This workshop contains quiz questions and exercises to help cement your learning in this hour.

Quiz

1. Why should you use JavaScript's `===` equality operator over `==`?

2. Why have third-party developers created testing modules in addition to the assert module?

3. What are some of the advantages of writing tests for your code?

Quiz Answers

1. JavaScript has two equality operators. The first, `==`, performs type coercion and can lead to unexpected results. The second, `===`, checks that values are the same value and the same type. It is generally recommended to use the triple equals equality operator.

2. The assert module provides a basic testing framework for Node.js. It can be improved in some areas, however, including test reporting, testing asynchronous code, and using a BDD or TDD style.

3. Writing tests allows you to be sure that the code works the way you are expecting. It also allows other developers to understand how code should work and provides a set of repeatable tests that can be run when you change or refactor your code.

Exercises

1. Read through the documentation for Node's assert module at http://nodejs.org/docs/latest/api/assert.html. You can write a lot of good tests with this module! Take some time to understand the difference between JavaScript's comparison methods and how this relates to the assert module.

2. Extend example01 to add some more tests that allow you to use `assert.equal()` and `assert.strictEqual()`. Compare `'0'` and `'false'` and `'false'` and `'null'` to understand how JavaScript treats these.

3. Explore the test folder for Node.js on Github and how the assert module is used to test itself at https://github.com/joyent/node/blob/master/test/simple/test-assert.js. Do not worry if you do not understand all of the tests, but try and understand at least a few.

Deploying Node.js Applications

What You'll Learn in This Hour:

▶ What cloud hosting and Platform as a Service (PaaS) mean

▶ Deploying to Heroku

▶ Deploying to Cloud Foundry

▶ Deploying to Nodester

Ready to Deploy!

Before too long, you will want to deploy your Node.js project so you can share it with the world and become rich and famous! You need to find somewhere to host your Node.js application on the Web. If you have UNIX skills, you may want to take on this task yourself, but more likely you just want to deploy rather than build and maintain a server. In this hour, you see how you can deploy your site to a number of cloud hosting providers for Node.js.

Hosting in the Cloud

You may have heard the term *cloud computing*, which describes the delivery of computing services via the Internet. Some examples of cloud computing include

▶ Hosting files on Amazon S3

▶ Sharing files on multiple computers with Dropbox

▶ Accessing your email on the Internet with services like Gmail

▶ Automatic backups to services like iCloud

The basic idea of cloud computing is that data is not stored on your own hardware but instead on someone else's hardware and that you use the Internet to access data. There are many advantages to cloud computing:

▶ You are not responsible for running and maintaining services.

▶ It is quicker to get up and running with cloud services than to build your own infrastructure.

▶ It is generally cheaper.

▶ You can outsource bits of your infrastructure to providers that you lack skills to provide.

Many developers do not have the skills to build and maintain web servers, so using a cloud provider can offer many advantages:

▶ You are not responsible for building the server.

▶ You are not responsible for the network.

▶ Hosting specialists have created a service for you.

Hosting in the cloud essentially means that you develop the application, point it at a cloud hosting provider, deploy, and forget about it. The term used to describe services that provide deployment and hosting solutions is *Platform as a Service (PaaS)*.

These services take care of the end-to-end process of deploying and hosting your website, often including many other services that result from hosting like backups and databases. There are a lot of players in the Node.js PaaS market, many of whom provide a free hosting service for Node.js applications.

In this hour, you use a simple Express application as the example application to deploy. Of course, you are welcome to deploy your own application if you have one!

▼ TRY IT YOURSELF

If you have downloaded the code examples for this book, this code is hour11/example01.

Here is an example Node.js application:

1. Download the code examples and open the hour11/example01 folder. You should see a simple Express application.

2. Install the dependencies for the application:

```
npm install
```

3. Open a browser at http://127.0.0.1:3000.

4. You should see the example application. This is the application you will deploy in this hour (see Figure 11.1).

FIGURE 11.1
The example Express application you will deploy in this hour

Heroku

Heroku was one of the first Platform as a Service (PaaS) providers to gain popularity among developers. The service is designed around a Git-based workflow, so if you are familiar with Git for version control, then deployment is very simple. The service was originally designed to host Ruby applications, but Heroku has since added support for Node.js, Clojure, Java, Python, and Scala. For the basic service, Heroku is free.

Signing Up for Heroku

To use the Heroku service, you must first sign up for an account. To do this, follow these steps:

1. Visit https://api.heroku.com/signup, where you are asked to enter an email address (see Figure 11.2).

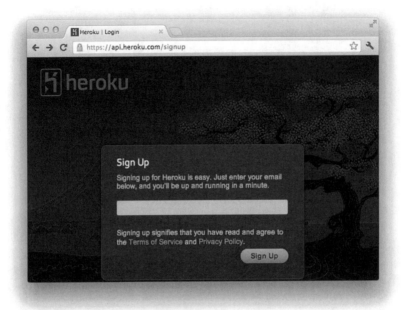

FIGURE 11.2
Signing up for Heroku

2. Once you successfully enter an email address, you are invited to check your email for a confirmation link.

3. Open your email, follow the provided Heroku link, and you are invited to choose a password.

4. Install the Heroku toolbelt by following the instructions at http://devcenter.heroku.com/articles/quickstart#step_2_install_the_heroku_toolbelt. This provides a command-line utility that allows you to deploy sites to Heroku.

5. Once you complete the installation for your platform, the final thing to do is to log in to your account. To complete the process, run `heroku login` from the terminal where you are asked to enter your credentials. Notice that if this is the first time you have logged in, an SSH public key is generated for you. This is how Heroku manages access to the service.

```
heroku login
Enter your Heroku credentials.
Email: george@shapeshed.com
Password:
Could not find an existing public key.
Would you like to generate one? [Yn]
```

```
Generating new SSH public key.
Uploading ssh public key /Users/george/.ssh/id_rsa.pub
```

That's it—you have a Heroku account and are ready to deploy!

BY THE WAY

SSH Keys Are an Alternative to Passwords

SSH keys are commonly used to grant users access to servers. They can be used in certain configurations to allow access to a server without a password. Many PaaS providers make use of public keys.

TRY IT YOURSELF ▼

Follow these steps to sign up for a Heroku account:

1. Sign up for a Heroku account at http://api.heroku.com/signup.

2. Follow the link in your email and choose a password.

3. Install the installer for your platform from http://devcenter.heroku.com/articles/quickstart#step_2_install_the_heroku_toolbelt.

4. Open a terminal window and log in to Heroku.

```
heroku login
```

Preparing Your Application for Heroku

Now that you have an account and your computer is set up for Heroku, you can deploy your application. To enable your example Express application to work, you must make one small change to it, as Heroku randomly assigns the port number that the application will run on.

In the app.js file at the top of the file, add a line to set the port correctly if the site is on Heroku:

```
var port = process.env.PORT || 3000;
```

Then replace the following line

```
app.listen(3000);
```

With the following

```
app.listen(port);
```

This sets the port correctly if the application is running on Heroku but continues to use port 3000 if the application is not on Heroku (or your local machine).

Heroku uses a tool called Foreman to manage processes, and a Procfile declares what should be run. To deploy your app to Heroku, you must also add a file called Procfile in the root of your application that looks like this:

```
web: node app.js
```

▼ TRY IT YOURSELF

If you have downloaded the code examples for this book, this code is hour11/example02.

Here's how to prepare a Node.js application for deployment to Heroku:

1. Make a copy of the Express application provided in the code examples at hour11/example01.

2. At the top of the app.js file, add the following line:
   ```
   var port = (process.env.PORT || 3000);
   ```

3. Remove the following line from app.js:
   ```
   app.listen(3000);
   ```

4. Replace it with the following line:
   ```
   app.listen(port);
   ```

5. In the root of the application, add a file called Procfile and add the following content:
   ```
   web: node app.js
   ```

6. Install the dependencies with the following:
   ```
   npm install
   ```

7. Start the application to check that it runs OK:
   ```
   node app.js
   ```

Deploying Your Application to Heroku

You are now ready to deploy your application! If you are using your own application rather than the example Express application supplied, note that you need to use a package.json file to declare your dependencies as Heroku uses this too.

To use Heroku, you must use Git, a version control tool. Git was installed by the Heroku installer, so if you installed that, you already have it on your system! Many developers in the Node.js community use Git for managing source code.

Heroku recommends that you do not add your node_modules folder to Git, so this can be achieved by creating a .gitignore file with the following contents:

```
node_modules
```

Now you can create a git repository and add your source code by running the following commands from the root of your application.

```
git init
git add .
git commit -m 'initial commit'
```

Next, the application is created on Heroku. The cedar stack is declared as this is the one that supports Node.js.

```
heroku create --stack cedar
```

This creates the site for you and automatically sets up everything you need to deploy. You will see some output like this:

```
Creating afternoon-light-5818... done, stack is cedar
http://afternoon-light-5818.herokuapp.com/ | git@heroku.com:afternoon-light-5818.
git
Git remote heroku added
```

Finally, you can deploy your application with the following command:

```
git push heroku master
```

After that, you should be able to visit the URL that was generated in the Heroku create step and see your site!

TRY IT YOURSELF ▼

To deploy a Node.js application to Heroku, follow these steps:

1. Return to your example Express application.

2. Create a Git repository with the following commands:

   ```
   git init
   git add .
   git commit -m 'initial commit'
   ```

3. Create the application on Heroku with the following command. Note the URL that was returned from this command:

   ```
   heroku create --stack cedar
   ```

4. Publish the site to Heroku with the following command:

```
git push heroku master
```

5. Visit the URL that you noted earlier. You should see your site deployed!

If you need to update your site in the future, commit the new files to Git and then push to Heroku:

```
git push heroku master
```

Cloud Foundry

Cloud Foundry is another PaaS provider for Node.js. One major difference between Cloud Foundry and other services is that it does not rely on Git, so if you are not keen on using Git as part of your deployment process, this may be a good choice for you.

Signing Up for Cloud Foundry

To register for the service, visit https://my.cloudfoundry.com/signup and enter your details (see Figure 11.3). You then receive a confirmation link that invites you to select a password.

FIGURE 11.3
Signing up for Cloud Foundry

Cloud Foundry requires that you have vmc, a command-line tool for interacting with the service, installed on your system. This requires Ruby and RubyGems to be installed on your system. For many, this may be a turn-off from using this service, but Cloud Foundry does provide comprehensive documentation on getting everything installed at http://start.cloudfoundry.com/tools/vmc/installing-vmc.html.

DID YOU KNOW?

Cloud Foundry Is Open Source

The Cloud Foundry platform is Open Source and can be used to create your own private cloud. This means you could run an instance of the Cloud Foundry software on your own servers if you wanted to! By using Cloud Foundry's own servers, though, you don't have to run your own server.

TRY IT YOURSELF ▼

To create a Cloud Foundry account, follow these steps:

1. Sign up for a Cloud Foundry account at https://my.cloudfoundry.com/signup.

2. Follow the link in your email and add a password.

3. Install vmc and related software following the instructions at http://start.cloudfoundry.com/tools/vmc/installing-vmc.html.

Preparing Your Application for Cloud Foundry

To prepare your application for Cloud Foundry, you need to make some amends to the app.js file. If you completed the Heroku example, you should work on a fresh copy of the example application that you can find in the code examples at hour11/example01.

Like Heroku, Cloud Foundry assigns the port number dynamically, so the app.js file needs to be updated to reflect that. At the top of the app.js file, the following is added:

```
var port = (process.env.VMC_APP_PORT || 3000);
```

Next, the line that reads

```
app.listen(3000);
```

Is amended to read

```
app.listen(port);
```

▼ TRY IT YOURSELF

If you have downloaded the code examples for this book, this code is hour11/example03.

Here's how to prepare a Node.js application for deployment to Cloud Foundry:

1. Make a copy of the Express application provided in the code examples at hour11/example01.

2. At the top of the app.js file, add the following line:

```
var port = (process.env.VMC_APP_PORT || 3000);
```

3. Remove the following line from app.js:

```
app.listen(3000);
```

4. Replace it with the following line:

```
app.listen(port);
```

5. Install the dependencies with the following:

```
npm install
```

6. Start the application to check that it runs OK:

```
node app.js
```

Deploying Your Application to Cloud Foundry

To deploy the application, the vmc tool is used. This is a command-line tool for deploying sites to Cloud Foundry. First, the target is set to the Cloud Foundry servers:

```
vmc target api.cloudfoundry.com
```

Next, you must add your login credentials:

```
vmc login
```

This prompts you for a username and password and lets you know if it has been successful:

```
Attempting login to [http://api.cloudfoundry.com]
Email: george@shapeshed.com
Password: ********
Successfully logged into [http://api.cloudfoundry.com]
```

Cloud Foundry does not support installing node modules via npm, so you must ensure that these are installed before you publish your site. If you haven't already done so, run the following:

```
npm install
```

There is currently a bug in vmc, so after running `npm install`, you must also run the following:

```
rm -r node_modules/.bin/
```

To deploy the site from the root directory for your project, run the following:

```
vmc push
```

This prompts you for a number of questions and then informs you if the app was successfully deployed:

```
Would you like to deploy from the current directory? [Yn]: y
Application Name: yourappname
Application Deployed URL [yourappname.cloudfoundry.com]:
Detected a Node.js Application, is this correct? [Yn]: Y
Memory Reservation (64M, 128M, 256M, 512M, 1G) [64M]:
```

You can then access your application at http://*yourappname*.cloudfoundry.com, where *yourappname* is whatever you chose to call your application.

If you need to update your application in the future, you may do so by changing the directory to the folder that contains your source code and running

```
vmc update yourappname
```

TRY IT YOURSELF ▼

Here's how to deploy a Node.js Application to Cloud Foundry:

1. Return to your example Express application.

2. Set the target for vmc to the Cloud Foundry servers:

   ```
   vmc target api.cloudfoundry.com
   ```

3. Enter your login credentials:

   ```
   vmc login
   ```

4. Ensure that all dependencies are installed from npm:

   ```
   npm install
   ```

5. Apply the fix for the bug in vmc:

   ```
   rm -r node_modules/.bin/
   ```

6. Deploy the site:

   ```
   vmc push
   ```

7. Visit the URL shown in the output. You should see your site deployed!

Nodester

Nodester is another Platform as a Service provider for Node.js. It is also open source software. The service is currently completely free! Nodester claims that you can deploy a Node.js application in 1 minute!

Signing Up for Nodester

To use the Nodester service, you must first sign up for an account. To do this, follow these steps:

1. Request a Registration Coupon by visiting http://nodester.com/ and entering your email address (see Figure 11.4). Registration coupons are sent out periodically by the maintainers of Nodester, so you may have to wait a few days to receive your coupon.

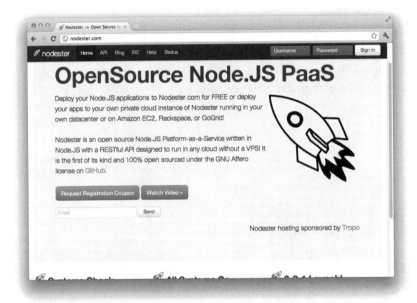

FIGURE 11.4
Requesting a token from Nodester

2. Once you have received your coupon, you can create an account. First, you need to install the nodester command-line tool from npm:

```
npm install nodester-cli -g
```

3. Nodester makes use of cURL to send requests in. For many developers, this may be too technical, but if you are familiar with cURL, you can create your account with the following cURL request:

```
curl -X POST -d
"coupon=yourcoupon&user=youruser&password=123&email=your@email.com&rsakey=ssh-
➥ rsa
AAAA..." http://nodester.com/user
```

4. If you don't have cURL installed on your system or you don't want to use cURL, you can also enter this information via a form at http://nodester.com/help.html. One piece of information that you need to enter is your RSA key. If you are on a UNIX-type (OSX or Linux) system, you can generate this with the following command:

```
ssh-keygen -t rsa -C "your@email.com"
```

5. If you are on Windows, you can install Git for Windows from the installer here: http://code.google.com/p/msysgit/downloads/list. A full walkthrough on installing this software is available at http://help.github.com/win-set-up-git/. Once you have this installed, you can run

```
ssh-keygen -t rsa -C "your@email.com"
```

6. Once you have generated your RSA key using either method, it will output where the file has been saved. To use Nodester, you need to open the file id_rsa.pub and copy the contents. You can either add the contents to the cURL command noted in step 3 or paste it into the form at http://nodester.com/help.html.

7. Once you have an account, you can set up your local machine for deploying applications to Nodester. Note here that *<username>* and *<password>* should be replaced with your own credentials.

```
nodester user <username> <password>
nodester info verifying credentials
nodester info user verified..
nodester info writing user data to config
```

TRY IT YOURSELF ▼

To sign up for a Nodester account, follow these steps:

1. Request a Nodester coupon from http://nodester.com.

2. Once you receive the coupon, generate an RSA key if you need to:

```
ssh-keygen -t rsa -C "your@email.com"
```

3. Complete the registration process either with a cURL request or by completing the form at http://nodester.com/help.html:

```
curl -X POST -d "coupon=yourcoupon&user=youruser&password=123&email=your@
➥ email.com&rsakey=ssh-rsa AAAA..." http://nodester.com/user
```

4. Ensure you have installed the Nodester CLI on your local machine:

```
npm install nodester-cli -g
```

5. Set up your local machine for Nodester:

```
nodester user <username> <password>
```

Preparing Your Application for Nodester

To create a new application on Nodester, run the following command:

```
nodester app create yourapp app.js
```

In this command, the name of the application is set to be yourapp, and the main Node.js file is declared as app.js. Next, the application is set up for deployment on Nodester:

```
nodester app init yourapp
```

This creates a remote Git repository on Nodester and sets up your local machine. It also starts a Hello World application, so if you visit http://yourapp.nodester.com, you will see something! You should also see that a new folder of "yourapp" (or whatever you called it) has been added to your file system. If you look inside this folder, you see a single file of app.js with the Hello World application. To publish your example Express site, simply copy the code into this folder. If you have completed either the Heroku or Cloud Foundry examples, make sure you use a copy of the code from the code examples that can be found in hour11/example01.

As with Heroku and Cloud Foundry, the port number that your site runs on is assigned dynamically, so the app.js file must be updated to reflect this. At the top of the file, the following line needs to be added:

```
var port = process.env.app_port || 3000;
```

Delete the line that reads as follows:

```
app.listen(3000);
```

Replace this line with

```
app.listen(port);
```

Deploying Your Application to Nodester

To install the dependencies on Nodester from the "yourapp" folder, run the following:

```
nodester npm install
```

This command reads your package.json file and installs any packages.

Finally, you can add the files to Git and push to publish your site!

```
git add .
git commit -m 'adding site files'
git push origin master
```

If you open a browser at http://yourapp.nodester.com, where "yourapp" is the name of your application, you should see your site!

TRY IT YOURSELF

If you have downloaded the code examples for this book, this code is hour11/example04.

To deploy a Node.js application to Nodester, follow these steps:

1. Create a new Nodester application. Replace *yourapp* with a name for your application:

```
nodester app create yourapp app.js
```

2. Initialize the Nodester application. Replace *yourapp* with whatever you chose to call the application in step 1:

```
nodester app init yourapp
```

3. Copy the files from the code examples at hour11/example01 into the folder created during step 2. The folder will be called whatever you chose to replace *yourapp* with.

4. At the top of the app.js file, add the following line:

```
var port = process.env.app_port || 3000;
```

5. Remove the following line from app.js:

```
app.listen(3000);
```

6. Replace it with the following line:

```
app.listen(port);
```

7. Install the dependencies with the following:

```
nodester npm install
```

8. Add the files to the git repository:

```
git add .
git commit -m 'adding site files'
```

9. Push the files to publish the site:

```
git push origin master
```

10. Visit the URL shown in the output. You should see your site deployed!

Other PaaS Providers

The marketplace for Node.js hosting is growing fast, and there are other service providers that you might want to use:

- ▶ **Nodejitsu**—http://nodejitsu.com/
- ▶ **Cure**—http://cure.willsave.me/
- ▶ **Joyent**—http://node.de
- ▶ **Windows Azure**—https://www.windowsazure.com

A full list of Node.js hosting providers is maintained at https://github.com/joyent/node/wiki/Node-Hosting.

Summary

This hour explored the idea of hosting your Node.js application in the cloud. You were introduced to Heroku, Cloud Foundry, and Nodester, all of which are Node.js PaaS providers. You then walked through how to deploy to each of these platforms and saw that some follow a Git workflow for deployment, whereas Cloud Foundry does not. You saw that with each provider, small changes need to be made to your main application (in the example, it is app.js) for your application to run on these services. Finally, you learned that there are many PaaS providers for Node.js!

Q&A

Q. **Which PaaS provider should I use?**

A. The PaaS provider that you choose depends on what your application does and how many users you estimate will be using it. Nodester is great for quickly prototyping and sharing applications with users and other developers. It does not currently cost you anything to use Nodester, but in my experience, the uptime on Nodester cannot be guaranteed. Heroku is another free service that allocates a certain amount of RAM (Random Access Memory) to your Node.js process. If your application becomes very popular, you may find that you need to add more processes, at which point you will need to pay. Both Heroku and Nodester rely on Git, and while it is encouraged that you version your source code in Git, you may not be doing this. If you do not want to use Git, then Cloud Foundry may be a good choice for you.

Q. **What about databases?**

A. In the example Express application that you deployed, there was no data store. Most Platform as a Service providers provide access to databases one way or another. Heroku supports PostgreSQL and a large number of other data stores through third-party add-ons. Cloud Foundry supports MongoDB, MySQL, PostgreSQL, RabbitMQ, and Redis. Nodester does not provide a data store, but you can also use many of the third-party services available through Heroku.

Q. **What about WebSockets?**

A. Support for WebSockets varies between providers. At the time of writing, Heroku and CloudFoundry do not support WebSockets, but Nodester does. For the latest situation, consult https://github.com/joyent/node/wiki/Node-Hosting.

Q. **Can I host Node.js sites on my own server?**

A. If you have UNIX or Windows Administration skills, you can provision a VPS (Virtual Private Server), install Node.js, and begin hosting Node.js sites. This is not covered in this hour, but the following URL is a good place to get started: http://howtonode.org/deploying-node-upstart-monit.

Workshop

This workshop contains quiz questions and exercises to help cement your learning in this hour.

Quiz

1. What does PaaS stand for?
2. Which PaaS providers discussed in this hour are open source?
3. When should you use your own hosting over PaaS?

Quiz Answers

1. PaaS stands for Platform as a Service, meaning an entire hosting platform is provided for developers with no requirement for developers to become involved with systems administration.

2. Cloud Foundry and Nodester are both open source projects, so if you want to change the way they work, you can fork the code. Also if you find bugs or issues, you are encouraged to file an issue on the GitHub projects (https://github.com/nodester and https://github.com/cloudfoundry).

3. Although many large production sites run on top of PaaS providers, you may want to have your hosting environment exactly the way you want it. If you want full control, you can create your own server, but the tradeoff is that you need to invest some time in building and maintaining the server and possess the relevant skills.

Exercises

1. For each of the PaaS providers in this hour, make a small change to your Node.js application and publish the change.

2. Do some research on the Internet into Node.js hosting providers. Try to understand the publishing process for each and note the costs for using the service.

3. If you have a Node.js application that you have written, however small it is, choose a Node.js PaaS provider and publish your site.

PART IV

Intermediate Sites with Node.js

Introducing Socket.IO

What You'll Learn in This Hour:

▶ What Socket.IO is and how you can use it

▶ Connect clients to a Socket.IO-enabled Node.js server

▶ Send data from the server to clients

▶ Create real-time applications

Now for Something Completely Different

Up to this point, you have learned the fundamentals of how to create basic applications with Node.js. Socket.IO is a module for Node.js that exposes some of the things that make Node.js different from other frameworks and languages. In this hour, you see how Node.js, Socket.IO, and WebSockets can create real-time web applications—a hugely exciting possibility for web development!

Brief History of the Dynamic Web

Historically, the Web was not designed to be dynamic. It was designed around documents and being able to read a single document at a time. The cycle of a user requesting a web page from a browser, getting a response, and the browser displaying the page is the basis for the design of many technologies that power the Web. Over time, developers wanted to do more than display just documents, and JavaScript has always been at the center of developers pushing what a web page can do.

During the late 1990s and early 2000s, the term DHMTL (Dynamic Hypertext Markup Language) came into being. This described the ability to change parts of a page using JavaScript, HTML, and CSS to make a web page more interactive, or dynamic. This introduced things like tickers, showing and hiding parts of a page, and simple animations. DHTML was primarily a behavioral term; it covered how a user interacted with a web page and what happened when that interaction happened. The Web Standards community later adopted the term DOM

(Document Object Model) Scripting to describe manipulating web pages in a responsible way that degraded gracefully if certain things were not available in a browser.

The next big development for dynamic web pages was Ajax (Asynchronous JavaScript and XML) that, like DHTML, describes a range of technologies including JavaScript, XML, HTML, and CSS. Ajax enabled developers to request data from a server without refreshing a web page. This meant that new data could be requested from a server on certain events like a user clicking a button. As the entire web page does not need to be refreshed, it leads to a much more interactive, dynamic experience.

Perhaps the most well-known application to be created using real-time technologies was Gmail, Google's web-based email service. This refreshed entire parts of the page when a user was reading email, replacing it with new data without reloading the page using a technology known as Comet. This was the first application to support real-time streaming in multiple browsers and really challenged what was technically possible in browsers. Today, Ajax and related technologies continue to be used heavily across the Web to pull data dynamically into web pages and add dynamic functionality. Examples include

▶ Embeddable widgets that show data from other websites and services

▶ Web-based chat clients (like Campfire)

▶ Validating data with a server without a page refresh

▶ Simple games between players on the Web

No doubt Ajax will continue to be extremely useful in creating dynamic web pages in the future, but in some areas, it is greatly lacking. Ajax works well for requesting data from a server, but what if the server wants to push data out to browsers? Ajax technologies do not easily support pushing data to clients, although some techniques like Comet have made this possible. Two-way data flow is possible using Ajax technologies, but you need to jump through a lot of hoops, and it works differently depending on which browser is being used.

WebSockets are a response to the problem of enabling two-way real-time communication between servers and clients. Instead of trying to make existing technologies do this job through complex setups that do not always work in all browsers, the idea was to go back to basics and design a standard that developers could use to create applications in a consistent manner. The basic idea of WebSockets is to keep a persistent connection open between a web server and a browser. This allows either the server or the browser to push data whenever they want to. Because the connection is persistent, the exchange of data is very fast leading to the term real-time. WebSockets do not support features like reconnection handling or heartbeats, but libraries like Socket.IO are able to provide these as well as abstract some cross-browser issues.

Initially, this is a lot to take in, but during this hour, you see examples of Socket.IO and WebSockets in action that make this clear.

Socket.IO

Socket.IO is a module for Node.js that provides an easy way of communicating via WebSockets. The WebSocket protocol is complicated and to write an application from scratch that supports WebSockets would take a long time. Socket.IO provides both server and client components, so you just need one module to add WebSockets support to your application. Socket.IO also solves issues of browser support (not all browsers support WebSockets) and enables real-time communication across almost all commonly used browsers. Socket.IO has been designed extremely well and makes the process of bringing real-time communication to your application very simple. If you want to do anything involving real-time communication between a web server and a browser, Node.js and Socket.IO are a perfect fit!

Basic Socket.IO Example

Socket.IO works on both the server and the client. To use it, you must add it to your server-side JavaScript (Node.js) and your client-side JavaScript (jQuery, etc.). This is because communication can be both ways, so Socket.IO needs to work on both sides. In the following example, you learn about building the server side first. In Listing 12.1, Node.js is used to serve a single HTML file.

Listing 12.1   Serving a File with Node.js

```
var http = require('http');
var fs = require('fs');

var server = http.createServer(function (req, res) {
    fs.readFile('./index.html', function(error, data) {
      res.writeHead(200, { 'Content-Type': 'text/html' });
      res.end(data, 'utf-8');
    });
  }).listen(3000, "127.0.0.1");
console.log('Server running at http://127.0.0.1:3000/');
```

The server should be familiar to you from the Hello World example you saw in previous hours. The difference here is that Node.js's File System module is used to read the HTML file before sending it. To add Socket.IO functionality to this server, the Socket.IO library must be included and then attached to the server.

```
var io = require('socket.io').listen(server);
```

This binds Socket.IO to the server, effectively making real-time communication available to any client connecting to the server. Now that the server is Socket.IO enabled, some code is needed to allow Socket.IO to respond to certain events and messages from clients. Socket.IO listens for many events including clients connecting and disconnecting. In this example, a message is logged to the terminal whenever a client connects or disconnects. A connection would be whenever a Socket.IO-enabled page is loaded in a browser. A disconnection would be the same browser page being closed. In Listing 12.2, the server logs these events to the console.

Listing 12.2   Adding Socket.IO Functionality to a Server

```
io.sockets.on('connection', function (socket) {
  console.log('User connected');
  socket.on('disconnect', function () {
    console.log('User disconnected');
  });
});
```

The Socket.IO server is now complete and ready to receive connections from the client side. For clients (or browsers) to be able to connect to the server, they must use the client-side JavaScript library that ships with Socket.IO and then connect to the server. The server is serving a single index.html file, and this needs to be connected to the server. This can be achieved by adding the following lines to index.html:

```
<script src="/socket.io/socket.io.js"></script>
<script>
  var socket = io.connect('http://127.0.0.1:3000');
</script>
```

This includes a single JavaScript file that allows the client (or browser) to communicate with the server. Note this can be any server, but in this case, it is connected to the Node.js server running at 127.0.0.1 on port 3000.

DID YOU KNOW?

Socket.IO Serves the Client-Side Library Automatically

You may have noticed that in the client-side code, there is a JavaScript file socket.io.js. If you are running your server and client on the same server, the Socket.IO library will serve this automatically for you. This contains all the necessary code for the browser to connect to the server and send and receive messages.

▼ TRY IT YOURSELF

If you have downloaded the code examples for this book, this code is hour12/example01.

Follow these steps to connect a Socket.IO server and client:

1. Create a new folder called socket.io.

2. Within the socket.io folder, create a new file called package.json and add the following content to declare Socket.IO as a dependency:

```
{
  "name":"socketio_example",
  "version":"0.0.1",
  "private":true,
  "dependencies":{
    "socket.io":"0.8.7"
  }
}
```

3. Within the socket.io folder, create a new file called app.js with the following content:

```
var http = require('http');
var fs = require('fs');

var server = http.createServer(function (req, res) {
    fs.readFile('./index.html', function(error, data) {
      res.writeHead(200, { 'Content-Type': 'text/html' });
      res.end(data, 'utf-8');
    });
  }).listen(3000, "127.0.0.1");
console.log('Server running at http://127.0.0.1:3000/');

var io = require('socket.io').listen(server);

io.sockets.on('connection', function (socket) {
  console.log('User connected');
  socket.on('disconnect', function () {
    console.log('User disconnected');
  });
});
```

4. Within the socket.io folder, create a new file called index.html with the following content:

```
<!DOCTYPE html>
<html>
  <head>
    <title>Socket.IO Example</title>
  </head>
  <body>
    <h1>Socket.IO Example</h1>
    <script src="/socket.io/socket.io.js"></script>
    <script>
      var socket = io.connect('http://127.0.0.1:3000');
    </script>
  </body>
</html>
```

5. Install the dependencies by running the following from a terminal:

```
npm install
```

6. Start the server by running the following from a terminal:

```
node app.js
```

7. Open a browser at http://127.0.0.1:3000.

8. You should see a page showing "Socket.IO Example."

9. Examine the server logs in the terminal and you should see "User connected."

10. Open another browser tab at http://127.0.0.1:3000.

11. You should see another "User connected" message in the server logs.

12. Close the browser tab you have been using to browse http://127.0.0.1:3000.

13. You should see "User disconnected" in the server logs.

This example demonstrates how Socket.IO can listen for certain events when clients do things like connecting and disconnecting. You take this further in the next example, where this data sent back to the clients.

Sending Data from the Server to Clients

In the first example, you used Socket.IO to log when new clients connect and disconnect from a simple Socket.IO server. But, what about sending data to the browsers that have connected? To send data to a single client from the server side looks like this:

```
io.sockets.on('connection', function (socket) {
  socket.emit('message', { text: 'You have connected!' });
});
```

Note that in this example, Socket.IO is sending a JavaScript object, so if your requirements were more complex, you can use a more sophisticated data structure.

This code needs to be added to the server side of the application. This sends data out to each new client whenever a client connects. If instead you want to send a message to every client currently connected to the server, you can also send a broadcast message. To broadcast some data to all connected clients looks like this:

```
io.sockets.on('connection', function (socket) {
  socket.broadcast.emit('message', { text: 'A new user has connected' });
});
```

This is similar, but instead sends the message to all connected clients other than the one that has just connected. Notice that the message is once again sent as a JavaScript object under the `'message'` event. The term `'message'` can be anything, but it is important as you will need to set up the client side to listen for a `'message'` event when data is received. You do not have to send data as a JavaScript object; you can also just send text if you want, but using a JavaScript object makes it easier to use the data on the client side.

On the client side (or browser), the following JavaScript is included to first connect to the Socket.IO server and then to listen for data being received on the `'message'` event.

```
var socket = io.connect('http://127.0.0.1:3000');
socket.on('message', function (data) {
  alert(data.text);
});
```

Using these features and some client-side JavaScript, it is possible to create a real-time counter for the number of connected clients on a Socket.IO-enabled server. The idea is that when the server is started, a counter starts at zero. When a client connects to the server, it increases by one. When a client disconnects, it decreases by one. Socket.IO's messaging can be used to update all clients with the number of clients on the server in real-time as clients connect and disconnect. Think of it as real-time analytics of the visitors to your site!

To achieve this, a simple JavaScript variable can be used to hold the number of users on the server. When the server boots, the number of users will be zero:

```
var counter = 0;
```

This can then be used in conjunction with Socket.IO's events to increase and decrease the counter when clients join and leave, using JavaScript increment and decrement functions:

```
counter++; // This increases the count by one.
counter--; // This decreases the count by one.
```

Now that the server has a count of the number of clients on the server, the clients themselves can be updated using Socket.IO to send the data to all clients using `socket.emit.broadcast`. In this example, this data is sent under the `'users'` event, since it relates to the number of users.

```
socket.broadcast.emit('users', { number: count });
```

This works well when a client disconnects, but when a new client connects, they would not receive an update, because `socket.emit.broadcast` does not go to the connecting client. To resolve this, an additional `socket.emit` message is sent as the same `'users'` event to the connecting client:

```
socket.emit('users', { number: count });
```

The Socket.IO part of the Node.js server now looks like Listing 12.3.

Listing 12.3 A Real-Time Counter with Socket.IO

```
var io = require('socket.io').listen(server);
io.sockets.on('connection', function (socket) {
  count++;
  socket.emit('users', { number: count });
  socket.broadcast.emit('users', { number: count });
  socket.on('disconnect', function () {
    count--;
    socket.broadcast.emit('users', { number: count });
  });
});
```

The server sends the number of connected users to clients! But how do we show this to the users? Some client-side JavaScript needs to be added to listen for the `'users'` event to receive and display the data. This can be achieved with a small amount of Socket.IO code and some JavaScript to update the DOM.

Listing 12.4 Handling Events on the Client

```
<script src="/socket.io/socket.io.js"></script>
<script>
var socket = io.connect('http://127.0.0.1:3000');
var count = document.getElementById('count');
socket.on('users', function (data) {
  count.innerHTML = data.number
});
</script>
```

When a `'users'` event is received, the number received is used to update a paragraph with an id of count within the HTML page. Conveniently, the syntax for receiving and sending message on the client side and server side is the same.

To make the number appear correctly, a paragraph tag with an id of count must be added to the HTML.

```
<p id="count"></p>
```

The server is now set up to receive connection and disconnection events from clients and to increment and decrement a counter. It is also able to broadcast this information to all connected clients in real-time. With a little client-side JavaScript, connected clients can use this data to update the views for users so they can see the number of connected users. So, it is time to fire up a browser and see data flowing back and forth!

If you have downloaded the code examples for this book, this code is hour12/example02.

The following steps demonstrate a real-time Socket.IO counter:

1. Create a new folder called realtime_counter.

2. Within the realtime_counter folder, create a new file called package.json and add the following content to declare Socket.IO as a dependency:

```
{
    "name":"socketio_example",
    "version":"0.0.1",
    "private":true,
    "dependencies":{
        "socket.io":"0.8.7"
    }
}
```

3. Within the realtime_counter folder, create a new file called app.js with the following content:

```
var http = require('http');
var fs = require('fs');
var count = 0;

var server = http.createServer(function (req, res) {
    fs.readFile('./index.html', function(error, data) {
        res.writeHead(200, { 'Content-Type': 'text/html' });
        res.end(data, 'utf-8');
    });
}).listen(3000, "127.0.0.1");
console.log('Server running at http://127.0.0.1:3000/');

var io = require('socket.io').listen(server);

io.sockets.on('connection', function (socket) {
    count++;
    console.log('User connected. ' + count + ' user(s) present.');
    socket.emit('users', { number: count });
    socket.broadcast.emit('users', { number: count });
    socket.on('disconnect', function () {
        count--;
        console.log('User disconnected. ' + count + ' user(s) present.');
        socket.broadcast.emit('users', { number: count });
    });
});
```

4. Within the socket.io folder, create a new file called index.html with the following content:

```
<!DOCTYPE html>
<html lang="en">
  <head>
    <meta charset="utf-8" />
    <title>Socket.IO Example</title>
  </head>
  <body>
    <h1>Socket.IO Example</h1>
    <h2>How many users are here?</h2>
    <p id="count"></p>
    <script src="/socket.io/socket.io.js"></script>
    <script>
      var socket = io.connect('http://127.0.0.1:3000');
      var count = document.getElementById('count');
      socket.on('users', function (data) {
        console.log('Got udpate from the server');
        console.log('There are ' + data.number + ' users');
        count.innerHTML = data.number
      });
    </script>

  </body>
</html>
```

5. Install the dependencies by running the following from a terminal:

```
npm install
```

6. Start the server by running the following from a terminal:

```
node app.js
```

7. Open a browser at http://127.0.0.1:3000.

8. You should see a page showing "Socket.IO Example" and that one user is on the server.

9. Open another browser tab at http://127.0.0.1:3000.

10. You should see that two users are now on the server. Switch to the other tab, and you should see that this has also been updated to two users (see Figure 12.1).

11. Close one of the browser tabs you have open. You should see the number of users on the server drop to 1.

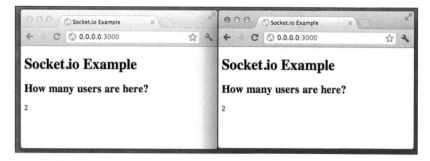

FIGURE 12.1
A real-time counter with Socket.IO

Broadcasting Data to Clients

The real-time counter shows how data on the number of clients can be pushed out to clients in real-time. But what if you want to enable communicating between clients? You might have a scenario where you want to add chat functionality or perhaps a game where you need to send messages across clients.

To allow clients to communicate with each other, you need to first send a message from a client to the server and then push that message out to clients from the server. The process is as follows:

1. Clients connect to Socket.IO Node.js server.

2. A single client sends a message to the server.

3. The server receives the message.

4. The server broadcasts the message to all other clients.

You have already seen in the last example that you can broadcast messages to clients from a Socket.IO server:

```
socket.broadcast.emit('message', { text: "This goes to everyone!" });
```

You also saw that you can send messages from a server to single clients:

```
socket.emit('message', { text: "This goes to a single client });
```

The code for sending messages from clients to the server is exactly the same! The difference from the real-time counter example is that the message initiates from the client side and from client-side JavaScript. So, on the client side (or browser), there must be a way for users to add a message and submit it to the server. One way this can be achieved is to create a form and then use some JavaScript to capture whatever a user puts into the form and send it to the server. In this example, jQuery is used, but if you prefer to write this in vanilla JavaScript, you could do so. The form to capture a message is a standard HTML form:

```
<form id="message-form" action="#">
  <textarea id="message" rows="4" cols="30"></textarea>
  <input type="submit" value="Send message" />
</form>
```

This is used by some client-side JavaScript to capture the contents of the form and send it to the server:

```
<script src="https://ajax.googleapis.com/ajax/libs/jquery/1.7.1/jquery.min.js"></
➥script>
<script src="/socket.io/socket.io.js"></script>
<script>
  var socket = io.connect('http://127.0.0.1:3000');
  var message = document.getElementById('message');
  $(message.form).submit(function() {
    socket.emit('message', { text: message.value });
    return false;
  });
  socket.on('broadcast', function (data) {
    $('form').after('<p>' + data.text + '</p>');
  });
</script>
```

What's happening in this JavaScript?

▶ The jQuery library is included followed by the Socket.IO library.

▶ The browser is instructed to connect to the Socket.IO server at http://127.0.0.1:3000.

▶ Using jQuery's submit() method a listener is added for whenever a user submits the form.

▶ A message is sent to the Socket.IO server, and the contents of the text area is sent as the message.

▶ A return false statement is added so that the form is not submitted in the browser window.

In the real-time counter example, some code was added to receive the message on the client side. In this example, you must set up some code to receive the message on the server. The functionality we want to achieve is

▶ The message is received from the client.

▶ The message is immediately broadcast to all other clients, but not the one that has sent it.

You may already know that you can use `socket.broadcast.emit` for this. This broadcasts a message to all clients other than the one that sent it. You can achieve this with just a short piece of code on the server side:

```
io.sockets.on('connection', function (socket) {
  socket.on('message', function (data) {
  socket.broadcast.emit('push message', data);
  });
});
```

Now whenever the server receives a message, it pushes it to all clients other than the one that sent it in real-time! You will see that this is sent under the broadcast event. The name `'push message'` can be anything, but it will be used on the client side to listen for new messages of this type. The example is almost complete, but currently there is no way for the client to display a message that has been pushed from the server. To receive the messages, we need to create some client-side JavaScript that

▶ Listens for the `'push message'` event

▶ Captures the data received

▶ Writes it to the DOM or page so the user can read it

Adding the following code to the client side completes the example:

```
socket.on('push message', function (data) {
  $('form').after('<p>' + data.text + '</p>');
});
```

With a small amount of code, when a broadcast event is received, the data is passed into an anonymous function that uses jQuery's `after()` method. This inserts data into the DOM at the point after the element given. In this case, the data is inserted after the form and is included between two paragraph tags. We now have a complete cycle for a message going through a simple messaging server:

1. A client connects to the Socket.IO-enabled Node.js server.

2. The client submits a message and clicks Submit.

3. The message is sent to the server.

4. The server broadcasts the message to all other clients.

5. The clients update the web page with the contents of the message.

▼ TRY IT YOURSELF

If you have downloaded the code examples for this book, this code is hour12/example03.

The following steps show how Socket.IO can be used to send messages between clients:

1. Create a new folder called simple_messaging.

2. Within the simple_messaging folder, create a new file called package.json and add the following content to declare Socket.IO as a dependency:

```
{
  "name":"socketio_example",
  "version":"0.0.1",
  "private":true,
  "dependencies":{
    "socket.io":"0.8.7"
  }
}
```

3. Within the simple_messaging folder, create a new file called app.js with the following content:

```
var http = require('http');
var fs = require('fs');

var server = http.createServer(function (req, res) {
 fs.readFile('./index.html', function(error, data) {
    res.writeHead(200, { 'Content-Type': 'text/html' });
    res.end(data, 'utf-8');
  });
}).listen(3000, "127.0.0.1");
console.log('Server running at http://127.0.0.1:3000/');

var io = require('socket.io').listen(server);

io.sockets.on('connection', function (socket) {
  socket.on('message', function (data) {
    socket.broadcast.emit('push message', data);
  });
});
```

4. Within the simple_messaging folder, create a new file called index.html with the following content: ·

```
<html lang="en">
  <head>
    <meta charset="utf-8" />
    <title>Socket.IO Example</title>
  </head>
```

```
  <body>
    <h1>Socket.IO Example</h1>
    <form id="message-form" action="#">
      <textarea id="message" rows="4" cols="30"></textarea>
      <input type="submit" value="Send message" />
    </form>
    <script src="https://ajax.googleapis.com/ajax/libs/jquery/1.7.1/jquery.
➥ min.js"></script>
    <script src="/socket.io/socket.io.js"></script>
    <script>
      var socket = io.connect('http://127.0.0.1:3000');
      var message = document.getElementById('message');
      $(message.form).submit(function() {
        socket.emit('message', { text: message.value });
        return false;
      });
      socket.on('push message', function (data) {
        $('form').after('<p>' + data.text + '</p>');
      });
    </script>

  </body>
</html>
```

5. Install the dependencies by running the following from a terminal:

```
npm install
```

6. Start the server by running the following from a terminal:

```
node app.js
```

7. Open a browser at http://127.0.0.1:3000.

8. Open another browser tab at http://127.0.0.1:3000.

9. Enter a message in the text box and click Submit.

10. In the other browser tab, you should see the message appear.

11. Send a message back by entering a message in the text box and clicking Submit.

12. You should see the message appear in the other window (see Figure 12.2).

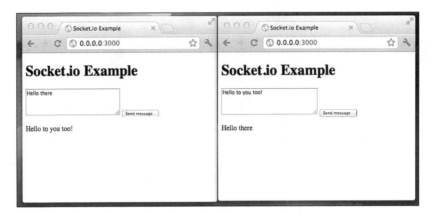

FIGURE 12.2
Sending a message between Socket.IO clients

Bi-Directional Data

In the real-time counter and messaging server examples, you have seen how to send data from the server to clients and from the clients to the server. You have sent data bi-directionally (both ways), and this is a key feature of Socket.IO and WebSockets that you should understand. What WebSockets enables is a way for clients and servers to push data to each other whenever they want to. This really changes the landscape of the Web and the types of applications that you can create for the browser. At the same time, as a browser is sending a message to the server, the server might be sending the client a message, too. Other clients might be updating the server, and clients may be joining and leaving the server. You can see that even in a small example, many events are happening! JavaScript is a perfect fit for this. It is an event-driven language, and, given that Node.js brings server-side networking to the party, you can see how JavaScript is set to become the darling of these types of application.

To cement the theory of sending data both ways, the final example in this hour demonstrates the flow of data between client and server and how events can be used to respond with more messages. In computing, the term *PING* is a request to a service or server to tell the requestor that it is up or alive. The expected response is PONG. If you think of a game of table tennis, the ball is hit over the net and then it is hit back—ping-pong! You use this idea to explore message flow in Socket.IO by sending a message requesting a PONG response from the other end.

On the server side, the example

1. Sends a PONG response when it receives a PING.

2. Logs a message to the terminal when it receives a PONG response.

3. Sends a PING message to clients every 10 seconds.

On the client side, the example

1. Sends a PONG response when it receives a PING.

2. Logs a message to the console when it receives a PONG response.

3. Sends a PING message to the server when a user clicks a Submit button.

Before you get into the code for this functionality, it is important to understand that these events can happen at any time and in any order. The messages are bi-directional, after all! To achieve the server-side functionality, the Socket.IO code looks like Listing 12.5.

Listing 12.5   Demonstrating Messaging in Socket.IO

```
io.sockets.on('connection', function (socket) {
  socket.on('ping', function (data) {
    console.log('Received PING. Sending PONG..');
    socket.emit('pong', { text: 'PONG' });
  });
  socket.on('pong', function (data) {
    console.log('Received PONG response. PONG!');
   });
  setInterval(function() {
    console.log('Sending PING to client..');
    socket.emit('ping', { text: 'PING' });
  }, 10000);
});
```

Two listener events are created to listen for 'ping' and 'pong' events. If a 'ping' event is received, it responds with a PONG message. If a 'pong' event is received, it logs it to the terminal. To send a message to a client every 10 seconds, setInterval() is used. This simply repeats something as often as you specify (in this case, 10,000 milliseconds or 10 seconds). On the client side, the functionality is almost exactly the same other than the 'ping' event is triggered by a user clicking a Submit button.

```
<script src="https://ajax.googleapis.com/ajax/libs/jquery/1.7.1/jquery.min.js"></
script>
<script src="/socket.io/socket.io.js"></script>
<script>
  var socket = io.connect('http://127.0.0.1:3000');
  socket.on('ping', function (data) {
    console.log('Received PING. Sending PONG..');
    socket.emit('pong', { text: 'PONG' });
  });
  socket.on('pong', function (data) {
    console.log('Received PONG response. PONG!');
  });
  $('#ping').click(function() {
```

```
    console.log('Sending PING to server..')
    socket.emit('ping', { text: 'PING' });
  });
</script>
```

What's happening in this JavaScript?

▶ The jQuery library is included, followed by the Socket.IO library.

▶ The browser is instructed to connect to the Socket.IO server at http://127.0.0.1:3000.

▶ Using jQuery's `submit()` method, a listener is added for whenever a user submits the form.

▶ Two listeners are created to respond to the `'ping'` and `'pong'` events. The ping event responds with a pong. The `'pong'` event logs the event to the browser console.

▶ To allow a user to send a PING, jQuery's `click()` method is used to listen for a click event on an HTML button with an id of ping. Whenever this is clicked, a ping message is sent to the server.

The HTML button to capture the click and send a ping to the server is simple:

```
<button id="ping">Send PING to server</button>
```

The example completes a ping-pong messaging cycle. If you can understand how this is working, you understand Socket.IO messaging. It is easier to understand by watching messages go back and forth, so fire up a browser!

▼ TRY IT YOURSELF

If you have downloaded the code examples for this book, this code is hour12/example04.

Follow these steps to watch dynamic messaging with Socket.IO:

1. Create a new folder called ping_pong.

2. Within the ping_pong folder, create a new file called package.json and add the following content to declare Socket.IO as a dependency:

```
{
  "name":"socketio_example",
  "version":"0.0.1",
  "private":true,
  "dependencies":{
    "socket.io":"0.8.7"
  }
}
```

3. Within the ping_pong folder, create a new file called app.js with the following content:

```
var http = require('http');
var fs = require('fs');

var server = http.createServer(function (req, res) {
  fs.readFile('./index.html', function(error, data) {
    res.writeHead(200, { 'Content-Type': 'text/html' });
    res.end(data, 'utf-8');
  });
}).listen(3000, "127.0.0.1");
console.log('Server running at http://127.0.0.1:3000/');

var io = require('socket.io').listen(server);

io.sockets.on('connection', function (socket) {
  socket.on('ping', function (data) {
    console.log('Received PING. Sending PONG..');
    socket.emit('pong', { text: 'PONG' });
  });
  socket.on('pong', function (data) {
    console.log('Received PONG response. PONG!');
  });
  setInterval(function() {
    console.log('Sending PING to client..');
    socket.emit('ping', { text: 'PING' });
  }, 10000);
});
```

4. Within the ping_pong folder, create a new file called index.html with the following content:

```
<!DOCTYPE html>
<html lang="en">
  <head>
    <meta charset="utf-8" />
    <title>Socket.IO Example</title>
  </head>
  <body>
    <h1>Socket.IO Example</h1>
    <button id="ping">Send PING to server</button>
    <script src="https://ajax.googleapis.com/ajax/libs/jquery/1.7.1/jquery.
➥min.js"></script>
    <script src="/socket.io/socket.io.js"></script>
    <script>
      var socket = io.connect('http://127.0.0.1:3000');
      socket.on('ping', function (data) {
        console.log('Received PING. Sending PONG..');
        socket.emit('pong', { text: 'PONG' });
```

```
          });
          socket.on('pong', function (data) {
            console.log('Received PONG response. PONG!');
          });
          $('#ping').click(function() {
            console.log('Sending PING to server..')
            socket.emit('ping', { text: 'PING' });
          });
      </script>
    </body>
  </html>
```

5. Install the dependencies by running the following from a terminal:

   `npm install`

6. Start the server by running the following from a terminal:

   `node app.js`

7. Open Firefox, Chrome, or Safari at http://127.0.0.1:3000 and open a console window.

8. Watch the browser console as `'ping'` events are received from the server and `'pong'` responses are sent (see Figure 12.3).

9. In the browser window, click the Submit button to send a `'ping'` to the server.

10. Watch the terminal log to see that a `'ping'` has been received and a `'pong'` has been returned (see Figure 12.3).

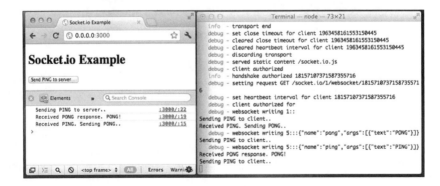

FIGURE 12.3
Message ping-ponging between server and client

Summary

In this hour, you saw one of the things that really makes Node.js different. You saw how using Socket.IO can create applications that allow communications between the server and clients in real-time! You learned how to send data from the server to the client, and then from the client to the server. You understood how to receive data on both the server and the client and how to use client-side JavaScript to display the data to users. In the final example, you understood how messages can trigger other messages and how the flow of messages can be bi-directional. You learned much of the theory behind Socket.IO in this hour, and you have all the tools you need to build the real-time Web!

Q&A

Q. Are WebSockets supported in all browsers?

A. The short answer is no. At the time of writing, the WebSockets standard is still in Editor's Draft so the standard is not finished. Many browser vendors have already implemented WebSockets, although some have disabled the feature due to security concerns. Although it is expected that support for WebSockets will become standard across all browsers, support for WebSockets cannot be expected at the time of writing. The good news is that Socket.IO accounts for WebSockets support not being available in all browsers. If WebSockets support is available, Socket.IO will choose that. If it is not, Socket.IO will try to use Adobe Flash Sockets, Ajax long polling, Ajax multipart streaming, Forever iFrame, or JSONP polling. You do not need to understand what these are as Socket.IO handles these seamlessly, although you can choose which transports to enable if you need to. This means that if you use Socket.IO, you can expect support from a broad range of browsers. At the time of writing, Socket.IO browser support is listed as follows: Internet Explorer 5.5+, Safari 3+, Google Chrome 4+, Firefox 3+, Opera 10.61+, iPhone Safari, iPad Safari, Android WebKit, and WebOs WebKit. Pretty impressive!

Q. Can I connect across different domains?

A. Yes, you can. If you have experience using Ajax, you may know that to enable cross-domain requests, you must use additional techniques. You do not need these when using Socket.IO. It just works!

Q. What is the difference between Ajax and Socket.IO?

A. Socket.IO provides a great deal more functionality than Ajax, namely the ability to easily push data out to clients in real-time. If WebSockets are available, then the connection between the client and server will be persistent. With Ajax, a connection needs to be established each time.

Q. **Should I use WebSockets or Ajax?**

A. WebSockets and Ajax serve different purposes, so it is difficult to say whether to use one or the other. Ajax is good for scenarios where data is requested by a browser every now and again and potentially needs to be cached. If you frequently need to send and receive data between the client and you have many clients, then WebSockets should be used. If you are building a networked application where clients can communicate with each other, WebSockets are a better choice.

Workshop

This workshop contains quiz questions and exercises to help cement your learning in this hour.

Quiz

1. What is the difference between push and pull messaging?

2. How well are WebSockets currently supported in browsers? (Hint: You can use http:// caniuse.com/ to help you.)

3. What is the advantage of using Socket.IO over plain WebSockets?

Quiz Answers

1. Push messaging means that new messages are pushed out to clients through a persistent connection. This means that a client does not have to make a request for new messages. By contrast, pull messaging means that the client has to check the server to see whether any new messages are available.

2. If you visit http://caniuse.com and type *WebSockets* into the Search box, you will see how well WebSockets are supported. Particularly on mobile devices, support for WebSockets can be patchy, adding more weight to the argument for using Socket.IO.

3. Socket.IO falls back to other transport methods if WebSockets are not available. This means that you can support more browsers in your application without writing any more code.

Exercises

1. Create a Socket.IO application that sends clients the message "You have connected!" when a new client connects.

2. Extend Exercise 1 to display the message to clients by writing some client-side JavaScript to receive the message.

3. Explore the client-side JavaScript debuggers available in Firefox, Safari, and Chrome. If you need to refresh your memory, these were covered in Hour 9, "Debugging Node.js Applications." If you do not have access to all of these browsers, just choose the ones that you have available on your system. Work through some of the examples in this hour and understand how you can use the debugger and console.log on the client-side to help develop Socket.IO applications.

A Socket.IO Chat Server

What You'll Learn in This Hour:

▶ Use Socket.IO with Express

▶ Add and maintain a list of nicknames

▶ Use callbacks with Socket.IO

▶ Send messages between connected users

▶ Create a fully featured chat server with Socket.IO

Express and Socket.IO

In Hour 12, "Introducing Socket.IO," you were introduced to Socket.IO and how it can be used to send messages in real-time between the browser and the server. In this hour, you see a practical application of Socket.IO—a browser-based chat server. This is another excellent use case for Node.js!

The chat server has the following features:

▶ It allows users to set a nickname.

▶ It displays a list of connected users.

▶ It broadcasts chat messages to all connected users.

In previous hours, you were introduced to Express, which is a web framework for Node.js. Express makes creating web applications simpler with Node.js, and, thankfully, it integrates well with Socket.IO. You can create Socket.IO applications just using the standard libraries that ship with Node.js, but using Express abstracts away many common issues and problems. To use Socket.IO with Express, you just need to bind Socket.IO to your Express server:

```
var app = module.exports = express.createServer(),
    io = require('socket.io').listen(app);
```

A simple Express Socket.IO server looks like this:

```
var app = module.exports = express.createServer(),
    io = require('socket.io').listen(app);


app.listen(3000);

app.get('/', function (req, res) {
  res.sendfile(__dirname + '/index.html');
});


io.sockets.on('connection', function (socket) {
  socket.emit('welcome', { text: 'OH HAI! U R CONNECTED!' });
});
```

This serves a single index.html file to the browser and sends a welcome message to clients when they connect. On the client side (or browser), the code is the same as the examples you saw in Hour 12. Within the index.html file that you are serving with Express, a listener is set up for the welcome event to receive the message and write it to the JavaScript console:

```
<script src="/socket.io/socket.io.js"></script>
<script>
  var socket = io.connect();
  socket.on('welcome', function (data) {
    console.log(data.text);
  });
</script>
```

▼ TRY IT YOURSELF

If you have downloaded the code examples for this book, this code is hour13/example01.

Follow these steps to create a basic Socket.IO server using Express:

1. Create a new folder called socket.io_express.

2. Within the socket.io_express folder, create a new file called package.json and add the following content to declare Socket.IO and Express as a dependencies:

```
{
  "name":"socket.io-express-example",
  "version":"0.0.1",
  "private":true,
  "dependencies":{
    "express":"2.5.4",
    "socket.io":"0.8.7"
  }
}
```

3. Within the socket.io_express folder, create a new file called app.js with the following content:

```
var app = module.exports = express.createServer(),
    io = require('socket.io').listen(app);

app.listen(3000);

app.get('/', function (req, res) {
  res.sendfile(__dirname + '/index.html');
});

io.sockets.on('connection', function (socket) {
  socket.emit('welcome', { text: 'OH HAI! U R CONNECTED!' });
});
```

4. Within the socket.io_express folder, create a new file called index.html with the following content:

```
<!DOCTYPE html>
<html lang="en">
  <head>
    <meta charset="utf-8">
    <title>Socket.IO Express Example</title>
  </head>
  <body>
    <h1>Socket.IO Express Example</h1>
    <script src="/socket.io/socket.io.js"></script>
    <script>
      var socket = io.connect();
      socket.on('welcome', function (data) {
        console.log(data.text);
      });
    </script>
  </body>
</html>
```

5. Install the dependencies by running the following from a terminal:

```
npm install
```

6. Start the server by running the following from a terminal:

```
node app.js
```

7. Open a browser at http://127.0.0.1:3000.

8. You should see a page showing "Socket.IO Express Example."

9. Open a browser JavaScript console.

10. You should see "OH HAI! U R CONNECTED!" (see Figure 13.1), which indicates that the browser is connected to the Socket.IO server and has received a message.

FIGURE 13.1
Using Socket.IO with Express

Adding Nicknames

Now that you have a basic Express server connected to Socket.IO, you can start adding features. The first feature is to allow users to set a nickname when they join the server. This works in the following way:

1. Users can enter a nickname into a form.

2. The nickname is sent to the server when the form is submitted.

3. The server checks that the nickname is unique.

4. If the nickname is already taken, the server notifies the client.

5. If the nickname does not already exist, it is added to a list of nicknames.

6. The server broadcasts the list of nicknames to all connected clients.

7. Clients receive the broadcast and update the list of nicknames.

Sending Nicknames to the Server

The first step is to add a form to the index.html file so that users can enter their nickname:

```
<form id="set-nickname">
  <label for="nickname">Nickname:</label>
  <input type="text" id="nickname" />
  <input type="submit" />
</form>
```

Now that there is a form, some client-side JavaScript can be used to capture the nickname when a user submits the form. jQuery's `submit()` method can be used to listen for the submit event on the form and capture the value in the input field and send it to the Socket.IO server:

```
<script src="https://ajax.googleapis.com/ajax/libs/jquery/1.7.1/jquery.min.js"></
➥ script>
<script src="/socket.io/socket.io.js"></script>
<script>
  var socket = io.connect();
  jQuery(function ($) {
    var nickname = $('#nickname');
    var setNicknameForm = $('#set-nickname');
    setNicknameForm.submit(function(event) {
      event.preventDefault();
      socket.emit('nickname', nickname.val());
    });
  });
</script>
```

Here's what's happening in this JavaScript:

1. The jQuery library is included from Google's Content Delivery Network.

2. The Socket.IO library is included to allow the page to connect to the Socket.IO server.

3. The page is connected to the Socket.IO server using `io.connect()`.

4. An anonymous function is created to wrap any jQuery functions that we are using on the page. This safety measure ensures that other libraries that may use the `$` variable or function can be used alongside jQuery.

5. jQuery's `submit()` method listens for the submit event on the form.

6. The form submission is prevented with `event.preventDefault()`.

7. jQuery's `val()` method is used to capture the nickname that the user has entered.

8. Socket.IO sends the nickname to the server using `socket.emit()`.

DID YOU KNOW?

Socket.IO Can Auto-Discover the Server

If your Socket.IO client and server are on the same server (as in this example), you do not need to specify the server when using `io.connect();`. Socket.IO will auto-discover this for you. If, however, you are connecting across origins, pass the URL into the `io.connect()` function (e.g., `io.connect('http://yourdomain.com/');`).

This pattern may be familiar to you from the last hour and hour12/example03 of the book's code examples. The code captures an input from a user and sends it to the Socket.IO server using client-side JavaScript. To receive the message, a listener needs to be added to the server-side code:

```
socket.on('nickname', function (data) {
  console.log('The server received the following nickname: ' + data);
});
```

This adds a listener for the `nickname` event and receives the data so that it can be used.

▼ TRY IT YOURSELF

If you have downloaded the code examples for this book, this code is hour13/example02.

To receive data from the client with Socket.IO, follow these steps:

1. Create a new folder called sending_nickname.

2. Within the sending_nickname folder, create a new file called package.json and add the following content to declare Socket.IO and Express as dependencies:

```
{
  "name":"socket.io-express-example",
  "version":"0.0.1",
  "private":true,
  "dependencies":{
    "express":"2.5.4",
    "socket.io":"0.8.7"
  }
}
```

3. Within the sending_nickname folder, create a new file called app.js with the following content:

```
var app = module.exports = express.createServer(),
    io = require('socket.io').listen(app);

app.listen(3000);

app.get('/', function (req, res) {
  res.sendfile(__dirname + '/index.html');
});

io.sockets.on('connection', function (socket) {
  socket.on('nickname', function (data) {
    console.log('The server received the following nickname: ' + data);
  });
});
```

4. Within the socket.io_express folder, create a new file called index.html with the following content:

```html
<!DOCTYPE html>
<html lang="en">
  <head>
    <meta charset="utf-8">
    <title>Socket.IO Express Example</title>
  </head>
  <body>
    <h1>Socket.IO Express Example</h1>
    <form id="set-nickname">
      <label for="nickname">Nickname:</label>
      <input type="text" id="nickname" />
      <input type="submit" />
    </form>
    <script src="https://ajax.googleapis.com/ajax/libs/jquery/1.7.1/jquery.
 min.js"></script>
    <script src="/socket.io/socket.io.js"></script>
    <script>
      var socket = io.connect();
      jQuery(function ($) {
        var nickname = $('#nickname');
        var setNicknameForm = $('#set-nickname');
        setNicknameForm.submit(function(event) {
          event.preventDefault();
          socket.emit('nickname', nickname.val());
        });
      });
    </script>
  </body>
</html>
```

5. Install the dependencies by running the following from a terminal:

```
npm install
```

6. Start the server by running the following from a terminal:

```
node app.js
```

7. Open a browser at http://127.0.0.1:3000.

8. You should see a page showing "Socket.IO Express Example."

9. Enter a nickname into the form and click the Submit button.

10. In the server logs, you should see that the server has received the nickname.

Managing the List of Nicknames

To date, the application can send a nickname from the browser to the server. But, this isn't very useful! The server needs a way to maintain a list of nicknames that are connected and to be able to remove nicknames from the list when they disconnect. Some simple JavaScript can be used here to set up an empty array to hold nicknames and then add and remove names when users connect and disconnect. On the server side, an empty array is created to hold the nicknames:

```
var nicknames = [];
```

JavaScript's push() method can then be employed when a nickname is received by the server to add it to the array:

```
io.sockets.on('connection', function (socket) {
  socket.on('nickname', function (data) {
    nicknames.push(data);
  });
});
```

In reality, some sanitization would be performed on the data received from the client, but this is omitted for brevity. Whenever a client disconnects from the server, the nickname of the user needs to be removed from the list. The neatest way to do this is to use the following snippet of JavaScript:

```
nicknames.splice(nicknames.indexOf("Item to remove"), 1);
```

This finds the item in the array and then removes it. This can be employed in the Socket.IO server to remove the nickname whenever a user disconnects. Socket.IO is able to set a variable for each client to allow the user to access the nickname in the disconnect event. The nickname event must be amended to set this variable so that it can be used later:

```
socket.on('nickname', function (data) {
  nicknames.push(data);
  socket.nickname = data;
});
```

Now that the client's nickname is available to the server with socket.nickname, this can be used to remove the nickname from the server whenever a user disconnects:

```
socket.on('disconnect', function () {
  if (!socket.nickname) return;
  if (nicknames.indexOf(socket.nickname) > -1) {
    nicknames.splice(nicknames.indexOf(socket.nickname), 1);
  }
});
```

It is a good idea here to check for the existence of socket.nickname first, as if it doesn't exist, an error will be thrown. Also if the nickname to be removed is not in the nicknames array, it could cause unwanted results. So, with some simple server-side JavaScript, we are now able to maintain a list of nicknames!

If you have downloaded the code examples for this book, this code is hour13/example03.

To manage nicknames on the server, follow these steps:

1. Create a new folder called managing_nicknames.

2. Within the managing_nicknames folder, create a new file called package.json and add the following content to declare Socket.IO and Express as a dependencies:

```
{
  "name":"socket.io-express-example",
  "version":"0.0.1",
  "private":true,
  "dependencies":{
    "express":"2.5.4",
    "socket.io":"0.8.7"
  }
}
```

3. Within the managing_nicknames folder, create a new file called app.js with the following content:

```
var app = require('express').createServer(),
    io = require('socket.io').listen(app),
    nicknames = [];


app.listen(3000);

app.get('/', function (req, res) {
  res.sendfile(__dirname + '/index.html');
});

io.sockets.on('connection', function (socket) {
  socket.on('nickname', function (data) {
    nicknames.push(data);
    socket.nickname = data;
    console.log('Nicknames are ' + nicknames);
  });
  socket.on('disconnect', function () {
    if (!socket.nickname) return;
    if (nicknames.indexOf(socket.nickname) > -1) {
```

```
            nicknames.splice(nicknames.indexOf(socket.nickname), 1);
        }
        console.log('Nicknames are ' + nicknames);
    });
});
```

4. Within the socket.io_express folder, create a new file called index.html with the following content:

```
<!doctype html>
<html lang="en">
  <head>
    <meta charset="utf-8">
    <title>Socket.IO Express Example</title>
  </head>
  <body>
    <h1>Socket.IO Express Example</h1>
    <form id="set-nickname">
      <label for="nickname">Nickname:</label>
      <input type="text" id="nickname" />
      <input type="submit" />
    </form>
    <script src="https://ajax.googleapis.com/ajax/libs/jquery/1.7.1/jquery.
➥ min.js"></script>
    <script src="/socket.io/socket.io.js"></script>
    <script>
      var socket = io.connect();
      jQuery(function ($) {
        var nickname = $('#nickname');
        var setNicknameForm = $('#set-nickname');
        setNicknameForm.submit(function(event) {
          event.preventDefault();
          socket.emit('nickname', nickname.val());
        });
      });
    </script>
  </body>
</html>
```

5. Install the dependencies by running the following from a terminal:

```
npm install
```

6. Start the server by running the following from a terminal:

```
node app.js
```

7. Open a browser at http://127.0.0.1:3000.

8. You should see a page showing "Socket.IO Express Example."

9. Enter a nickname into the form and click the Submit button.

10. In the server logs, you should see that the list of nicknames that the server currently has.

11. Open another browser tab, enter another nickname, and click Submit.

12. In the server logs, you should see that the nickname has been added to the list of nicknames.

13. Close a browser tab with the Socket.IO example.

14. In the server logs, you should see that the nickname has been removed from the list.

Using Callbacks for Validation

You may have noticed there are several problems with the current implementation of managing nicknames on the server. Bonus points if you noticed any of the following!

▶ Users can enter the same nickname more than once.

▶ There is no validation on the server side.

▶ Once a nickname has been successfully submitted, the form is still visible, so in theory another nickname could be submitted.

To enable the client side to display the right information to the user, a key technique of using Socket.IO is employed—a callback. A callback is a way for the server to return some information to the client after a message has been sent. Think of it as the client side asking, "Hey, how did that go? Was everything OK?" This allows the client side to know whether the nickname was already in the list of nicknames and act accordingly. Effectively, the client can receive an acknowledgment from the server that everything was as expected. The desired logic is as follows:

1. A user submits a nickname via the form from the client side.

2. The server receives the nickname message.

3. The server checks to see whether the nickname is already in the list of registered nicknames.

4. If the nickname is already in the list of nicknames, the server issues a callback that everything is not okay.

5. If the nickname is not in the list of nicknames, it is added to the list of nicknames and a callback is issued to the client side to say that everything is okay.

6. If the callback tells the client side that everything is okay, the nickname form is hidden.

On the client side, the code that has been used to send the nickname to the server looks like this:

```
var socket = io.connect();
jQuery(function ($) {
  var nickname = $('#nickname');
  var setNicknameForm = $('#set-nickname');
  setNicknameForm.submit(function(event) {
    event.preventDefault();
    socket.emit('nickname', nickname.val());
  });
});
```

This can be amended to take a callback that will receive data from the server side after the message has been received. This allows the client side to know how things went at the other end:

```
jQuery(function ($) {
  var nickname = $('#nickname');
  var setNicknameForm = $('#set-nickname');
  setNicknameForm.submit(function(event) {
    event.preventDefault();
    socket.emit('nickname', nickname.val(), function (data) {
      if (data) {
        console.log('Nickname set successfully');
        setNicknameForm.hide();
      } else {
        setNicknameForm.prepend('<p>Sorry - that nickname is already taken.</p>');
      }
    });
  });
});
```

If the server returns the callback as true, the nickname has successfully been added. The client side can use jQuery's hide() method to hide the form from the user. If, on the other hand, the server returns false, a message is shown to the user that the nickname has already been taken. The client side then uses jQuery's prepend() method to insert a paragraph into the DOM (Document Object Model) or page to tell the user the nickname has been taken. On the server side, some logic needs to be added to return true or false to the callback depending on whether the nickname was already in the list of nicknames:

```
socket.on('nickname', function (data, callback) {
  if (nicknames.indexOf(data) != -1) {
    callback(false);
  } else {
    callback(true);
    nicknames.push(data);
    socket.nickname = data;
    console.log('Nicknames are ' + nicknames);
  }
});
```

The anonymous function inside the nickname event now takes two arguments: the data received from the client (data) and a function (callback). The function is the callback function that will be returned to the client from the server. JavaScript's indexOf() function can be used on an array to return whether an item is already in an array. If the nickname is not in the array, a value of -1 will be returned so true or false can be set depending on a simple test to see whether the nickname is in the array. This is returned to the client side to either hide the form or tell the user that the nickname has been taken. Callbacks are an extremely powerful tool to use in messaging between client and server, and you should use them whenever you need the client side to know what happened to the data that it just sent.

```
          callback(true);
          nicknames.push(data);
          socket.nickname = data;
          console.log('Nicknames are ' + nicknames);
        }
    });
    socket.on('disconnect', function () {
      if (!socket.nickname) return;
      if (nicknames.indexOf(socket.nickname) > -1) {
        nicknames.splice(nicknames.indexOf(socket.nickname), 1);
      }
      console.log('Nicknames are ' + nicknames);
    });
});
```

4. Within the socket.io_express folder, create a new file called index.html with the following content:

```html
<!doctype html>
<html lang="en">
  <head>
    <meta charset="utf-8">
    <title>Socket.io Express Example</title>
  </head>
  <body>
    <h1>Socket.io Express Example</h1>
    <form id="set-nickname">
      <label for="nickname">Nickname:</label>
      <input type="text" id="nickname" />
      <input type="submit" />
    </form>
    <script src="https://ajax.googleapis.com/ajax/libs/jquery/1.7.1/jquery.
min.js"></script>
    <script src="/socket.io/socket.io.js"></script>
    <script>
      var socket = io.connect();
      jQuery(function ($) {
        var nickname = $('#nickname');
        var setNicknameForm = $('#set-nickname');
        setNicknameForm.submit(function(event) {
          event.preventDefault();
          socket.emit('nickname', nickname.val(), function (data) {
            if (data) {
              console.log('Nickname set successfully');
              setNicknameForm.hide();
            } else {
              setNicknameForm.prepend('<p>Sorry - that nickname is already
```

```
taken.</p>');
            }
        });
    });
});
    </script>
    </body>
</html>
```

5. Install the dependencies by running the following from a terminal:

   `npm install`

6. Start the server by running the following from a terminal:

   `node app.js`

7. Open a browser at http://127.0.0.1:3000.

8. You should see a page showing "Socket.IO Express Example."

9. Enter a nickname into the form and click the Submit button.

10. In the server logs, you should see the list of nicknames that the server currently has. You should also see a message logged to the browser JavaScript console that the nickname was successfully set (see Figure 13.2).

11. Open another browser tab, enter another nickname, and click Submit.

12. In the server logs, you should see your nickname in the list of nicknames that the server currently has. You should see that the form has been hidden on the client side and a message has been logged to the JavaScript console.

13. Open another browser tab, enter the same nickname, and click Submit.

14. You should see a message that the nickname has been taken (see Figure 13.3), indicating the server-side validation worked!

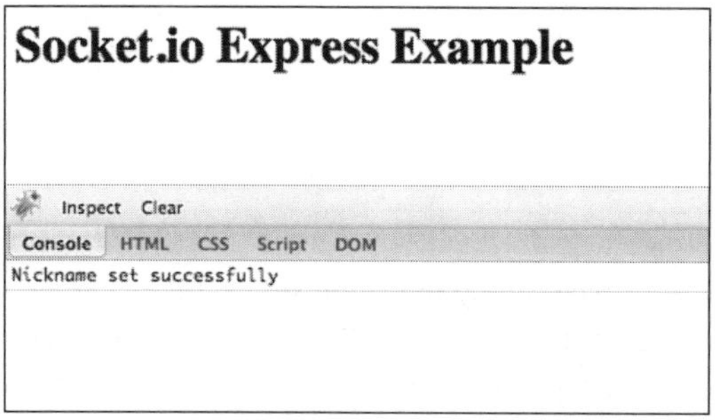

FIGURE 13.2
Using callbacks to set a nickname

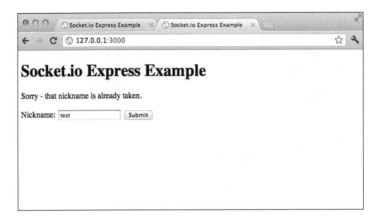

FIGURE 13.3
Using callbacks to validate a nickname

Broadcasting the List of Nicknames

Now that the logic for maintaining a list of nicknames is complete, the application needs to broadcast the list to clients so that users can see who is on the server. As you saw in Hour 12, broadcasting a message to all users is simple in Socket.IO, and we can add an emitter to the nickname event to send out the list of nicknames to clients:

```
io.sockets.emit('nicknames', nicknames);
```

On the client side, this can be received and then written to a page to show the user who is on the server. A simple JavaScript loop can be used to handle the data, iterating over the array and adding the nicknames to the DOM. To give the JavaScript somewhere to write the list of nicknames, an empty section tag is added to the HTML document with an id of "nicknames" containing and empty unordered list:

```
var nicknamesList = $('#nicknames ul');
socket.on('nicknames', function (data) {
  var html = '';
  for (var i = 0; i < data.length; i++) {
    html += '<li>' + data[i] + '</li>';
  }
  nicknamesList.empty().append(html);
});
```

When a 'nicknames' event is received by the client side, jQuery's empty() function is used to empty the unordered list within the section tag. This covers the scenario where there may be an existing list of nicknames from a previous update that is now stale. The data is displayed within the unordered list, so jQuery's append() function adds the data to the DOM. As the data is a

JavaScript array, it can be iterated (or looped) over. Whenever a new user joins the server, the server broadcasts a 'nicknames' event to all connected clients and the list of nicknames will be updated. By emitting the list of nicknames again when a user disconnects, the client side will also be updated whenever a user disconnects from the server.

If you want to try this code in a browser, this example is available in the code examples for this book as hour13/example05.

Adding Messaging

The application now has a list of nicknames on the server and updates clients when users join and leave the server. But users are not able to communicate with each other! To add messaging to the application another form must be added to the index.html file to allow users to submit messages. This is a standard HTML form:

```html
<form id="send-message">
  <textarea id="message"></textarea>
  <input type="submit" />
</form>
```

This form will be hidden with "display: none" in CSS until the nickname has been successfully set. After the nickname has been set successfully, the callback can be used to hide the nickname form and show the message form. The client-side JavaScript for submitting a nickname now looks like this:

```javascript
var nickname = $('#nickname');
var setNicknameForm = $('#set-nickname');
var messages = $('#messages');
setNicknameForm.submit(function(event) {
  event.preventDefault();
  socket.emit('nickname', nickname.val(), function (data) {
    if (data) {
      console.log('Nickname set successfully');
      setNicknameForm.hide();
      messages.show();
    } else {
      setNicknameForm.prepend('<p>Sorry - that nickname is already taken.</p>');
    }
  });
});
```

If the callback from the server indicates that the nickname was successfully added, the form to add a nickname is hidden using jQuery's hide() method, and the form to submit messages is shown using jQuery's show() method, effectively switching them out. Now that a form is visible to the user, some client-side JavaScript can then be added to listen for the submit event on the form and send the contents of the text area to the Socket.IO server. The form is also cleared and focus given to the form so that the user can enter another message if she wants:

```
var messageForm = $('#send-message');
var message = $('#message');
messageForm.submit(function(event) {
  event.preventDefault();
  socket.emit('user message', message.val());
  message.val('').focus();
});
```

On the server side, a listener is created to receive the 'user message' event and broadcasts it to all connected clients. This also uses socket.nickname that was set on the nickname event to send the nickname along with the message:

```
socket.on('user message', function (data) {
  io.sockets.emit('user message', {
    nick: socket.nickname,
    message: data
  });
});
```

Back on the client side, some client-side JavaScript is added to receive the broadcast of the message and display it to users. This receives the message and then writes the message to page using jQuery's append() method. Note that there is no need to parse the data received via Socket.IO. You can use it straightaway!

```
var messages = $('#messages');
socket.on('user message', function (data) {
  messages.append('<p><strong>' + data.nick + '</strong> ' + data.message + '</
  ➥ p>');
});
```

Finally, a little CSS is needed to hide the message form when the page initially loads. A few rudimentary styles are also added to display the list of nicknames on the right of the page, to make the text area box a little bigger and to add some padding between the nickname and the message:

```
<style>
  #send-message { display: none; }
  #nicknames { width: 300px; float: right; }
  #message { width: 300px; height: 100px; }
  #messages p strong { margin-right: 5px; }
</style>
```

If you have downloaded the code examples for this book, this code is hour13/example06.

Follow these steps to message between a server and client:

1. Create a new folder called messaging.

2. Within the messaging folder, create a new file called package.json and add the following content to declare Socket.IO and Express as a dependencies:

```
{
  "name":"socket.io-express-example",
  "version":"0.0.1",
  "private":true,
  "dependencies":{
    "express":"2.5.4",
    "socket.io":"0.8.7"
  }
}
```

3. Within the messaging folder, create a new file called app.js with the following content:

```
var app = require('express').createServer(),
    io = require('socket.io').listen(app),
    nicknames = [];

app.listen(3000);

app.get('/', function (req, res) {
  res.sendfile(__dirname + '/index.html');
});

io.sockets.on('connection', function (socket) {
  socket.on('nickname', function (data, callback) {
    if (nicknames.indexOf(data) != -1) {
      callback(false);
    } else {
      callback(true);
      nicknames.push(data);
      socket.nickname = data;
      console.log('Nicknames are ' + nicknames);
      io.sockets.emit('nicknames', nicknames);
    }
  });
  socket.on('user message', function (data) {
    io.sockets.emit('user message', {
      nick: socket.nickname,
      message: data
```

▼

```
      });
    });

    socket.on('disconnect', function () {
      if (!socket.nickname) return;
      if (nicknames.indexOf(socket.nickname) > -1) {
        nicknames.splice(nicknames.indexOf(socket.nickname), 1);
      }
      console.log('Nicknames are ' + nicknames);
      io.sockets.emit('nicknames', nicknames);
    });
  });
```

4. Within the messaging folder, create a new file called index.html with the following content:

```
<!doctype html>
<html lang="en">
  <head>
    <meta charset="utf-8">
    <title>Socket.IO Express Example</title>
    <style>
      #send-message { display: none; }
      #nicknames { width: 300px; float: right; }
      #message { width: 300px; height: 100px; }
      #messages p strong { margin-right: 5px; }
    </style>
  </head>
  <body>
    <h1>Socket.IO Express Example</h1>
    <form id="set-nickname">
      <label for="nickname">Nickname:</label>
      <input type="text" id="nickname" />
      <input type="submit" />
    </form>
    <form id="send-message">
      <textarea id="message"></textarea>
      <input type="submit" />
    </form>
    <section id="nicknames">
      <ul></ul>
    </section>
    <section id="messages">
    </section>
    <script src="https://ajax.googleapis.com/ajax/libs/jquery/1.7.1/jquery.
➥min.js"></script>
    <script src="/socket.io/socket.io.js"></script>
    <script>
      var socket = io.connect();
```

```
    jQuery(function ($) {
      var nickname = $('#nickname');
      var setNicknameForm = $('#set-nickname');
      var nicknamesList = $('#nicknames ul');
      var messageForm = $('#send-message');
      var message = $('#message');
      var messages = $('#messages');
      setNicknameForm.submit(function(event) {
        event.preventDefault();
        socket.emit('nickname', nickname.val(), function (data) {
          if (data) {
            console.log('Nickname set successfully');
            setNicknameForm.hide();
            messageForm.show();
          } else {
            setNicknameForm.prepend('<p>Sorry - that nickname is already
➥ taken.</p>');
          }
        });
      });
      messageForm.submit(function(event) {
        event.preventDefault();
        socket.emit('user message', message.val());
        message.val('').focus();
      });

      socket.on('nicknames', function (data) {
        var html = '';
        for (var i = 0; i < data.length; i++) {
          html += '<li>' + data[i] + '</li>';
        }
        nicknamesList.empty().append(html);
      });
      socket.on('user message', function (data) {
        messages.append('<p><strong>' + data.nick + '</strong> ' + data.
➥ message + '</p>');
      });
    });
  </script>
  </body>
</html>
```

5. Install the dependencies by running the following from a terminal:

```
npm install
```

6. Start the server by running the following from a terminal:

```
node app.js
```

7. Open a browser at http://127.0.0.1:3000.

8. You should see a page showing "Socket.IO Express Example."

9. Enter a nickname into the form and click Submit. You should see your nickname appear on the right of the screen.

10. In the server logs, you should see the list of nicknames the server currently has.

11. Open another browser tab, enter the same nickname, and click Submit. You should see two nicknames on the right of the screen.

12. Start chatting between tabs. You see your conversation appear in both tabs!

The chat server currently works well, but looks a little functional, to say the least. Because you are working in the browser, you have the full power of HTML and CSS at your disposal! Going into detail on layout and design is beyond the scope of this book, but if you need an example to whet your appetite, there is a more designed version of this chat server available in the code examples for this book in hour13/example07 (see Figure 13.4).

FIGURE 13.4
The chat application with some styling applied

Summary

In this hour, you learned how to create a fully featured chat server with Socket.IO. You learned how to use Socket.IO within Node.js applications that use the Express framework. You learned how to manage a list of nicknames on the server and how to use callbacks to return information on the outcome of sending data to the original sender. You also saw how to broadcast the list of nicknames and how to add messaging into the application. Most importantly, you learned how to use client-side and server-side JavaScript together to create a rich, real-time application!

Q&A

Q. I've noticed that more of the Socket.IO application logic is on the client side than the server side. Is this bad design?

A. A feature of single-page applications such as the chat server you created is that much of the application logic becomes client-side JavaScript. This is a paradigm shift from classical applications where most of the logic lived on the server and was used to send HTML to the browser. This design can also be known as "thick server, thin client" because most of the processing happens on the server. Modern JavaScript applications are flipping this idea around so that more logic is happening on the browser. This leads to a world of exciting possibilities but is not without problems. With a server, you can be 100% sure of the capabilities of the hardware and software being used. With browsers, you could be relying on a range of different JavaScript engines, CSS rendering capabilities, not to mention screen resolutions. Anyone who has been involved in front-end development knows of the pain of deploying to different browsers! Libraries like Socket.IO and jQuery abstract many of the differences between browsers for you. This is another argument for using libraries! It is not bad design, but it would be fair to say that it does bring some new challenges.

Q. Where can I host an application like this?

A. Because Socket.IO depends on WebSockets, you need to find a host that supports WebSockets. Not all Node.js PaaS hosts support WebSockets. At the time of writing, Nodester, Nodejitsu, Nodesocket, Cure, and Cloudnode support WebSockets.

Q. Can you share an Express session with a Socket.IO one?

A. Yes, you can. Many approaches use Redis (a key-value store) to store the Express session and give Socket.IO access to it. The implementation is beyond the scope of this hour.

Q. Could you add keyword banning and logging to this application?

A. Absolutely! You can hook into the Socket.IO event listeners to check messages for a list of banned words or to write the messages to a file or data store.

Workshop

This workshop contains quiz questions and exercises to help cement your learning in this hour.

Quiz

1. Do you have to use Express to use Socket.IO?

2. What happens to the list of nicknames if the server process is killed or dies?

3. Can you host your Socket.IO server and web application server in different places?

Quiz Answers

1. No. Socket.IO is independent from Express. Furthermore, Socket.IO abstracts WebSockets for you, so if you want to, you can write your own WebSockets server and handle the client-side code.

2. The list of nicknames is only persisted in memory in the examples in this hour, so if the process is killed or dies, the list of nicknames will be lost. You could use a key value store like Redis to hold this list if you wanted.

3. Yes. Although the Socket.IO server and web application are in the same process, in these examples, you can split them if you want.

Exercises

1. Using the knowledge that you learned in Hour 12, add a new feature to the application so that a message is posted to the chat window every time a user joins or leaves the server. Consult the code examples for the book and hour13/example07 for an approach to do this.

2. Experiment with adding some styling to the chat application. If you do not have any design skills, work with a friend or colleague who understands CSS and HTML to add some simple styling.

3. If you are looking for a challenge, add a new feature of private messaging to the application. This should function so a message can be sent between two connected clients rather than being broadcast to everyone on the server.

A Streaming Twitter Client

What You'll Learn in This Hour:

▶ Receive data from Twitter's streaming API

▶ Parse data received from Twitter's streaming API

▶ Push third-party data out to clients in real-time

▶ Create a real-time graph

▶ Discover whether there is more love or hate in the world by using real-time data from Twitter

Streaming APIs

In Hour 13, "A Socket.IO Chat Server," you learned how to create a chat server with Socket.IO and Express. This involved sending data from clients (or browsers) to the Socket.IO server and then broadcasting it out to other clients. In this hour, you learn about how Node.js and Socket.IO can also be used to consume data directly from the Web and then broadcast the data to connected clients. You will be working with Twitter's streaming Application Programming Interface (API) and pushing data out to the browser in real-time.

With Twitter's standard API, the process for getting data is as follows:

1. You open a connection to the API server.

2. You send a request for some data.

3. You receive the data that you requested from the API.

4. The connection is closed.

With Twitter's streaming API, the process is different:

1. You open a connection to the API server.

2. You send a request for some data.

3. Data is pushed to you from the API.

4. The connection remains open.

5. More data is pushed to you when it becomes available.

Streaming APIs allow data to be pushed from the service provider whenever new data is available. In the case of Twitter, this data can be extremely frequent and high volume. Node.js is a great fit for this type of scenario where large numbers of events are happening frequently as data is received. This hour represents another excellent use case for Node.js and highlights some of the features that make Node.js different from other languages and frameworks.

Signing Up for Twitter

Twitter provides a huge amount of data to developers via a free, publically available API. Many Twitter desktop and mobile clients are built on top of this API, but this is also open to developers to use however they want.

If you do not already have a Twitter account, you need one for this hour. You can sign up for an account for free at https://twitter.com/. It takes less than a minute! Once you have a Twitter account, you need to sign into the Twitter Developers website with your details at http://dev.twitter.com/. This site provides documentation and forums for anything to do with the Twitter API. The documentation is thorough, so if you want, you can get a good understanding of what types of data you can request from the API here.

Within the Twitter Developers website, you can also register applications that you create with the Twitter API. You create a Twitter application in this hour, so to register your application, do the following:

1. Click the link Create an App.

2. Pick a name for your application and fill out the form (see Figure 14.1). Application names on Twitter have to be unique, so if you find that the name has already been taken, choose another one.

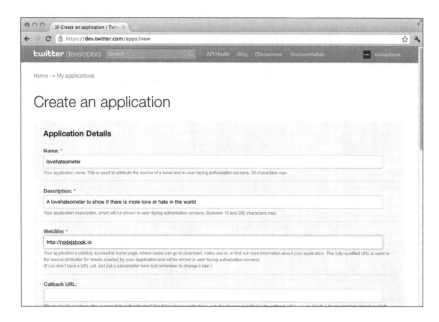

FIGURE 14.1
Creating a Twitter application

Once you create your application, you need to generate an access token and an access token secret to gain access to the API from your application.

3. At the bottom of the Details tab is a Create My Access Token button (see Figure 14.2). Click this button to create an access token and an access token secret.

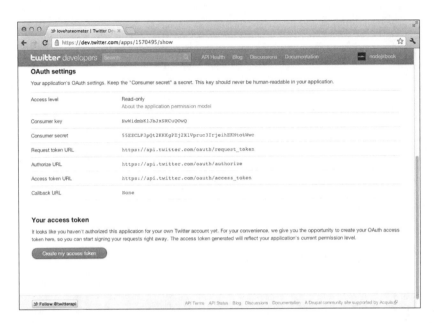

FIGURE 14.2
Requesting an access token

4. When the page refreshes, you see that values have been added for access token and access token secret (see Figure 14.3). Now you are ready to start using the API!

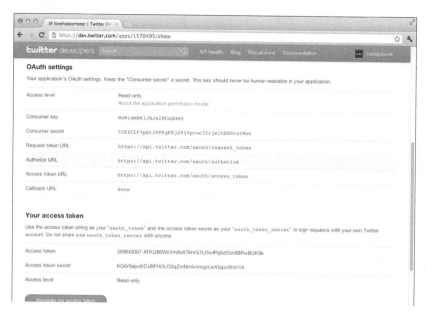

FIGURE 14.3
A successful creation of an access token

BY THE WAY

OAuth Is a Way of Allowing Access to Online Accounts

OAuth is an open standard for authentication, typically used within the context of web applications. It allows users to grant access to all or parts of an account without handing over a username or password. When a user grants an application access to their account, a unique token is generated. This can be used by a third-party services to access all or parts of a user's account. At any time, the user can revoke access and the token will no longer be valid so an application would no longer have access to the account.

Using Twitter's API with Node.js

Once you create your application within the Twitter Developers website and request an OAuth access token, you are ready to start using the Twitter API. An excellent Node.js module is available for interacting with the Twitter API called ntwitter. This module was initially developed by technoweenie (Rick Olson), then jdub (Jeff Waugh), and is now maintained AvianFlu (Charlie McConnell). All the authors have done an amazing job of abstracting the complexity of interacting with Twitter's API to make it trivial to get data and do things with it. You continue to use Express in this hour, so the package.json file for the application will include the Express and ntwitter modules.

```
{
  "name":"socket.io-twitter-example",
  "version":"0.0.1",
  "private":true,
  "dependencies":{
    "express":"2.5.4",
    "ntwitter":"0.2.10"
  }
}
```

The ntwitter module uses OAuth to authenticate you, so you must provide four pieces of information:

▶ Consumer key

▶ Consumer secret

▶ Access token key

▶ Access token secret

If you requested these when you were setting up the application in the Twitter Developers website, these will be available on the Details page for your application. If you did not request them when you set up the application, you need to do so now under the Details tab. Once you have the keys and secrets, you can create a small Express server to connect to Twitter's streaming API:

```
var app = require('express').createServer(),
    twitter = require('ntwitter');

app.listen(3000);

var twit = new twitter({
  consumer_key: 'YOUR_CONSUMER_KEY',
  consumer_secret: 'YOUR_CONSUMER_SECRET',
  access_token_key: 'YOUR_ACCESS_TOKEN_KEY',
  access_token_secret: 'YOUR_ACCESS_TOKEN_KEY'
});
```

Of course, you need to remember to replace the values in the example with your actual values. This is all you need to start interacting with Twitter's API! In this example, you answer the question, "Is there more love or hate in the world?" by using real-time data from Twitter. You request tweets from Twitter's streaming API that mention the words "love" or "hate" and perform a small amount of analysis on the data to answer the question. The ntwitter module makes it easy to request this data:

```
twit.stream('statuses/filter', { track: ['love', 'hate'] }, function(stream) {
  stream.on('data', function (data) {
    console.log(data);
  });
});
```

This requests data from the `'statuses/filter'` endpoint that allows developers to track tweets by keyword, location, or specific users. In this case, we are interested in the keywords `'love'` and `'hate'`. The Express server opens a connection to the API server and listens for new data being received. Whenever a new data item is received, it writes the data to the console. In other words, you can see the stream live for the keywords "love" and "hate" in the terminal.

If you have downloaded the code examples for this book, this code is hour14/example01.

To stream data from Twitter, follow these steps:

1. Create a new folder called express_twitter.

2. Within the express_twitter folder, create a new file called package.json and add the following content to declare ntwitter and Express as dependencies:

```
{
    "name":"socket.io-twitter-example",
    "version":"0.0.1",
    "private":true,
    "dependencies":{
        "express":"2.5.4",
        "ntwitter":"0.2.10"
    }
}
```

3. Within the express_twitter folder, create a new file called app.js with the following content. Remember to replace the keys and secrets with your own:

```
var app = require('express').createServer(),
    twitter = require('ntwitter');

app.listen(3000);

var twit = new twitter({
  consumer_key: 'YOUR_CONSUMER_KEY',
  consumer_secret: 'YOUR_CONSUMER_SECRET',
  access_token_key: 'YOUR_ACCESS_TOKEN_KEY',
  access_token_secret: 'YOUR_ACCESS_TOKEN_KEY'
```

```
  });

  twit.stream('statuses/filter', { track: ['love', 'hate'] }, function(stream) {
    stream.on('data', function (data) {
      console.log(data);
    });
  });
```

4. Install the dependencies by running the following from a terminal:

```
npm install
```

5. Start the server by running the following from a terminal:

```
node app.js
```

6. Watch the terminal; you should see data being received from Twitter's streaming API (see Figure 14.4). There is a lot of data, so expect it to move fast!

7. Kill the server pressing Ctrl+C in the terminal.

```
● ○ ○                    Terminal — node — 80×24
      notifications: null,
      profile_background_tile: false,
      follow_request_sent: null,
      profile_sidebar_fill_color: '252429',
      created_at: 'Sat Dec 11 15:04:33 +0000 2010',
      protected: false,
      default_profile_image: false,
      contributors_enabled: false,
      profile_sidebar_border_color: '181A1E',
      followers_count: 21,
      profile_image_url: 'http://a0.twimg.com/profile_images/1789738168/____norma
l.jpg',
      name: 'Noura',
      id_str: '225434395',
      favourites_count: 0,
      id: 225434395,
      lang: 'en',
      profile_use_background_image: true,
      utc_offset: -18000,
      url: null },
    in_reply_to_screen_name: null,
    id: 164010055543435260,
    entities: { user_mentions: [], urls: [], hashtags: [ [Object] ] } }
```

FIGURE 14.4
Streaming data to the terminal

Extracting Meaning from the Data

So far, you created a way to retrieve data in real-time from Twitter, and you saw a terminal window move very fast with a lot of data. This is good, but in terms of being able to understand the data, you are not able to answer the question set. To work toward this, you need to be able to parse the tweets received and extract information. Twitter provides data in JSON, a subset of JavaScript, and this is great news for using it with Node.js. For each response, you can simply use dot notation to retrieve the data that you are interested in. So, if you wanted to view the screen name of the user along with the tweet, this can be easily achieved:

```
twit.stream('statuses/filter', { track: ['love', 'hate'] }, function(stream) {
  stream.on('data', function (data) {
    console.log(data.user.screen_name + ': ' + data.text);
  });
});
```

Full documentation on the structure of the data received from Twitter is available on the documentation for the status element. This can be viewed online at https://dev.twitter.com/docs/api/1/get/statuses/show/%3Aid. Under the section "Example Request," you can see the data structure for a status response. Using dot notation on the data object returned from Twitter, you are able to access any of these data points. For example, if you want the URL for the user, you can use data.user.url. Here is the full data available for the user who posted the tweet:

```
"user": {
    "profile_sidebar_border_color": "eeeeee",
    "profile_background_tile": true,
    "profile_sidebar_fill_color": "efefef",
    "name": "Eoin McMillan ",
    "profile_image_url": "http://a1.twimg.com/profile_images/1380912173/Screen_
➡ shot_2011-06-03_at_7.35.36_PM_normal.png",
    "created_at": "Mon May 16 20:07:59 +0000 2011",
    "location": "Twitter",
    "profile_link_color": "009999",
    "follow_request_sent": null,
    "is_translator": false,
    "id_str": "299862462",
    "favourites_count": 0,
    "default_profile": false,
    "url": "http://www.eoin.me",
    "contributors_enabled": false,
    "id": 299862462,
    "utc_offset": null,
    "profile_image_url_https": "https://si0.twimg.com/profile_images/1380912173/
➡ Screen_shot_2011-06-03_at_7.35.36_PM_normal.png",
    "profile_use_background_image": true,
    "listed_count": 0,
    "followers_count": 9,
    "lang": "en",
    "profile_text_color": "333333",
    "protected": false,
    "profile_background_image_url_https": "https://si0.twimg.com/images/themes/
➡ theme14/bg.gif",
    "description": "Eoin's photography account. See @mceoin for tweets.",
    "geo_enabled": false,
    "verified": false,
```

```
  "profile_background_color": "131516",
  "time_zone": null,
  "notifications": null,
  "statuses_count": 255,
  "friends_count": 0,
  "default_profile_image": false,
  "profile_background_image_url": "http://a1.twimg.com/images/themes/theme14/
➥ bg.gif",
  "screen_name": "imeoin",
  "following": null,
  "show_all_inline_media": false
}
```

There is much more information available with each response including geographic coordinates, whether the tweet was retweeted, and more.

▼ TRY IT YOURSELF

If you have downloaded the code examples for this book, this code is hour14/example02.

To parse data from Twitter, follow these steps:

1. Create a new folder called parsing_twitter_data.

2. Within the parsing_twitter_data folder, create a new file called package.json and add the following content to declare ntwitter and Express as dependencies:

   ```
   {
     "name":"socket.io-twitter-example",
     "version":"0.0.1",
     "private":true,
     "dependencies":{
       "express":"2.5.4",
       "ntwitter":"0.2.10"
     }
   }
   ```

3. Within the express_twitter folder, create a new file called app.js with the following content. Remember to replace the keys and secrets with your own:

   ```
   var app = require('express').createServer(),
       twitter = require('ntwitter');

   app.listen(3000);

   var twit = new twitter({
     consumer_key: 'YOUR_CONSUMER_KEY',
   ```

```
consumer_secret: 'YOUR_CONSUMER_SECRET',
access_token_key: 'YOUR_ACCESS_TOKEN_KEY',
access_token_secret: 'YOUR_ACCESS_TOKEN_KEY'
});

twit.stream('statuses/filter', { track: ['love', 'hate'] }, function(stream) {
  stream.on('data', function (data) {
    console.log(data.user.screen_name + ': ' + data.text);
  });
});
```

4. Install the dependencies by running the following from a terminal:

```
npm install
```

5. Start the server by running the following from a terminal:

```
node app.js
```

6. Watch the terminal; you should see that now only the screen name of the user and the tweet are displayed (see Figure 14.5).

7. Kill the server by pressing Ctrl+C in the terminal.

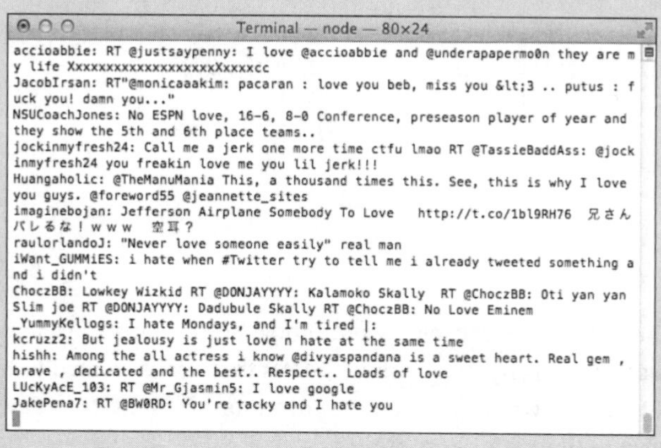

FIGURE 14.5
Parsing data received from Twitter

Pushing Data to the Browser

Now that data from Twitter is in a more digestible format, you can push this data out to connected browsers using Socket.IO and use some client-side JavaScript to display the tweets. This is similar to the patterns that you saw in Hours 12 and 13 where data is received by a

Socket.IO server and then broadcast to connected clients. To use Socket.IO, it must first be added as a dependency in the package.json file:

```
{
  "name":"socket.io-twitter-example",
  "version":"0.0.1",
  "private":true,
  "dependencies":{
    "express":"2.5.4",
    "ntwitter":"0.2.10",
    "socket.io":"0.8.7"
  }
}
```

Then, Socket.IO must be required in the main server file and instructed to listen to the Express server. This is exactly the same as the examples that you worked through in Hours 12 and 13:

```
var app = require('express').createServer(),
    twitter = require('ntwitter'),
    io = require('socket.IO').listen(app);
```

The streaming API request can now be augmented to push the data out to any connected Socket.IO clients whenever a new data event is received:

```
twit.stream('statuses/filter', { track: ['love', 'hate'] }, function(stream) {
  stream.on('data', function (data) {
    io.sockets.volatile.emit('tweet', {
      user: data.user.screen_name,
      text: data.text
    });
  });
});
```

Instead of logging the data to the console, you are now doing something useful with the data by pushing it out to connected clients. A simple JSON structure is created to hold the name of the user and the tweet. If you want to send more information to the browser, you could simply extend the JSON object to hold other attributes.

You may have noticed that, instead of using `io.sockets.emit` as you did in Hours 12 and 13, you are now using `io.sockets.volatile.emit`. This is an additional method provided by Socket.IO for scenarios where certain messages can be dropped. This may be down to network issues or a user being in the middle of a request-response cycle. This is particularly the case where high volumes of messages are being sent to clients. By using the `volatile` method, you can ensure that your application will not suffer if a certain client does not receive a message. In other words, it does not matter whether a client does not receive a message.

The Express server is also instructed to serve a single HTML page so that the data can be viewed in a browser.

```
app.get('/', function (req, res) {
  res.sendfile(__dirname + '/index.html');
});
```

On the client side (or browser), some simple client-side JavaScript is added to the index.html file to listen for new tweets being sent to the browser and display them to the user. The full HTML file is available in the example that follows:

```
<ul class="tweets"></ul>
<script src="https://ajax.googleapis.com/ajax/libs/jquery/1.7.1/jquery.min.js"></
➥ script>
<script src="/socket.io/socket.io.js"></script>
<script>
  var socket = io.connect();
  jQuery(function ($) {
    var tweetList = $('ul.tweets');
    socket.on('tweet', function (data) {
      tweetList
        .prepend('<li>' + data.user + ': ' + data.text + '</li>');
    });
  });
</script>
```

An empty unordered list is added to the DOM (Document Object Model), and this is filled with a new list item containing the screen name of the user and the tweet each time a new tweet is received. This uses jQuery's prepend() method to insert data received into a list item within the unordered list. This has the effect of creating a stream on the page.

Now, whenever Socket.IO pushes a new tweet event out the browser receives it and writes it to the page immediately. Instead of viewing the stream of tweets in a terminal, it can now be viewed in the browser!

TRY IT YOURSELF ▼

If you have downloaded the code examples for this book, this code is hour14/example03.

Here's how to stream Twitter data to a browser:

1. Create a new folder called socket.io-twitter-example.

2. Within the socket.io-twitter-example folder, create a new file called package.json and add the following content to declare ntwitter, Express, and Socket.IO as dependencies:

```
{
    "name":"socket.io-twitter-example",
    "version":"0.0.1",
    "private":true,
    "dependencies":{
```

```
"express":"2.5.4",
"ntwitter":"0.2.10",
"socket.io":"0.8.7"
    }
}
```

3. Within the socket.io-twitter-example folder, create a new file called app.js with the following content. Remember to replace the keys and secrets with your own:

```
var app = require('express').createServer(),
    twitter = require('ntwitter'),
    io = require('socket.io').listen(app);


app.listen(3000);

var twit = new twitter({
  consumer_key: 'YOUR_CONSUMER_KEY',
  consumer_secret: 'YOUR_CONSUMER_SECRET',
  access_token_key: 'YOUR_ACCESS_TOKEN_KEY',
  access_token_secret: 'YOUR_ACCESS_TOKEN_KEY'
});

twit.stream('statuses/filter', { track: ['love', 'hate'] }, function(stream) {
  stream.on('data', function (data) {
    io.sockets.volatile.emit('tweet', {
      user: data.user.screen_name,
      text: data.text
    });
  });
});

app.get('/', function (req, res) {
  res.sendfile(__dirname + '/index.html');
});
```

4. Within the Socket.IO-twitter-example, create a file called index.html and add the following contents:

```
<!doctype html>
<html lang="en">
  <head>
    <meta charset="utf-8">
    <title>Socket.IO Twitter Example</title>
  </head>
  <body>
    <h1>Socket.IO Twitter Example</h1>
    <ul class="tweets"></ul>
    <script src="https://ajax.googleapis.com/ajax/libs/jquery/1.7.1/jquery.
➥ min.js"></script>
```

```
<script src="/socket.io/socket.io.js"></script>
<script>
  var socket = io.connect();
  jQuery(function ($) {
    var tweetList = $('ul.tweets');
    socket.on('tweet', function (data) {
      tweetList
        .prepend('<li>' + data.user + ': ' + data.text + '</li>');
    });
  });
</script>
</body>
</html>
```

5. Install the dependencies by running the following from a terminal:

```
npm install
```

6. Start the server by running the following from a terminal:

```
node app.js
```

7. Open a browser window at http://127.0.0.1:3000.

8. You should see a stream of tweets in your browser (see Figure 14.6).

9. Kill the server by pressing Ctrl+C in the terminal.

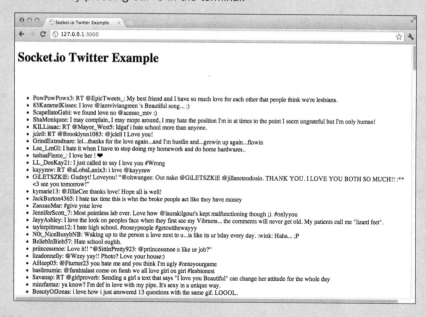

FIGURE 14.6
Streaming tweets to the browser

Creating a Real-Time Lovehateometer

Although the application can now stream tweets to a browser window, it is still not very useful. It is still impossible to answer the question of whether there is more love or hate in the world. To answer the question, you need a way to visualize the data. Assuming that the tweets received from the API are indicative of human sentiment, you set up several counters on the server that increment when the words "love" and "hate" are mentioned in the streaming data that is received. Furthermore, by maintaining another counter for the total number of tweets with either love or hate in them, you can calculate whether love or hate is mentioned more often. With this approach, it is possible to say—in unscientific terms—that there is x% of love and y% of hate in the world.

To be able to show data in the browser, you need counters on the server to hold:

▶ The total number of tweets containing "love" or "hate"

▶ The total number of tweets containing "love"

▶ The total number of tweets containing "hate"

This can be achieved by initializing variables and setting these counters to zero on the Node.js server:

```
var app = require('express').createServer(),
    twitter = require('ntwitter'),
    io = require('socket.io').listen(app),
    love = 0,
    hate = 0,
    total = 0;
```

Whenever new data is received from the API, the love counter will be incremented if the word "love" is found and so on. JavaScript's indexOf() string function can be used to look for words within a tweet and provides a simple way to analyze the content of tweets:

```
twit.stream('statuses/filter', { track: ['love', 'hate'] }, function(stream) {
  stream.on('data', function (data) {

    var text = data.text.toLowerCase();
    if (text.indexOf('love') !== -1) {
      love++
      total++
    }
    if (text.indexOf('hate') !== -1) {
      hate++
      total++
    }
  });
});
```

Because some tweets may contain both "love" and "hate," the total is incremented each time a word is found. This means that the total counter represents the total number of times "love" or "hate" was mentioned in a tweet rather than the total number of tweets.

Now that the application is maintaining a count of the occurrences of words this data can be added to the tweet emitter and pushed to connected clients in real-time. Some simple calculation is also used to send the values as a percentage of the total number of tweets:

```
io.sockets.volatile.emit('tweet', {
  user: data.user.screen_name,
  text: data.text,
  love: (love/total)*100,
  hate: (hate/total)*100
});
```

On the client side, by using an unordered list and some client-side JavaScript, the browser can receive the data and show it to users. Before any data is received from the server, the values are set to zero:

```
<ul class="percentage">
  <li class="love">0</li>
  <li class="hate">0</li>
</ul>
```

Finally, a client-side listener can be added to receive the tweet event and replace the percentage values with the ones received from the server. By starting the server and opening the browser, you can now answer the question!

```
<script src="https://ajax.googleapis.com/ajax/libs/jquery/1.7.1/jquery.min.js"></
➥ script>
<script src="/socket.io/socket.io.js"></script>
<script>
  var socket = io.connect();
  jQuery(function ($) {
    var tweetList = $('ul.tweets'),
        loveCounter = $('li.love'),
        hateCounter = $('li.hate');
    socket.on('tweet', function (data) {
      tweetList
        .prepend('<li>' + data.user + ': ' + data.text + '</li>');
      loveCounter
        .text(data.love + '%');
      hateCounter
        .text(data.hate + '%');
    });
  });
</script>
```

▼ TRY IT YOURSELF

If you have downloaded the code examples for this book, this code is hour14/example04.

To analyze data from Twitter's streaming API, follow these steps:

1. Create a new folder called percentages.

2. Within the percentages folder, create a new file called package.json and add the following content to declare ntwitter, Express, and Socket.IO as dependencies:

```
{
  "name":"socket.io-twitter-example",
  "version":"0.0.1",
  "private":true,
  "dependencies":{
    "express":"2.5.4",
    "ntwitter":"0.2.10",
    "socket.io":"0.8.7"
  }
}
```

3. Within the percentages folder, create a new file called app.js with the following content. Remember to replace the keys and secrets with your own:

```
var app = require('express').createServer(),
    twitter = require('ntwitter'),
    io = require('socket.io').listen(app),
    love = 0,
    hate = 0,
    total = 0;


app.listen(3000);


var twit = new twitter({
  consumer_key: 'YOUR_CONSUMER_KEY',
  consumer_secret: 'YOUR_CONSUMER_SECRET',
  access_token_key: 'YOUR_ACCESS_TOKEN_KEY',
  access_token_secret: 'YOUR_ACCESS_TOKEN_KEY'
});


twit.stream('statuses/filter', { track: ['love', 'hate'] }, function(stream) {
  stream.on('data', function (data) {
    var text = data.text.toLowerCase();
    if (text.indexOf('love') !== -1) {
      love++
      total++
    }
    if (text.indexOf('hate') !== -1) {
```

```
      hate++
      total++
    }
    io.sockets.volatile.emit('tweet', {
      user: data.user.screen_name,
      text: data.text,
      love: (love/total)*100,
      hate: (hate/total)*100
    });
  });
});

app.get('/', function (req, res) {
  res.sendfile(__dirname + '/index.html');
});
```

4. Within the percentages folder, create a file called index.html and add the following contents:

```
<!doctype html>
<html lang="en">
  <head>
    <meta charset="utf-8">
    <title>Socket.IO Twitter Example</title>
  </head>
  <body>
    <h1>Socket.IO Twitter Example</h1>
    <ul class="percentage">
      <li class="love">0</li>
      <li class="hate">0</li>
    </ul>
    <ul class="tweets"></ul>
    <script src="https://ajax.googleapis.com/ajax/libs/jquery/1.7.1/jquery.
➥ min.js"></script>
    <script src="/socket.io/socket.io.js"></script>
    <script>
      var socket = io.connect();
      jQuery(function ($) {
        var tweetList = $('ul.tweets'),
            loveCounter = $('li.love'),
            hateCounter = $('li.hate');
        socket.on('tweet', function (data) {
          tweetList
            .prepend('<li>' + data.user + ': ' + data.text + '</li>');
          loveCounter
            .text(data.love + '%');
          hateCounter
```

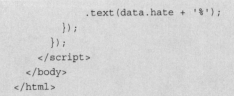

```
                .text(data.hate + '%');
            });
        });
    </script>
  </body>
</html>
```

5. Install the dependencies by running the following from a terminal:

   `npm install`

6. Start the server by running the following from a terminal:

   `node app.js`

7. Open a browser window at http://127.0.0.1:3000.

8. You should see a stream of tweets in your browser, along with the percentages being dynamically updated (see Figure 14.7).

9. Kill the server by pressing Ctrl+C in the terminal.

FIGURE 14.7
Dynamically updating percentage values

Adding a Real-Time Graph

The application is now able to answer the question. Hurray! In terms of visualization, though, it is still just data. It would be great if the application could generate a small bar graph that moved dynamically based on the data received. The server is already sending this data to the browser so this can be implemented entirely using client-side JavaScript and some CSS. The application has an unordered list containing the percentages, and this is perfect to create a simple bar graph. The unordered list will be amended slightly so that it is easier to style. The only addition here is to wrap the number in a span tag:

```
<ul class="percentage">
  <li class="love">
    <span>0</span>
  </li>
  <li class="hate">
    <span>0</span>
  </li>
</ul>
```

Some CSS can then be added to the head of the HTML document that makes the unordered list look like a bar graph. The list items represent the bars with colors of pink to represent love and black to represent hate:

```
<style>
  ul.percentage { width: 100% }
  ul.percentage li { display: block; width: 0 }
  ul.percentage li span { float: right; display: block}
  ul.percentage li.love { background: #ff0066; color: #fff}
  ul.percentage li.hate { background: #000; color: #fff}
</style>
```

Finally, some client-side JavaScript allows the bars (the list items) to be resized dynamically based on the percentage values received from the server:

```
<script src="https://ajax.googleapis.com/ajax/libs/jquery/1.7.1/jquery.min.js"></
➥ script>
<script src="/socket.io/socket.io.js"></script>
<script>
  var socket = io.connect();
  jQuery(function ($) {
    var tweetList = $('ul.tweets'),
        loveCounter = $('li.love'),
        hateCounter = $('li.hate'),
        loveCounterPercentage = $('li.love span'),
        hateCounterPercentage = $('li.hate span');
    socket.on('tweet', function (data) {
      loveCounter
```

```
        .css("width", data.love + '%');
      loveCounterPercentage
        .text(Math.round(data.love * 10) / 10 + '%');
      hateCounter
        .css("width", data.hate + '%');
      hateCounterPercentage
        .text(Math.round(data.hate * 10) / 10 + '%');
      tweetList
        .prepend('<li>' + data.user + ': ' + data.text + '</li>');
    });
  });
</script>
```

Whenever a new tweet event is received from Socket.IO, the bar graph is updated by dynamically setting the CSS width of the list items with the percentage values received from the server.
This has the effect of adjusting the graph each time a new tweet event is received. You have created a real-time graph!

▼ TRY IT YOURSELF

If you have downloaded the code examples for this book, this code is hour14/example05.

Follow these steps to visualize real-time data:

1. Create a new folder called realtime_graph.

2. Within the realtime_graph folder, create a new file called package.json and add the following content to declare ntwitter, Express, and Socket.IO as dependencies:

   ```
   {
     "name":"socket.io-twitter-example",
     "version":"0.0.1",
     "private":true,
     "dependencies":{
       "express":"2.5.4",
       "ntwitter":"0.2.10",
       "socket.io":"0.8.7"
     }
   }
   ```

3. Within the realtime_graph folder, create a new file called app.js with the following content.
   Remember to replace the keys and secrets with your own:

   ```
   var app = require('express').createServer(),
       twitter = require('ntwitter'),
       io = require('socket.io').listen(app),
       love = 0,
       hate = 0,
   ```

```
      total = 0;

app.listen(3000);

var twit = new twitter({
  consumer_key: 'YOUR_CONSUMER_KEY',
  consumer_secret: 'YOUR_CONSUMER_SECRET',
  access_token_key: 'YOUR_ACCESS_TOKEN_KEY',
  access_token_secret: 'YOUR_ACCESS_TOKEN_KEY'
});

twit.stream('statuses/filter', { track: ['love', 'hate'] }, function(stream) {
  stream.on('data', function (data) {

    var text = data.text.toLowerCase();
    if (text.indexOf('love') !== -1) {
      love++
      total++
    }
    if (text.indexOf('hate') !== -1) {
      hate++
      total++
    }

    io.sockets.volatile.emit('tweet', {
      user: data.user.screen_name,
      text: data.text,
      love: (love/total)*100,
      hate: (hate/total)*100
    });
  });
});

app.get('/', function (req, res) {
  res.sendfile(__dirname + '/index.html');
});
```

4. Within the realtime_graph folder, create a file called index.html and add the following
content:

```
<!doctype html>
<html lang="en">
  <head>
    <meta charset="utf-8">
    <title>Socket.IO Twitter Example</title>
    <style>
      ul.percentage { width: 100% }
```

▼

```
    ul.percentage li { display: block; width: 0 }
    ul.percentage li span { float: right; display: block}
    ul.percentage li.love { background: #ff0066; color: #fff}
    ul.percentage li.hate { background: #000; color: #fff}
  </style>
</head>
<body>
  <h1>Socket.IO Twitter Example</h1>
  <ul class="percentage">
    <li class="love">
      Love <span>0</span>
    </li>
    <li class="hate">
      Hate <span>0</span>
    </li>
  </ul>
  <ul class="tweets"></ul>
  <script src="https://ajax.googleapis.com/ajax/libs/jquery/1.7.1/jquery.
➥min.js"></script>
  <script src="/socket.io/socket.io.js"></script>
  <script>
    var socket = io.connect();
    jQuery(function ($) {
      var tweetList = $('ul.tweets'),
          loveCounter = $('li.love'),
          hateCounter = $('li.hate'),
          loveCounterPercentage = $('li.love span'),
          hateCounterPercentage = $('li.hate span');
      socket.on('tweet', function (data) {
        loveCounter
          .css("width", data.love + '%');
        loveCounterPercentage
          .text(Math.round(data.love * 10) / 10 + '%');
        hateCounter
          .css("width", data.hate + '%');
        hateCounterPercentage
          .text(Math.round(data.hate * 10) / 10 + '%');
        tweetList
          .prepend('<li>' + data.user + ': ' + data.text + '</li>');
      });
    });
  </script>
</body>
</html>
```

5. Install the dependencies by running the following from a terminal:

```
npm install
```

6. Start the server by running the following from a terminal:

```
node app.js
```

7. Open a browser window at http://127.0.0.1:3000.

8. You should see a stream of tweets in your browser, along with a real-time graph resizing based on data received (see Figure 14.8).

9. Kill the server by pressing Ctrl+C in the terminal.

FIGURE 14.8
A real-time graph

The application that you created provides a visual representation of whether there is more love than hate in the world based on real-time data from Twitter. Granted this is totally unscientific, but it does showcase the capabilities of Node.js and Socket.IO to receive large amounts of data and to push it out to the browser. With a little more CSS work, the application can be styled to look better (see Figure 14.9).

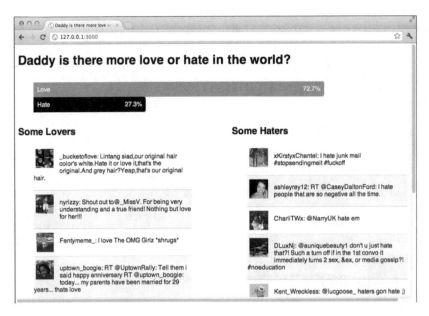

FIGURE 14.9
The finished application with additional styling

If you want to run this example yourself, this version is available in the code for this book as hour14/example06.

Summary

In this hour, you answered a fundamental question about human nature using Node.js, Twitter, and Socket.IO. Not bad for an hour's work! At the time of writing, there is more love in the world, so if you take nothing else from this hour, rejoice! You learned how a Node.js server can receive large amounts of data from a third-party service and push it out to the browser in real-time using Socket.IO. You saw how to manipulate the data to extract meaning from it and performed simple calculations on the data to extract percentage values. Finally, you added some client-side JavaScript to receive the data and create a real-time graph. This hour showcased many of the strengths of Node.js, including the ease that data can be sent between the server and browser, the ability to process large amounts of data, and the strong support for networking.

Q&A

Q. Are there other streaming APIs that I can use to create applications like this?

A. Yes. An increasing number of streaming APIs is becoming available to developers. At the time of writing, some APIs of interest include Campfire, Salesforce, Datasift, and Apigee, with many more expected to be created.

Q. How accurate is this data?

A. Not very. This data is based on the "statuses/filter" method from Twitter's streaming API. More information about what goes into this feed is available here https://dev.twitter.com/docs/streaming-api/methods. In short, do not base any anthropological studies on it.

Q. Can I save this data somewhere?

A. The application created in this hour does not persist data anywhere, so if the server is stopped, the counters and percentages are reset. Clearly, the longer that data can be collected, the more accurate the results. The application could be extended to store the counters with a data store that can handle high volumes of writes like Redis. This is outside the scope of this hour, though!

Workshop

This workshop contains quiz questions and exercises to help cement your learning in this hour.

Quiz

1. What is different about a streaming API?

2. What is OAuth?

3. Why is Node.js a good fit for working with streaming APIs?

Quiz Answers

1. A streaming API keeps the connection between client and server open and is able to push new data to the client when it becomes available. This enables applications to become real-time as data is pushed to the client as soon as it is availabie.

2. OAuth is a way for applications to grant access to data without exposing user credentials. Authorization is granted on a per-application basis and can be revoked at any time. If you have connected your Twitter account with any other services, you may be familiar with allowing other services to access your data. OAuth is used to achieve this.

3. As Node.js is designed around evented I/O, it can respond very well to new data being received from a streaming API. It can handle large amounts of data without needing huge amounts of memory. Because Node.js is JavaScript, it is easy to communicate with clients like browsers that understand JSON. Node.js is able to receive, process, and transmit large numbers of data events without needing many machines to process it on.

Exercises

1. Amend the example available in the book's code examples as hour14/example02 to display the user's real name and URL. Consult the data structure earlier in this hour to understand which attributes you need for this.

2. Amend the server to receive data from Twitter's streaming API based on some keywords that you are interested in. If there are more than two keywords, update the application to show more than two bars on the graph.

3. Think about how you could create an application to provide visualizations of different streaming Twitter datasets. Remember that you can limit your query by location, certain users, and keywords. Some examples to get you started:

   ▶ Do people talk more about beer or wine in London?

   ▶ How often do famous people use the words "me" or "you"?

   ▶ Are the Beatles more popular than the Rolling Stones?

JSON APIs

What You'll Learn in This Hour:

▶ What an API is

▶ What JSON is and how you can use it with Node.js

▶ Retrieving data from third-party APIs

▶ Creating a simple JSON API

APIs

An Application Programming Interface (API) is a means to create an interface between different software components. On the Web, this usually means making data from your website or service available to third parties or applications on devices like mobiles or tablets.

Node.js is extremely well suited for creating APIs for a number of reasons:

▶ It is able to handle a large number of concurrent connections and has a low memory footprint.

▶ It is written in JavaScript, so creating JSON (JavaScript Object Notation) APIs is easy.

▶ The first-class HTTP support in Node.js makes creating APIs simple.

APIs follow the same client and server model that a web browser and a web server follow. Consider a user loading a web page in a browser:

▶ A user requests a web page using browser (or client).

▶ The server returns the web page and any related media (images, video, etc.) to the browser.

▶ The browser renders the web page for the user.

With an API, the process is the same, but all that a user is interested in is data, so a server will return data in the requested format. As you work with APIs, you will hear the terms "client" and "server" used regularly. A client refers to something interacting with or getting data from an API. This might be something like a mobile app on an iPhone or Android device. A server refers to something that sends data to a client upon request. Node.js can be used to create both API clients and servers.

Some reasons that you might want to create an API server include

▶ To make data public and allow other developers to use it

▶ To allow devices like mobiles, tablets, and billboards to interact with your service

Some reasons that you might want to create an API client include

▶ So you can write software to interact with a third-party service like Twitter or Facebook

▶ So you can automate tasks with third-party services

▶ So you can integrate external data with your product

JSON

JavaScript Object Notation (JSON) is a lightweight data exchange format. It was discovered by Douglas Crockford and is intended to be used as an alternative to Extensible Markup Language (XML). Historically, XML has been favored as a means to exchange data. With requirements to exchange data in the context of the Web, XML was felt to be lacking in terms of creating data structures and that it was too heavyweight for the job at hand. Originally XML was designed to exchange documents. JSON was designed specially for data exchange. For many web developers, JSON has strong advantages over XML; JSON is

▶ Easy to read

▶ Easy to parse especially if you are using JavaScript

▶ A good choice for complex or simple data structures

▶ An excellent format for data exchange

▶ Well supported with parsers available for most languages

▶ Generally smaller in size than XML

In the last few years, JSON has emerged as the data exchange format of choice for web developers, and many large web businesses such as Twitter, Flickr, and Facebook have created JSON APIs that allow third-party developers rich access to data. JSON began to be preferred by developers who started to use Ajax to request data from third-party services. Consuming JSON as a data format with JavaScript is much simpler than XML so the popularity of JSON began to rise.

Today, single-page web applications are becoming popular. These applications make heavy usage of JavaScript and Ajax to fetch data and display it on the page. The direction of web technologies points to one thing—that JavaScript is going to become more important and that JSON is going to be the data format of choice for data APIs. Node.js is the perfect choice for creating APIs in this context. As Node.js is JavaScript based, it is simple to create, send, and consume JSON data. If you need to create a JSON-based API, you should use Node.js!

JSON looks like this:

```
{
  "name": "Darth Vader",
  "occupation": "Dark Lord of the Sith",
  "home": "Tatooine"
}
```

It is a subset of JavaScript so should be familiar to you if you understand a little JavaScript. After the opening brackets comes a key and then a value associated with that key. Values can be any of the following:

▶ String

▶ Number

▶ Object

▶ Array

▶ True or false

▶ Null

Commas are used to separate key/value pairs and allow key/value pairs to be nested to create more complex data structures. Consider this abbreviated example of a JSON response from the Twitter API:

```
{
  "name": "Twitter API",
  "description": "The Real Twitter API. I tweet about API changes, service issues
and happily answer questions about Twitter and our API. Don't get an answer? It's
on my website.",
  "time_zone": "Pacific Time (US & Canada)",
  "profile_background_image_url": "http://a3.twimg.com/profile_background_
images/59931895/twitterapi-background-new.png",
  "friends_count": 20,
  "statuses_count": 2404,
```

```
  "status": {
    "coordinates": null,
    "created_at": "Wed Dec 22 20:08:02 +0000 2010",
    "id_str": "17672734540570624",
    "text": "Twitter downtime - Twitter is currently down. We are aware of the
problem and working on it. http://t.co/37zl2jI",
    "retweet_count": 30,
    "in_reply_to_status_id_str": null,
  },
  "following": true,
  "screen_name": "twitterapi"
}
```

The status key shows how you can nest data and create more complex structures. Data structures can be created however you need them to be created, and most developers find that JSON is much simpler to read than XML.

WATCH OUT

Keys and Strings Must Be in Double Quotes

To be valid, JSON keys and strings must be in double quotes. If you are using a module to generate your JSON, this will likely be handled for you. If you are writing JSON by hand, remember to use double quotes. For more information, see http://simonwillison.net/2006/oct/11/json/.

Sending JSON Data with Node.js

To send data as JSON in Node.js, you must set the header to application/json. This header tells clients that JSON is being sent and is important as many clients rely on this to work out how to use the data:

```
var http = require('http');
http.createServer(function (req, res) {
  res.writeHead(200, {'Content-Type': 'application/json'});
  res.end('{"name": "Darth Vader","occupation": "Dark Lord of the Sith","home":
➡"Tatooine"}');
}).listen(3000, "127.0.0.1");
console.log('Server running at http://127.0.0.1:3000/');
```

▼ TRY IT YOURSELF

If you have downloaded the code examples for this book, this code is hour15/example01.

Follow these steps to send JSON with Node.js:

1. Create a file called app.js and copy the following code into it:

```
var http = require('http');
http.createServer(function (req, res) {
  res.writeHead(200, {'Content-Type': 'application/json'});
  res.end('{"name": "Darth Vader","occupation": "Dark Lord of the
➥ Sith","home": "Tatooine"}');
}).listen(3000, "127.0.0.1");
console.log('Server running at http://127.0.0.1:3000/');
```

2. Run the script:

```
node app.js
```

3. Using Google Chrome, open http://127.0.0.1:3000.

4. Click the HTTP Headers icon (you learned how to install this in Hour 8, "Persisting Data") to see that it is JSON.

5. You should see that the Content-Type is correctly set to application/json (see Figure 15.1).

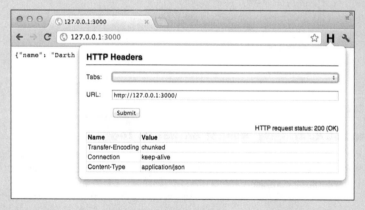

FIGURE 15.1
Sending JSON with Node.js

Creating JSON from JavaScript Objects

Often, you may be working with JavaScript objects that you want to send as JSON. Examples of things you might want to return include

▶ Database records

▶ Data calculated on the server side

▶ A combination of different data sources combined on the server side

Within Node.js, it is possible to create JSON from JavaScript objects using `JSON.stringify`. This allows you to convert JavaScript objects easily to JSON. Suppose that you have a simple JavaScript object:

```
var obj = {
  name : "Officer",
  surname : "Dibble"
}
```

This can be converted to JSON easily using `JSON.stringify`:

```
JSON.stringify(obj);
```

Using this approach, you can then send the JSON as before:

```
var http = require('http');
var obj = {
  name : "Officer",
  surname : "Dibble"
}
http.createServer(function (req, res) {
  res.writeHead(200, {'Content-Type': 'application/json'});
  res.end(JSON.stringify(obj));
}).listen(3000, "127.0.0.1");
console.log('Server running at http://127.0.0.1:3000/');
```

DID YOU KNOW?

You Can Use JSON.stringify in Most Browsers, Too

You can also use JSON.stringify to convert JavaScript objects to JSON in most browsers. It is available from Internet Explorer 7 and has good support in mobile browsers. For a full matrix of browser support, see http://caniuse.com/json.

▼ TRY IT YOURSELF

If you have downloaded the code examples for this book, this code is hour15/example02.

Follow these steps to convert JavaScript objects to JSON:

1. Create a file called app.js and copy the following code into it:

```
var http = require('http');
var obj = {
  name : "Officer",
  surname : "Dibble"
}
http.createServer(function (req, res) {
```

```
    res.writeHead(200, {'Content-Type': 'application/json'});
    res.end(JSON.stringify(obj));
}).listen(3000, "127.0.0.1");
console.log('Server running at http://127.0.0.1:3000/');
```

2. Run the script:

```
node app.js
```

3. Using Google Chrome open http://127.0.0.1:3000.

4. Click the HTTP Headers icon (you learned how to install this in Hour 8) to see that it is JSON (see Figure 15.2).

5. You should see the data sent as a JSON string to the browser.

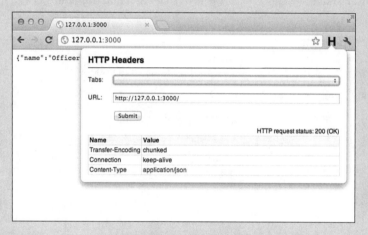

FIGURE 15.2
Converting JavaScript object to JSON

Consuming JSON Data with Node.js

Now that you have created a simple JSON-based web service, you can write a client to consume the data and do something with it. For this, you use a standard Node.js HTTP client and parse the data that you receive using JSON.parse.

The JSON.parse method parses a JSON string, reconstructing the original JavaScript object. You can see this at work by extending the earlier example to first convert a JavaScript object to JSON and then convert it back again:

```
var obj = {
  name : "Officer",
  surname : "Dibble"
```

```
}

console.log('JavaScript object:');
console.log(obj);

var json = JSON.stringify(obj);
console.log('JavaScript object to JSON:');
console.log(json);

var parsedJson = JSON.parse(json);
console.log('JSON to JavaScript object:');
console.log(parsedJson);
```

This example demonstrates how easy it is to convert a JavaScript object to JSON and back again. This is the reason that JavaScript developers love JSON as a data format!

▼ TRY IT YOURSELF

If you have downloaded the code examples for this book, this code is hour15/example03.

Follow these steps to parse JSON data:

1. Create a file called app.js and copy the following code into it:

```
var obj = {
  name : "Officer",
  surname : "Dibble"
}

console.log('JavaScript object:');
console.log(obj);

var json = JSON.stringify(obj);
console.log('JavaScript object to JSON:');
console.log(json);

var parsedJson = JSON.parse(json);
console.log('JSON to JavaScript object:');
console.log(parsedJson);
```

2. Run the script:

```
node app.js
```

3. You should see the data being logged to the terminal as a JavaScript object, then JSON, and then back to a JavaScript object.

The example is theoretical, but you can quickly see how see how easy it is to consume JSON with Node.js by working with a third-party data provider. Node.js makes it easy to fetch data and JSON.parse makes it simple to use the data. In the following example, a simple HTTP client is created to query the Twitter Search API for the latest tweets about Node.js. This returns JSON that can then be parsed and used:

```
var http = require('http');
var data = "";
var tweets = "";

var options = {
  host: 'search.twitter.com',
  port: 80,
  path: '/search.json?q=%23node.js'
};

var request = http.get(options, function(res){
  res.on('data', function(chunk){
    data += chunk
  });
  res.on('end', function(){
    tweets = JSON.parse(data);
    for (var i=0; i<tweets.results.length; i++) {
      console.log(tweets.results[i].text)
    }
  });
  res.on('error', function(e){
    console.log("There was an error: " + e.message);
  });
})
```

In this example, when the response from Twitter is complete, the raw data is parsed using JSON.parse. Then each tweet is outputted to the terminal within a loop. In a real-world application, you might save this data to a database or send it to a browser here.

This small script is a good example of how powerful retrieving data from APIs can be. This script could be extended to save the data so that it could be analyzed at a later date or so that the search term could be set dynamically. With a few lines of code, you can make Twitter's search data available to your application.

If you have downloaded the code examples for this book, this code is hour15/example04.

Follow these steps to parse JSON data from Twitter's API:

1. Create a file called app.js and copy the following code into it:

```
var http = require('http');
var data = "";
var tweets = "";

var options = {
  host: 'search.twitter.com',
  port: 80,
  path: '/search.json?q=%23node.js''
};

var request = http.get(options, function(res){
  res.on('data', function(chunk){
    data += chunk
  });
  res.on('end', function(){
    tweets = JSON.parse(data);
    for (var i=0; i<tweets.results.length; i++) {
      console.log(tweets.results[i].text)
    }
  });
  res.on('error', function(e){
    console.log("There was an error: " + e.message);
  });
})
```

2. Run the script:

```
node app.js
```

3. After a short pause, you should see the 15 latest tweets about Node.js outputted to your terminal.

BY THE WAY

There Are Thousands of APIs!

There are thousands of free, publically available APIs on the Web that give developers a wealth of data in JSON format. Some large organizations that publish data via APIs include the U.S. and U.K. governments and The World Bank. You can also get data from sites like Rotten Tomatoes for your film and video needs, Google Maps for maps, GitHub for source code, and many more. The possibilities are literally endless!

Creating a JSON API with Node.js

Now that you know a little more about JSON and how to work with it in Node.js, you see how to create a JSON-based API so that other developers can interact with your service. You modify the Express application that you created in Hour 8 to make it a JSON-based API and make your data available outside the browser.

The application that you created in Hour 8 had the following features:

▶ The ability to create, update, delete, and read tasks.

▶ Tasks are stored in MongoDB.

▶ Tasks can be updated from the browser.

This is great, but what about when someone wants to create an Android or iPhone application? Or perhaps you want a third-party piece of software to be able to update your tasks list? If for example you are tracking issues in a GitHub project, you might want any issues that are added into the project to be automatically added to your tasks list. This is where you need an API!

Sending Data as JSON in Express

Express has excellent support for working with JSON and provides many conveniences over the HTTP module in the Node.js Standard Library. There are two ways that you can send JSON data with Express and both take care of converting to JSON and setting headers correctly for you. The first is res.send():

```
var ingredients = [
  { name: 'eggs' },
  { name: 'flour' },
  { name: 'milk' }
];

app.get('/', function(req, res, next){
  res.send(ingredients);
});
```

If you were to perform a curl request on this route, you would get the following back:

```
HTTP/1.1 200 OK
X-Powered-By: Express
Content-Type: application/json; charset=utf-8
Content-Length: 127
Connection: keep-alive

[{"name":"eggs"},{"name":"flour"},{"name":"milk"}]
```

The response shows that Express performs a number of things for you here:

▶ The response code is set to 200.

▶ The Content-Type header is correctly set to `application/json`.

▶ The JavaScript object is converted a JSON string.

▼ TRY IT YOURSELF

If you have downloaded the code examples for this book, this code is hour15/example05.

Follow these steps to serve JSON data with Express:

1. Create a file called package.json and copy the following code into it:

```
{
  "name":"express-json",
  "version":"0.0.1",
  "private":true,
  "dependencies":{
    "express":"2.5.4"
  }
}
```

2. Create a second file called app.js and copy the following code into it:

```
var express = require('express')

var app = module.exports = express.createServer();

var rebels = [
  { name: 'Han Solo' },
  { name: 'Luke Skywalker' },
  { name: 'C-3PO' },
  { name: 'R2-D2' },
  { name: 'Chewbacca' },
  { name: 'Princess Leia' }
];

app.get('/', function(req, res, next){
  res.send(rebels);
});

app.use(express.errorHandler({ dumpExceptions: true, showStack: true }));

app.listen(3000);
console.log("Express server listening on port %d in %s mode", app.address().
➥ port, app.settings.env);
```

3. Install the dependencies:

```
npm install
```

4. Run the script:

```
node app.js
```

5. Using Google Chrome, open http://127.0.0.1:3000.

6. You should see a list of Rebel Alliance members as JSON. Check the headers using the HTTP Headers extension (see Figure 15.3).

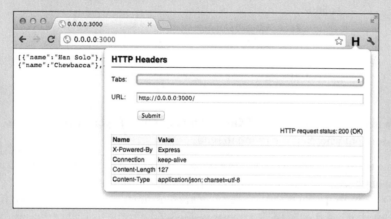

FIGURE 15.3
Sending JSON with Express

The second way you can tell Express to send JSON is by using `res.json()`. This is almost identical to `res.send()`:

```
var ingredients = [
  { name: 'eggs' },
  { name: 'flour' },
  { name: 'milk' }
];

app.get('/', function(req, res, next){
  res.json(ingredients);
  res.end();
});
```

This sets the response code and content type, and converts to JSON just as `res.send()` does. So what is the difference between these two methods?

In Express, res.send is designed to be a high-level response utility that allows you to pass all manner of objects into it. This could be a number of things:

▶ An empty response

▶ Some JSON

▶ Some HTML

▶ Some plain text

▶ Nothing with a 404 response

In code, these look like this:

```
res.send();
res.send({ greeting: 'OHAI!' });
res.send('<p>some html</p>');
res.send('text', { 'Content-Type': 'text/plain' }, 201);
res.send(404);
```

You can see that you can send a lot of different things using res.send and that it is clever enough to work out what you are trying to send.

If you choose to use res.json(), you are explicitly saying I want to send JSON and nothing else. This might be a good option if you know you only ever want to send JSON or if you need to send a string as JSON. Using the res.send() method assumes that you are sending HTML if you give it a string. But using res.json() allows you to send a string as JSON. If this is confusing, just use res.send(). It will almost always do what you want!

Building the Application

To understand creating a JSON API with Node.js, you build a simple API similar to the tasks application created in Hour 8. This allows you to create, read, update, and delete records. Based on the testing tools you learned in Hour 10, "Testing Node.js Applications," you follow a behavior driven development approach, so writing tests first and then writing code to make those tests pass. You use MongoDB as the data store as you did in Hour 8.

WATCH OUT

Make Sure That MongoDB Is Running

To follow these examples, you need to ensure MongoDB is running on your machine. If you need a refresher, refer to Hour 11, "Deploying Node.js Applications."

If you have downloaded the code examples for this book, this code is hour15/example06.

To create a JSON API with Node.js, follow these steps:

1. Create a new folder called json_api.

2. Within the new folder, create a file called app.js and enter the following content. This sets up a basic Express application with a Mongoose model for tasks and development and test environments:

```
var express = require('express');
var mongoose = require('mongoose');

var Schema = mongoose.Schema;
var ObjectId = Schema.ObjectId;

var Task = new Schema({
  task : {
    type: String,
    required: true,
  },
  created_at: { type: Date, default: Date.now },
  updated_at : Date
});

var Task = mongoose.model('Task', Task);

var app = module.exports = express.createServer();

app.configure(function(){
  app.use(express.bodyParser());
  app.use(express.methodOverride());
  app.use(app.router);
});

app.configure('development', function(){
  app.use(express.errorHandler({ dumpExceptions: true, showStack: true }));
  mongoose.connect('mongodb://localhost/todo_development');
  app.listen(3000);
});

app.configure('test', function() {
  app.use(express.errorHandler({ dumpExceptions: true, showStack: true }));
  mongoose.connect('mongodb://localhost/todo_test');
  app.listen(3001);
});

console.log("Express server listening on port %d in %s mode", app.address().
➥ port, app.settings.env);
```

3. Within the json_api folder, create a file called package.json and enter the following content:

```
{
  "name":"json_api",
  "version":"0.0.1",
  "private":true,
  "dependencies":{
    "express":"2.5.3",
    "mongoose":">= 2.3.1"
  },
  "scripts":{
    "test":"./node_modules/.bin/mocha"
  },
  "devDependencies":{
    "mocha":"0.3.x"
  }
}
```

4. Within the json_api folder, create a folder called test.

5. Finally, install the dependencies, and you will be all set up!

```
npm install
```

Following the behavior-driven development approach, you first write tests for what you want the API to do. The first thing you want is a route to return all tasks. This will be accessible at /api/v1/tasks. The behavior of this can be described to make it clear:

▶ It should return a 200 response.

▶ It should return tasks as JSON.

In Mocha, this looks like this:

```
describe('api v1', function(){
  describe('GET /api/v1/tasks', function(){
    it('should return at 200 response code')
    it('should return JSON')
  })
})
```

Remember that without a callback, a mocha test is passed so effectively it remains pending. This is a useful exercise when you are thinking about an API. Using this technique, you first describe the behavior of the API before you write a line of code. For many developers, this leads to a clearer definition of how this piece of software should work.

Once you have described how the API should work, you can write some tests to ensure that it actually does work as expected:

```
var http = require('http');
var assert = require('assert');
var app = require('../app.js');

describe('api v1', function(){
  describe('GET /api/v1/tasks', function(){
    it('should return a 200 response', function(done){
      http.get({ path: '/api/v1/tasks', port: 3001 }, function(res){
        assert.equal(res.statusCode,
          200,
          'Expected: 200 Actual: ' + res.statusCode );
        done();
      })
    })
    it('should return JSON', function(done){
      http.get({ path: '/api/v1/tasks', port: 3001 }, function(res){
        assert.equal(res.headers["content-type"],
          "application/json; charset=utf-8",
          'Expected: application/json; charset=utf-8 Actual: ' + res.
➥headers["content-type"]);
        done();
      })
    })
  })
})
```

In these two tests, we use the *assert* module from Node.js's standard library to first check that the response code is 200 and that JSON is returned.

TRY IT YOURSELF ▼

If you have downloaded the code examples for this book, this code is hour15/example07.

To test a JSON API with Mocha, follow these steps:

1. Returning to your json_api project in the test folder, create a file called tasks.js and add the following content:

```
var http = require('http');
var assert = require('assert');
var app = require('../app.js');

describe('api v1', function(){
  describe('GET /api/v1/tasks', function(){
    it('should return a 200 response', function(done){
      http.get({ path: '/api/v1/tasks', port: 3001 }, function(res){
        assert.equal(res.statusCode,
          200,
```

```
                         'Expected: 200 Actual: ' + res.statusCode );
                done();
             })
          })
       it('should return JSON', function(done){
          http.get({ path: '/api/v1/tasks', port: 3001 }, function(res){
             assert.equal(res.headers["content-type"],
                "application/json; charset=utf-8",
                'Expected: application/json; charset=utf-8 Actual: ' + res.
  ➥headers["content-type"]);
             done();
          })
       })
    })
})
```

2. Run the tests. You should see that they fail:

```
NODE_ENV=test npm test
```

3. In the app.js, just before the last line, add the following code:

```
app.get('/api/v1/tasks', function(req, res, next){
  Task.find({}, function (err, docs) {
    res.send(docs);
  });
});
```

4. Run the tests. You should see that they pass:

```
✔ 2 tests complete
```

This is a good example of Behavior Driven Development. First, you described how you wanted the API to behave and then wrote some tests for it. You saw those tests failing and then added some code to the application so that the tests passed. This approach is good for a number of reasons:

▶ You clearly define how you want the application to behave before you write the code.

▶ You have a repeatable set of tests for the future when you add new features.

▶ Once you have the tests passing, you know the application works!

You have created the route that returns a list of tasks, but you still need routes for creating, editing, and deleting tasks. For brevity's sake, the Behavior Driven Development description followed by the implementation code are given here.

Here is the route for creating a new task:

```
describe('POST /api/v1/tasks', function(){
  it('should return at 200 response code on success')
  it('should return JSON')
  it('should return at 422 response code if there is a validation error')
})
```

Here is the route for showing a single task:

```
describe('GET /api/v1/tasks/:id', function(){
  it('should return at 200 response code on success')
  it('should return JSON')
  it('should return at 404 response code if the task doesn't exist')
})
```

Here is the route for updating a task:

```
describe('PUT /api/v1/tasks/:id', function(){
  it('should return at 200 response code on success')
  it('should return JSON')
  it('should return at 404 response code if the task doesn't exist')
  it('should return at 422 response code if there is a validation error')
})
```

Here is the route for deleting a task:

```
describe('DELETE /api/v1/tasks/:id', function(){
  it('should return at 200 response code on success')
  it('should return JSON')
  it('should return at 404 response code if the task doesn't exist')
})
```

Think about how the API should function. Are there any other things you would add here? Going through this process is also useful for documentation. At some point, you will need to share your API with other developers, and going through these steps makes it easy to write documentation.

The normal process here would be to write tests for these descriptions first and then write code to make the tests pass just as we did before. For brevity's sake, you will not be going into the tests for each of these actions, although you are encouraged to explore them outside this hour.

Here is the implementation for each route. It follows closely the techniques you used in Hour 8. First, create a new task:

```
app.post('/api/v1/tasks', function(req, res){
  var doc = new Task(req.body.task);
  doc.save(function (err) {
    if (!err) {
```

```
      res.send(doc);
    } else {
      res.send(err, 422);
    }
  });
});
```

As you saw in Hour 8, this sets up a route to accept a post request and expects data like `task[task]=feed the dog`. If the task saves successfully, it is returned as a JSON object with a 200 response.

Here is the implementation for getting a single task by id:

```
app.get('/api/v1/tasks/:id', function(req, res){
  Task.findById(req.params.id, function (err, doc){
    if (doc) {
      res.send(doc);
    } else {
      res.send(404);
    }
  });
});
```

This searches for a record in MongoDB with the id supplied. If it is found, it is returned as a JSON object. If it is not found, a 404 response is sent.

Here is the implementation for updating a single task by id:

```
app.put('/api/v1/tasks/:id', function(req, res){
  Task.findById(req.params.id, function (err, doc){
    if (!doc) {
      res.json(404)
    } else {
      doc.updated_at = new Date();
      doc.task = req.body.task.task;
      doc.save(function (err) {
        if (!err) {
          res.send(doc);
        } else {
          res.send(err, 422);
        }
      });
    }
  });
});
```

This searches for a record by id and updates the record based on the data sent in the PUT request. If there is a validation error, a 422 response is returned. If no document is found with the id, a 404 response is returned.

Here is the implementation for deleting a task:

```
app.del('/api/v1/tasks/:id', function(req, res){
  Task.findById(req.params.id, function (err, doc){
    if (doc) {
      doc.remove(function() {
        res.send(200)
      });
    } else {
      res.json(404)
    }
  });
});
```

This searches for a record by id, deletes it if found, and returns a 404 response if it is not found.

If you have downloaded the code examples for this book, the completed code for the API is available in hour15/example08.

This is a simplistic API (there is no authentication!), but it demonstrates how easy it is to create JSON APIs with Node.js.

Summary

In this hour, you were introduced to the idea of APIs and JSON as a format for data exchange. You saw how to send JSON data with Node.js and how easy it is to consume JSON with Node. js. You were introduced to the idea of API clients and servers. First with the Twitter example, you created a simple API client to fetch the latest Node.js tweets; then you created a simple API for tasks.

You really only scratched the surface of what Node.js can do with APIs in this hour, but hopefully you saw enough to convince you that creating API clients and servers is straightforward and powerful in Node.js. Coupled with the excellent performance and scalability of Node.js, APIs are an excellent use case for the technology.

Q&A

Q. **Why JSON and not XML?**

A. JSON has become very popular with web developers, especially those that use JavaScript. When working with Node.js and JavaScript, it makes sense to use JSON as a data format. Furthermore, in the context of the Web, JavaScript is now being used on the server and client side. It makes sense to keep the data exchange format within the JavaScript family if you are using JavaScript. It is faster to parse and easier to use. You'll find that most of the Node.js community likes JSON. If you do want to use XML or another data format, you can absolutely do that. It is just not covered in this hour.

Q. **Is JSON smaller and faster than XML?**

A. Typically JSON does result in a smaller amount of data than would be found with XML. Many servers compress data before it is sent to the client, so in reality the difference in data size is negligible.

Q. **Can I really use data that is published by third-party APIs?**

A. Generally the answer is yes. Particularly with public data (e.g., governments and public bodies), the data is effectively owned by taxpayers so it should be in the public domain. Many organizations have seen amazing things created by publishing their data in an API. Some APIs do have licensing restrictions particularly around commercial usage. If in doubt, review the license information for the API or get in touch with the API provider directly.

Workshop

This workshop contains quiz questions and exercises to help cement your learning in this hour.

Quiz

1. Why might you want to create an API?

2. What are some of the advantages of JSON over XML?

3. If you are writing JSON by hand, how can you ensure it is valid?

Quiz Answers

1. You might create an API as you want to provide access to data so that it can be used. It can be a private API, meaning that only you or whomever you give access to can use it. It can also be a public API, meaning that anyone can use it.

2. JSON is a great choice if you are using Node.js since it is easy to parse JSON. It is a lightweight data format that can handle complex data structures and is well supported by browsers too.

3. A number of online tools allow you to quickly validate your JSON. These tools ensure that handwritten JSON will not break scripts, so it is recommended that you validate handwritten JSON. Two popular sites are http://jsonlint.com/ and http://jsonformatter.curiousconcept. com/.

Exercises

1. Visit www.programmableweb.com/apis/directory and browse the list of APIs. Filter the data format to JSON and explore the list. Imagine what you could do with all this data!

2. Write a client to fetch some Node.js repositories from GitHub. Perform a GET request on the following URL: https://api.github.com/legacy/repos/search/node. Parse and output the JSON in the response.

3. In the Tasks API that you created, review the file in test/tasks.js. Try to understand the purpose of writing tests in this manner and complete a test that checks for a 200 response. If you are feeling ambitious, complete the test suite!

PART V

Exploring the Node.js API

The Process Module

What You'll Learn in This Hour:

▶ What a process is

▶ Sending signals to a process

▶ Creating executable scripts with Node.js

▶ Passing arguments to a process

What Processes Are

Whenever you run anything on a computer, you are running a process. If you have a browser open, you have at least one and probably more than one process running for the browser to do its work. As you have learned, Node.js runs on one process, so when you run a Node.js program, it runs on a single process. Operating systems assign processes an id that is sometimes referred to as the *pid* or *process id*. This is a unique number assigned to the process for as long as it is alive.

With the Process module, Node.js allows developers to discover the process id of a script. In the following example, the script does nothing more than write the process id to the terminal. The Process module does not need to be required like other scripts as all the information is already available in the existing process!

```
console.log(process.pid);
```

If you run this script from the console, you see the process id printed out:

```
node process.js
32204
```

Running the script more than once, you will notice that each time it is run, a new process id is assigned to it:

```
node process.js
32634
node process.js
```

```
32639
node process.js
32643
```

This may seem trivial, but it is important to understand that whenever a process is run, it is assigned a unique process id. In this example, the process id is only assigned for a short period. When the script has finished printing the process id, it exits and the process no longer exists.

▼ TRY IT YOURSELF

If you have downloaded the code examples for this book, this code is hour16/example01.

Follow these steps to discover a process id:

1. Create a file called app.js and copy the following code into it:

```
console.log(process.pid);
```

2. Run the script:

```
node process.js
```

3. Note the process id or PID that is shown.

4. Run the script again a number of times.

5. You should see that the pid number changes each time you run it (see Figure 16.1).

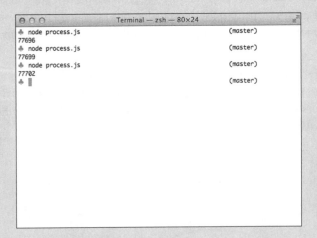

FIGURE 16.1
Each process has a unique process identifier.

Many Processes Are Running on Your Computer

At any one time, many processes are running on your computer. If you are on Mac OSX or Linux, open a terminal and run the command ps aux to see a list. On a windows machine, open a command prompt and run the command tasklist /v. All these processes are running to keep your computer running and you, as the user of the computer, happy.

Exiting and Errors in Processes

The Process module provides an event for whenever the process is exited:

```
process.on('exit', function ()
  // Do something when the script exits
});
```

This is useful if you need to perform some cleanup operations when a script exits like closing connections, or if you need to log some information. The Process module also provides an 'uncaughtException' event for an exception that isn't handled by your script:

```
process.on('uncaughtException', function (err) {
  console.error(err.stack);
});
```

One usage of this event would be to catch uncaught exceptions and send them to an email address. This allows you as the developer to be aware of any issues in your application that you have not accounted for in your normal error handling, leading to more stable robust scripts. This is exactly what the third-party node-exception-notifier module does (https://github.com/saschagehlich/node-exception-notifier/), and although the source code is written in CoffeeScript, you can see how this event is used in the code to send an exception notification. It should be noted that code execution within this event cannot be fully relied upon.

You might also choose to use this event to notify an exception-logging service like Airbrake (http://airbrake.io/). This service maintains a log of uncaught exceptions so that developers can review and close off exceptions. A third-party node-airbrake module does just this and catches the uncaughtException event and sends it to the service (https://github.com/felixge/node-airbrake/).

Processes and Signals

On UNIX type systems (Mac OSX or Linux), processes can receive signals. These allow a process to respond in a certain way. One of the most common signals is SIGINT. This is shorthand for sending the Interrupt signal. You have already been using this signal by pressing Ctrl+C to stop a Node.js process. You did this in the Hello World Node.js server, for example.

The Process module allows Node.js scripts to listen for these signals and respond to them accordingly. The SIGINT is issued to say that the process should be stopped but gives a process the opportunity to clean up before exiting.

To demonstrate a SIGINT signal being received, a short Node.js script can be created to show a signal being received:

```
process.stdin.resume();

process.on('SIGINT', function() {
  console.log('Got a SIGINT. Exiting');
  process.exit(0);
});
```

The first line of the script prevents the script from exiting as it initializes reading from `stdin` so it does not exit. If the line was not present, the script would finish and the process would end. Receiving signals in Node.js follows the familiar callback pattern of an anonymous function that is called when the process receives a signal. If this script is run and then Ctrl+C is pressed on the keyboard, a SIGINT is sent to the process and the script shows that a SIGINT was received before exiting:

```
node process.js
[Press Ctrl-C on your keyboard]
Got a SIGINT. Exiting.
```

▼ TRY IT YOURSELF

If you have downloaded the code examples for this book, this code is hour16/example02.

Follow these steps to handle a SIGINT signal in the Process module:

1. Create a file called process.js and copy the following code into it:

   ```
   process.stdin.resume();

   process.on('SIGINT', function() {
     console.log('Got a SIGINT. Exiting');
     process.exit(0);
   });
   ```

2. Run the script:

   ```
   node process.js
   ```

3. Press Ctrl+C on your keyboard.

4. You should see "Got a SIGINT. Exiting."

In this simple example, the script received a SIGINT, logged that it had been received, and then exited. A more practical use of receiving a SIGINT is to clean up anything related to a process before it exits. This might be closing connections, writing to a log file, or even doing something to another process.

Sending Signals to Processes

On UNIX type systems, you can send a signal to a process with the `kill` command. The `kill` command is given the process id that you want to send a signal to. By default, it sends a SIGTERM, indicating that the process should be terminated immediately:

```
kill [process_id]
```

The `kill` command can also send other signals too. In the last example, you saw how a process can be sent a SIGINT by pressing Ctrl+C on the keyboard. The `kill` command can also send a SIGINT:

```
kill -s SIGINT [process_id]
```

Using the Process module, it is possible to set up listeners for these signals and to respond accordingly:

```
process.on('SIGINT', function() {
  console.log('Got a SIGINT. Exiting');
  process.exit(0);
});

process.on('SIGTERM', function() {
  console.log('Got a SIGTERM. Exiting');
  process.exit(0);
});

setInterval(function() {
  // This keeps the process running
}, 10000);

console.log('Run `kill ' + process.pid + '` to send a SIGTERM')
console.log('Run `kill -s SIGINT ' + process.pid + '` to send a SIGINT')
```

In this example, the script listens for the SIGINT and SIGTERM signals. The `setInterval` at the end keeps the script running. Without it, the script would exit. If this file is saved as process.js, the script can be run with the following command:

```
node process.js
```

The script outputs the process id so that signals can be sent to it using the `kill` command from another terminal.

▼ TRY IT YOURSELF

If you have downloaded the code examples for this book, this code is hour16/example03.

Here's how to handle other signals in the Process module:

1. Create a file called process.js and copy the following code into it:

```
process.on('SIGINT', function() {
  console.log('Got a SIGINT. Exiting');
  process.exit(0);
});

process.on('SIGTERM', function() {
  console.log('Got a SIGTERM. Exiting');
  process.exit(0);
});

setInterval(function() {
  // This keeps the process running
}, 10000);

console.log('Run `kill ' + process.pid + '` to send a SIGTERM')
console.log('Run `kill -s SIGINT ' + process.pid + '` to send a SIGINT')
```

2. Run the script:

```
node process.js
```

3. Note the output and run the kill command on the first line of the output to demonstrate a SIGTERM:

```
kill [process_id]
```

4. You should see that the script is terminated.

5. Start the script in the background again:

```
node process.js &
```

6. Send the script a SIGINT signal, as shown by the output of running the script:

```
kill -s SIGINT [process_id]
```

7. You should see that the script receives the SIGINT and exits.

DID YOU KNOW?

Exit Statuses Matter

When exiting a script, it is important to give the correct exit status as other scripts may be interacting with it. If a script has executed successfully, it exits with a status of 0. If it exits with a status of 1, there was an error. The Process module provides a simple way to correctly exit scripts with `'process.exit()'`.

Creating Scripts with Node.js

The Process module helps to create small scripts with Node.js. When you run commands from the terminal, you are running an executable. The code that gets executed can be a binary or a script written in a range of scripting languages. So, it can be a script written with Node.js! There are a couple of steps for creating a script that can be run from the command line.

The first is to add a Node.js shebang to the top of the script. The word "shebang" may be new to you, but it is just a line that tells the operating system where to find the binary that should be used to run the script. This also means that you can call the file whatever you want, and you do not need the .js extension to identify what type of file it is. For Node.js, the shebang looks like as follows:

```
#!/usr/bin/env node
```

Once you have placed the shebang on the first line of script, the script also needs to be made executable. On Mac OSX or Linux, this can be achieved with the following command:

```
chmod +x yourscript.js
```

With the shebang in place and ensuring the script is executable, you can run the script as follows:

```
./yourscript.js
```

Note that you do not need to add the node command before you run the script because this is encapsulated in the shebang. A simple Node.js script is

```
#!/usr/bin/env node
console.log('my first node script!');
```

If this file is saved as script, it can be made executable and then run to see the output:

```
chmod +x script
./script
my first node script!
```

▼ TRY IT YOURSELF

If you have downloaded the code examples for this book, this code is hour16/example04.

Follow these steps to create an executable script with Node.js:

1. Create a file called script and copy the following code into it:

```
#!/usr/bin/env node
console.log('my first node script!');
```

2. Make the script executable:

```
chmod +x script
```

3. From the same directory as the script, run the following command to execute the script:

```
./script
```

4. You should see the output from your script (see Figure 16.2).

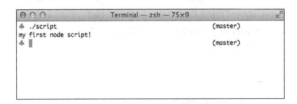

FIGURE 16.2
Running a simple Node.js script

Passing Arguments to Scripts

The Process module supports being able to pass arguments to a script, and this is available as an array in process.argv. The following script logs any arguments to the console:

```
#!/usr/bin/env node
console.log(process.argv);
```

If this script is run with no arguments, you see that the first two items of the array are already populated with 'node' and the path to the script:

```
[ 'node',
  '/Users/george/script' ]
```

If you pass arguments to the script, these are shown after these elements in the array:

```
./script one two three
[ 'node',
```

```
'/Users/george/script'
'one',
'two',
'there' ]
```

Using arguments scripts can become very flexible and very useful. You might want to write a script that fetches data from a public API, for example. The following example demonstrates how you can write a short Node.js script to fetch search results from Twitter's search API and show it in the console:

```
#!/usr/bin/env node

var http = require('http');

if (!process.argv[2]) {
  console.error('A search term is required');
  process.exit(1);
}

var options = {
  host: 'search.twitter.com',
  path: '/search.json?q=' + process.argv[2]
};

http.get(options, function(res) {
  var data = "";
  var json;
  res.on("data", function (chunk) {
    data += chunk;
  });
  res.on("end", function () {
    json = JSON.parse(data);
    for (i = 0; i < json.results.length; i++) {
      console.log(json.results[i].text)
    }
    process.exit(0);
  });
}).on('error', function(e) {
  console.log("Error fetching data: " + e.message);
  process.exit(1);
});
```

The HTTP module that you were introduced to in Hour 5, "HTTP," is used to fetch data from Twitter's publically available JSON search API. This returns a series of search results as JSON data from the search term given as a query. When the data comes back from Twitter's servers, the script parses the JSON and then loops through the results logging the text to the console.

Scripts like this are useful, because they can be executed by computers at regular intervals as well as by humans from the terminal. Furthermore scripts like this can be glued together with other scripts to provide more complex functionality. Given Node.js strengths in network programming, it is an excellent choice if you need to automate doing things with networks, and the Process module provides most of the tools you need to create scripts.

▼ TRY IT YOURSELF

If you have downloaded the code examples for this book, this code is hour16/example05.

Follow these steps to use arguments with executable scripts:

1. Create a file called script and copy the following code into it:

```
#!/usr/bin/env node

var http = require('http');

if (!process.argv[2]) {
  console.error('A search term is required');
  process.exit(1);
}

var options = {
  host: 'search.twitter.com',
  path: '/search.json?q=' + process.argv[2]
};

http.get(options, function(res) {
  var data = "";
  var json;
  res.on("data", function (chunk) {
    data += chunk;
  });
  res.on("end", function () {
    json = JSON.parse(data);
    for (i = 0; i < json.results.length; i++) {
      console.log(json.results[i].text)
    }
    process.exit(0);
  });
}).on('error', function(e) {
  console.log("Error fetching data: " + e.message);
  process.exit(1);
});
```

2. Make the script executable:

```
chmod +x script
```

3. From the same directory as the script file, run the script:

```
./script
```

4. You should see the script prompting you for a search term argument.

5. Run the script again with an argument:

```
./script node.js
```

6. You should see tweets about node.js returned from Twitter's search API (see Figure 16.3).

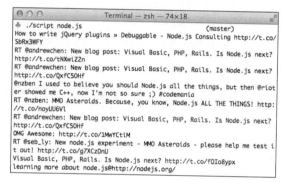

FIGURE 16.3
Passing arguments to a Node.js script

Summary

In this hour, you were introduced to the Process module. You saw how it provides a number of tools for developers to create and interact with Node.js processes. You saw how it is possible to send UNIX signals to Node.js scripts and how to create small, executable scripts with Node.js. You can build on top of this knowledge to create network scripts with Node.js that can be used and automated to solve many problems.

Q&A

Q. **What types of things can I use the Process module for?**

A. The Process module is particularly useful for creating scripts with Node.js. It can provide information on the environment that the script is running in and allows signals to be sent to a process. It also allows scripts to set the correct exit status allowing other scripts to interact with them correctly. It is useful for most programming that you do with Node.js, though, as everything is based on a process!

Q. **Should I use Node.js for scripts over say Ruby, Python, or Bash?**

A. Node.js excels at network programming, so if you are doing anything involving networks in your scripts, Node.js is an excellent choice. Node.js isn't designed to be a general scripting language, so if you have experience with other programming languages, you may find that your purposes are better suited by another language. As always, pick the right tool for the job.

Q. **Can I use system commands in Node.js scripts?**

A. Yes. You see how to do this in Hour 17, "The Child Process Module."

Q. **Are there any modules available to help write Node.js scripts?**

A. Yes. Commander is one Node.js module designed to ease developing command-line scripts: https://github.com/visionmedia/commander.js. There is also the cli module at https://github.com/chriso/cli. More modules are available that can be found at http://search.npmjs.org/.

Workshop

This workshop contains quiz questions and exercises to help cement your learning in this hour.

Quiz

1. Do you need to do anything to use the Process module in your scripts?

2. Why might you want to send signals to scripts?

3. How can you make sure a process stays up?

Quiz Answers

1. No. The Process module is a global object in Node.js, so you are able to use it without adding anything to your scripts.

2. Signals are used in UNIX and UNIX-type systems to provide a way for processes to communicate with each other. They can be used to make a process terminate, suspend, or restart. Signals are a POSIX standard meaning they are used by many other programs. Using signals in Node.js allows you to integrate with other UNIX tools if you want.

3. You might have realized that if you are working with a process, you may be placing a heavy reliance on that script running. On UNIX type systems, you can run scripts in the background, meaning you don't have to keep a terminal window open. There are also a number of tools on UNIX like monit and upstart to help you monitor processes and restart them if necessary. There are also tools created with Node.js to help with this. One of the most popular ones is forever (https://github.com/nodejitsu/forever/), which ensures a script runs continuously.

Exercises

1. Open a terminal and run `ps aux` on **Mac OSX or Linux** or `tasklist /v` on **Windows. Try to understand what these processes relate to. You might see the name of a program running on your machine. Understand that there are many processes running on your machine and that any Node.js process is just one of these.**

2. Write a short command-line script that takes two arguments that should be two numbers. The script should multiply the two numbers and output the answer to the terminal. Think about the types of validation that you need to do on the inputted data.

The Child Process Module

What You'll Learn in This Hour:

▶ What child processes are

▶ Creating child processes with Node.js

▶ Running a system command using a child process

▶ Managing child processes

What Is a Child Process?

In Hour 16, "The Process Module," you saw how Node.js provides a module to allow you to run and manage a Node.js process. You may also need to create child processes from your Node.js process, and the Child Process module gives you the tools you need to do this. A child process is simply one created by another process. The process that created the child process is referred to as the parent. A parent can have many child processes, but a child process can only have one parent. Some scenarios where you might want to consider using a child process include the following:

▶ You need to calculate a complex equation.

▶ You need to use a system-based tool outside Node.js to manipulate some data.

▶ You are performing any operation that is resource intensive or takes a long time to complete.

▶ You want to perform some cleanup operations.

In terms of a parent process interfacing with a child process, it can stream data through stdin (standard input), stdout (standard input), or sterr (standard error). Initially, this may be confusing, but this will become clear. To demonstrate how Node.js can communicate with a child process, open a terminal and type

```
ping bbc.co.uk
```

You see a series of responses indicating how long the server took to respond. The `ping` command has nothing to do with Node.js. It is a tool on both Windows- and UNIX-type systems that allows you to see whether a host or gateway is up by asking for an echo response. The `ping` command allows you say, "Hey server! Are you up?" If it is up, it responds, and the `ping` command shows you some statistics about how long the round-trip took. Like most terminal-based programs, ping expects some input and to send some output. If you are interested in using the ping program within Node.js, you can do so by spawning a child process and listening for the standard output of the child process.

The first way to create a child process in Node.js is to use the `spawn()` method. This takes a few arguments:

▶ **Command**—The command that you want to run

▶ **Arguments**—Any arguments that you want to give to the command

▶ **Options**—Things like the working directory and environment variables

In the case of using the ping utility, `ping` is the command and `'bbc.co.uk'` is the argument, so spawning a child process with the ping utility is as follows:

```
var spawn = require('child_process').spawn;
var ping = spawn('ping', ['bbc.co.uk']);
```

This starts a child process, and as you saw when you ran the `ping` command from your terminal, this returns some output to the terminal or stdout (standard output). To be able to use the data within your Node.js script, a listener must be added to the child process to handle data that is received at standard output. Note here that you must specify the encoding of the data or the raw stream will be shown:

```
ping.stdout.setEncoding('utf8');
ping.stdout.on('data', function (data) {
  console.log(data);
});
```

Now if this script is run, a child process will be spawned and the standard output will be available to the parent process and shown in the terminal:

```
PING bbc.co.uk (212.58.241.131): 56 data bytes
64 bytes from 212.58.241.131: icmp_seq=0 ttl=245 time=16.115 ms

64 bytes from 212.58.241.131: icmp_seq=1 ttl=245 time=396.518 ms
```

If you have downloaded the code examples for this book, this code is hour17/example01.

Follow these steps to create a child process in Node.js:

1. Create a file called app.js and copy the following code into it:

```
var spawn = require('child_process').spawn;
var ping = spawn('ping', ['bbc.co.uk']);
ping.stdout.setEncoding('utf8');
ping.stdout.on('data', function (data) {
  console.log(data);
});
```

2. Run the script:

```
node app.js
```

3. You should see the output from the child process in your terminal (see Figure 17.1).

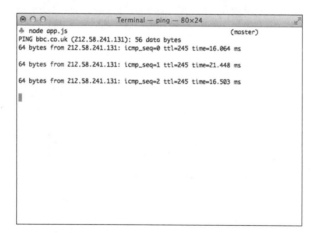

FIGURE 17.1
Spawning and outputting the results of a child process

This simple but powerful technique gives you access to any software that you have on your operating system. An example of where this might be useful is in encoding a video file from an upload. The industry standard tool for encoding videos is ffmpeg. This is an open source software that can be compiled and run from the command line. It is not part of Node.js, but using the Child Process module, Node.js can access it and use it to create a server that accepts a file and encodes it using ffmpeg. Note that if you are spawning multiple CPU intensive processes, you may have to use a job queue or distribute the processing across more than one computer to prevent your machine from running out of resources.

Killing a Child Process

A parent process can send a kill signal to the child process. This is similar to the kill messages you saw in Hour 16 with the Process module. To kill a child process, the Child Process module provides the `kill()` method. It is possible to pass in the type of message that you want the kill message to send. If you do not pass anything, the SIGTERM signal is be sent. The example that you just created can now be amended to send a kill signal from the parent to the child process. The parent can also listen for the exit event of the child and do something with it. In this example, because the child process is killed, it does not show the output of the `ping` command:

```
var spawn = require('child_process').spawn;
var ping = spawn('ping', ['bbc.co.uk']);

ping.stdout.setEncoding('utf8');
ping.stdout.on('data', function (data) {
  console.log(data);
});

ping.on('exit', function (code, signal) {
  console.log('child process was killed with a '+ signal + ' signal');
});

ping.kill('SIGINT');
```

▼ TRY IT YOURSELF

Follow these steps to kill a child process:

1. Create a file called app.js and copy the following code into it:

```
var spawn = require('child_process').spawn;
var ping = spawn('ping', ['bbc.co.uk']);

ping.stdout.setEncoding('utf8');
ping.stdout.on('data', function (data) {
  console.log(data);
});

ping.on('exit', function (code, signal) {
  console.log('child process was killed with a '+ signal + ' signal');
});

ping.kill('SIGINT');
```

2. Run the script:

```
node app.js
```

3. You should see the child process being killed by the parent process.

Communicating with a Child Process

The Child Process module also provides another method for creating child processes that are Node.js processes that also provide the capability for the parent and child process to have a communication channel. This method is called `fork()` and is used for creating child Node.js processes. If you are interacting with system commands, use `spawn()`. The overhead of using `fork()` is that each child process is an entire new instance of V8. The Node.js documentation notes that you should assume a startup time of 30 milliseconds and for 10MB of memory to be used for each process. So you can only start as many child processes as you have memory on your machine!

For this example, assume you have a parent process and a single child process that you need to communicate with. Using the `fork()` method is slightly different from `spawn()`, so creating the child process now looks as follows:

```
var fork = require('child_process').fork;
var child = fork(__dirname + '/child.js');
```

The child is now expected to be a Node.js module or program of some description. Using the `fork()` method, the parent can communicate with the child process. This can be useful for passing data around or letting either process know about changes in state. To send a message to the child from the parent looks like this:

```
child.send({ message: 'Hello child!' });
```

In the child process, this message can be listened for and handled:

```
process.on('message', function(m) {
  console.log('child process received message:', m);
});
```

The child process can also send messages back to the parent:

```
process.send({ message: 'Hello parent!' });
```

Putting all this together, the parent Node.js program looks as follows:

```
var fork = require('child_process').fork;
var child = fork(__dirname + '/child.js');
```

```
child.on('message', function(m) {
  console.log('parent process received message:', m);
});

child.send({ message: 'Hello child!' });
```

The corresponding child.js program looks like this:

```
process.on('message', function(m) {
  console.log('child process received message:', m);
});

process.send({ message: 'Hello parent!' });
```

Now when the parent process is run, it creates the child process and messages will be sent back and forth:

```
child process received message: { message: 'Hello child!' }
parent process received message: { message: 'Hello parent!' }
```

▼ TRY IT YOURSELF

If you have downloaded the code examples for this book, this code is hour17/example03.

Follow these steps to use fork() and messaging between processes:

1. Create a new file called parent.js and copy in the following content:

```
var fork = require('child_process').fork;
var child = fork(__dirname + '/child.js');

child.on('message', function(m) {
  console.log('parent process received message:', m);
});

child.send({ message: 'Hello child!' });
```

2. Create another new file called child.js and paste in the following content:

```
process.on('message', function(m) {
  console.log('child process received message:', m);
});
```

3. Run the parent process:

```
node parent.js
```

4. You should see the communication between the parent and child processes in your terminal (see Figure 17.2).

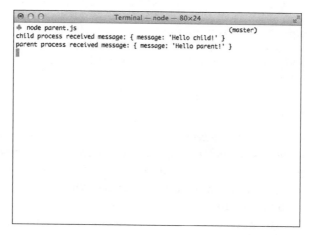

FIGURE 17.2
Communicating between a parent and child process

The Cluster Module

A common requirement in relation to child processes is to scale an application to the number of processors available on a computer. This means that there will be one child process for each of the processors on a machine and a parent (or master) process to manage them. In this context, child processes are often also known as worker processes. Node.js has a module specifically for this to allow a program to create child processes in a cluster and for a single parent process to handle requests coming in to a program before handing them off to a child process. A practical example of this is the Hello World web server. The Cluster module provides an easy way to scale a Node.js program to the number of processors available on a machine:

```
var cluster = require('cluster');
var http = require('http');
var cpus = 2;

if (cluster.isMaster) {
  console.log('Master process started with PID:', process.pid);

  for (var i = 0; i < cpus; i++) {
    cluster.fork();
  }

  cluster.on('death', function(worker) {
    console.log('worker ' + worker.pid + ' died');
    cluster.fork();
  });
```

```
} else {
  console.log('Worker process started with PID:', process.pid);
  http.createServer(function (req, res) {
    res.writeHead(200, {'Content-Type': 'text/plain'});
    res.end('Hello World\n');
  }).listen(3000);
}
```

The Cluster module starts a master process (sometimes also referred to as the parent process) and can be used to start as many child processes as you tell it to. The `fork()` method is also available in the Cluster module, and this actually builds on top of the `fork()` method available in the Child Process module, so has many of the same features. When this example runs, it creates child processes relative to the number of CPUs available on your machine—in this case, two. These processes will be created as a child (or worker) processes to serve the Hello World HTTP server. The master process listens for a worker process dying and responds to that event (in this case, restarting a new worker).

WATCH OUT

Be Careful About Sessions

If your application uses sessions, you need to be careful when using the Cluster module. If you store sessions in memory, they will not be shared across workers. To resolve this, you can store sessions in something like Redis to ensure that worker processes share sessions.

▼ TRY IT YOURSELF

If you have downloaded the code examples for this book, this code is hour17/example04.

Follow these steps to use the Cluster module to create child processes:

1. Create a new file called app.js and paste in the following content:

```
var cluster = require('cluster');
var http = require('http');
var cpus = 2;

if (cluster.isMaster) {
  console.log('Master process started with PID:', process.pid);

  for (var i = 0; i < cpus; i++) {
    cluster.fork();
  }

  cluster.on('death', function(worker) {
    console.log('worker ' + worker.pid + ' died');
```

```
      cluster.fork();
   });

} else {
   console.log('Worker process started with PID:', process.pid);
   http.createServer(function (req, res) {
      res.writeHead(200, {'Content-Type': 'text/plain'});
      res.end('Hello World\n');
   }).listen(3000);
}
```

2. Start the server:

   `node app.js`

3. You should see that one master and two child processes are started.

4. Note the pid of one of the child processes and in another terminal window or tab issue a kill signal to the child process:

   `kill [pid number of child process]`

5. Back in the terminal window running the server, you should see that the process died and that the master process started another child process (see Figure 17.3).

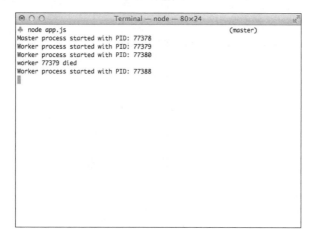

FIGURE 17.3
The Cluster module starting a pool of workers and restarting a worker that died

Summary

In this hour, you learned about the Child Process module. You saw how to create a child process and how to run a system command in Node.js using a child process. You saw how it is possible for a parent process to kill a child process and how to send signals to child processes. You learned about the `fork()` method that allows you to create child Node.js processes and how to communicate between Node.js processes. Finally, you saw how to use the Cluster module to child processes and scale your application to number of cores available on your server.

Q&A

Q. Should I be using system commands rather than trying to write JavaScript with Node.js?

A. Yes. Sometimes, you will come up against a problem that has already been solved with a mature, stable solution in another programming language or a system tool. The example of using ffmpeg to process videos is a good one where using another tool to solve a problem is going to be much more stable and vastly quicker than trying to write the code yourself.

Q. Are there any problems with using child processes and system tools?

A. Portability is the main issue. If you write code for one operating system, there is no guarantee that when the code is run on another operating system that a particular system tool or piece of software will be available. If portability is going to be an issue for the software that you write, think carefully about using system-level tools.

Q. Do I need to use child processes?

A. Child processes should be used for specific purposes like being able to use system tools, completing a long-running process, or scaling an application to the number of processors on a computer. For the majority of programming requirements, programming with a single process is all you need.

Workshop

This workshop contains quiz questions and exercises to help cement your learning in this hour.

Quiz

1. When should you use `spawn()`, and when should you use `fork()`?
2. What do you need to watch out for when you use `spawn()`?
3. When should you use the Cluster module over the Child Process module?

Quiz Answers

1. You should use `spawn()` when you want to use a system command. Use `fork()` to create another Node.js process.

2. If you are using a system command when you are developing, you may find that when you deploy your application that the system command is either not available or called something different. If you use `spawn()`, make sure that Node.js has access to the command when you deploy your application. If you are using Platform as a Service provider, it is likely that system commands will not be available to you.

3. You should use the Cluster module if you have a pool of child or worker processes that you want a master process to manage. If you need to scale your application to take advantage of the cores available on your machine, the Cluster module provides a simple way to do that.

Exercises

1. Find another system program that you use from the command line and modify the code example that you can find at hour17/example01 to output the results to the console. Try to understand how arguments passed to the child process affect the output.

2. Extend the example that you can find in hour17/example03 to add further messaging between the parent and child script in hour17/example01 by having the child script read the contents of a file and sending the contents of the file as a message to the parent.

3. Experiment with the example available as hour17/example04 to add more worker processes. Try sending kill signals to the worker processes. What happens if you send a kill signal to the master process?

The Events Module

What You'll Learn in This Hour:

▶ Using the Events module

▶ Emitting and listening for events

▶ How the Events module works with network programming

▶ Adding and removing events dynamically

Understanding Events

As you have learned, Node.js is opinionated about the best way to approach concurrency. It suggests that using an event loop (sometimes referred to as an event queue) is an efficient way to support asynchronous code and address the issue of concurrency. For developers coming from procedural, imperative languages this can be a paradigm shift, and many developers refer to programming around events as "programming inside out."

The Events module is central to Node.js, and many other modules use it to structure functionality around events. As Node.js runs on a single thread, any synchronous code is blocking so an event loop can become blocked if there is a long-running piece of code. To write code effectively with Node.js, you must think carefully about your style of programming and follow some simple rules:

▶ **Don't block**— Node.js is single threaded, so everything else halts if code is blocking.

▶ **Return fast**— Operations should return fast. If they are unable to return fast, they should be moved off into a separate process.

The Events module provides a simple way to structure code around events whether they are controlled by you or more likely that they come from the network somewhere. The Events module allows developers to set up listeners and handlers for events. If you are already using client-side JavaScript, creating listeners and handlers may be familiar to you. In client-side JavaScript, you can set up a listener for a click event and then perform something when that event happens:

```
var target = document.getElementById("target");
target.addEventListener('click', function () {
  alert('Click event fired. Target was clicked!');
}, false);
```

If you are more familiar with jQuery, this is how the code would look in jQuery:

```
$("#target").click(function() {
  alert('Click event fired. Target was clicked!');
});
```

Both pieces of code are doing the same thing. They are setting up an event listener for the click event on an HTML element with the id of 'target'. When the click event happens, the event is said to be fired, and an event listener handles the event by showing an alert. The way that an event is handled is defined by the function within the listener. In these examples, the event is emitted by a human controlling a mouse. When the mouse is clicked, the event is fired.

▼ TRY IT YOURSELF

If you have downloaded the code examples for this book, this code is hour18/example01.

Follow these steps to fire events in JavaScript:

1. Create a file called index.html and copy the following code into it:

```
<!DOCTYPE html>
<html lang="en">
  <head>
    <meta charset="utf-8" />
    <title>JavaScript Events</title>
  </head>
  <body>
  <h1>JavaScript Events</h1>
  <button id="target">Click me</button>
  <script type="text/javascript">
    var target = document.getElementById('target');
    target.addEventListener('click', function () {
      alert('Click event fired. Target was clicked!');
    }, false);
  </script>
  </body>
</html>
```

2. Open index.html in a web browser.

3. Click the button and fire the click event.

4. Notice that, as the event is fired, the alert is shown (see Figure 18.1).

FIGURE 18.1
A click event being fired and handled by an event listener

Events in Node.js are more commonly network events and include things like

▶ A response from a web server

▶ Data being read from a file

▶ Data returning from a database

Including the Events module in your code is similar to other modules with the familiar requiring of the module. To use the module, however, you must create a new instance of EventEmitter:

```
var EventEmitter = require('events').EventEmitter;
var ee = new EventEmitter();
```

Once you have added this to your code, you can start to add events and listeners. The Events module is actually simple, and if you can understand emitting events and listening to events, you are a long way to understanding how it works. If you have required the Events module and created a new instance of EventEmitter(), you can emit an event as follows:

```
ee.emit('message', 'This emits a message');
```

The first argument is a string to describe the event and allow you to match it up with a listener. You can use anything here. Once you have labeled your event, you can add more arguments. You can have more than one argument if you need it, and these will be passed into the listener when the event is received. In this case, the second argument is a string.

To receive the message, you must add a listener. This listens for the event and handles it when it is fired. In this case, the second argument of emit() is passed into the anonymous function as data so that it may be used:

```
ee.on('message', function(data) {
  console.log(data);
});
```

To explore this further, suppose that you are James Bond and have a requirement to show a secret message and make it self-destruct in 5 seconds. By emitting and listening for events, a short Node.js script can do this easily:

```
var EventEmitter = require('events').EventEmitter;
var secretMessage = new EventEmitter();

secretMessage.on('message', function(data) {
  console.log(data);
});

secretMessage.on('self destruct', function() {
    console.log('BANG!! The message is destroyed!');
});

secretMessage.emit('message', 'This is a secret message. It will self destruct in 5
➥ seconds..');

setTimeout(function(){
  secretMessage.emit('self destruct');
}, 5000);
```

In the script, there are two events emitted and two listeners. The message event happens as soon as the script is run and is handled by the 'message' handler. A setTimeout emits another event after 5 seconds and sends the 'self destruct' event. Note that there are no additional arguments here—as additional arguments are optional. If you run this script, you see the following:

```
This is a secret message. It will self destruct in 5 seconds..
[ 5 seconds later ... ]
BANG!! The message is destroyed!
```

▼ TRY IT YOURSELF

If you have downloaded the code examples for this book, this code is hour18/example02.

Follow these steps to emit and listen for events:

1. Create a file called app.js and copy the following code into it:

```
var EventEmitter = require('events').EventEmitter;
var secretMessage = new EventEmitter();
```

```
secretMessage.on('message', function(data) {
  console.log(data);
});

secretMessage.on('self destruct', function() {
    console.log('BANG!! The message is destroyed!');
});

secretMessage.emit('message', 'This is a secret message. It will self destruct
➥ in 5 seconds..');

setTimeout(function(){
  secretMessage.emit('self destruct');
}, 5000);
```

2. Run the script:

```
node app.js
```

3. You should see the following output after a 5-second pause before the second line:

```
This is a secret message. It will self destruct in 5 seconds..
BANG!! The message is destroyed!
```

DID YOU KNOW?

EventEmitter **Is Used Everywhere in Node.js**

EventEmitter is used in many other modules to handle events in Node.js. You may recognize EventEmitter being used when you are reading files, creating an HTTP server, or working with Streams. The code is relatively small, so if you understand how to read JavaScript, it can be found here: https://github.com/joyent/node/blob/master/lib/events.js. It is a small piece of code with a big part to play in how Node.js works!

Demonstrating Events Through HTTP

Node.js approaches data being moved around networks or I/O operations as events and the Events module is used extensively to support asynchronous programming. A good example to look at in terms of networked events is Twitter's streaming API. This allows developers to keep a connection to the Twitter API open and receive data as it happens.

When you use either the HTTP or HTTPS module in Node.js, you are actually using an instance of EventEmitter and several events have been defined for you to make interacting with HTTP servers possible.

Thinking about getting data from Twitter's streaming API, it makes sense to structure this around events. Suppose you are obsessed with chocolate and you want to listen to the API for tweets about chocolate in real-time. Because the streaming API allows you to keep a connection open, you can do this and the API will push new data to you when it becomes available. Because the HTTP and HTTPS modules in Node.js are instances of `EventEmitter`, you can listen for the data event to do something with it as soon as it is received:

```
var https = require('https');
var username = 'YOUR_TWITTER_USERNAME';
var password = 'YOUR_TWITTER_PASSWORD';
var json;

var options = {
  host: 'stream.twitter.com',
  auth: username + ":" + password,
  path: '/1/statuses/filter.json?track=chocolate',
  method: 'POST'
};

var req = https.request(options, function(res) {
  res.setEncoding('utf8');
  res.on('data', function (data) {
    json = JSON.parse(data);
    console.log('New data event!');
    console.log(json.text);
  });
});

req.end();
```

This is a simple HTTPS client, similar to the ones that you saw in Hour 5, "HTTP," in the HTTP module. What you should be concerned with here is the following line in the client:

```
res.on('data', function (data) {
```

This is an event listener straight from Events module and allows the client to receive the data when the event happens and do something with it. In this case, the event that fires the listener is a network event. It is the Twitter API that fires this event as new data is received. In this context, you can see how the Event module can be used to handle network events that can occur at any time and respond to them as soon as they arrive. Dealing with network events and I/O operations that are often outside the control of a script and using events as a way to manage this is one of the core principles of Node.js.

If you have downloaded the code examples for this book, this code is hour18/example03.

The following steps demonstrate events with streaming data:

1. Create a file called app.js and copy the following code into it:

```
var https = require('https');
var username = 'YOUR_TWITTER_USERNAME';
var password = 'YOUR_TWITTER_PASSWORD';
var json;

var options = {
  host: 'stream.twitter.com',
  auth: username + ":" + password,
  path: '/1/statuses/filter.json?track=chocolate',
  method: 'POST'
};

var req = https.request(options, function(res) {
  res.setEncoding('utf8');
  res.on('data', function (data) {
    json = JSON.parse(data);
    console.log('New data event!');
    console.log(json.text);
  });
});

req.end();
```

2. Change the username and password variables to your own Twitter username and password.

3. Run the script:

```
node app.js
```

4. You should see new data events arriving at the server and being handled by the event listener (see Figure 18.2).

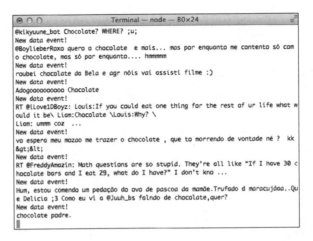

FIGURE 18.2
Listening for events from a network event

Playing Ping-Pong with Events

To gain a fuller understanding of how events can build a program, you create a ping-pong example. In computing terms, a ping is a request to something else (such as a server) to ask it whether it is alive. Using the Events module, you can create a self-referencing script that sends ping and pong messages back and forth to itself. The purpose here is to illustrate that event listeners can also be event emitters and that this technique can be used to let event listeners fire off other events:

```
var EventEmitter = require('events').EventEmitter;
var pingPong = new EventEmitter();

setTimeout(function(){
  console.log('Sending first ping');
  pingPong.emit('ping');
}, 2000);

pingPong.on('ping', function() {
  console.log('Got ping');
  setTimeout(function(){
    pingPong.emit('pong');
  }, 2000);
});

pingPong.on('pong', function() {
  console.log('Got pong');
  setTimeout(function(){
```

```
    pingPong.emit('ping');
  }, 2000);
});
```

This script makes heavy use of `setTimeout`, which executes something else after a certain period of time. In reality, this might be a network operation or something that you may not know exactly when it will return. In the script, the first `setTimeout` starts the game and emits a ping message. There are two listeners for `ping` and `pong`, and these both respond by sending a message back after 2 seconds. When the script is run, the events create an infinite loop and send messages back and forth until you stop the script:

```
Sending first ping
Got ping
Got pong
Got ping
Got pong
```

The simple idea that you can use one event to fire off another one allows complex functionality to be created, especially where a cascade of events occurs. In this context, you can see how the Events module can be used to build complex network programs that respond to network or I/O events.

TRY IT YOURSELF ▼

If you have downloaded the code examples for this book, this code is hour18/example04.

Follow these steps to emit events with event listeners:

1. Create a new file called parent.js and paste in the following content:

```
var EventEmitter = require('events').EventEmitter;
var pingPong = new EventEmitter();

setTimeout(function(){
  console.log('Sending first ping');
  pingPong.emit('ping');
}, 2000);

pingPong.on('ping', function() {
  console.log('Got ping');
  setTimeout(function(){
    pingPong.emit('pong');
  }, 2000);
});

pingPong.on('pong', function() {
  console.log('Got pong');
```

```
        setTimeout(function(){
          pingPong.emit('ping');
        }, 2000);
    });
```

2. Run the script:

   ```
   node app.js
   ```

3. Watch how messages are sent back and forth between event handlers and understand that the event handler is also an emitter. This keeps the ping-pong going (see Figure 18.3).

FIGURE 18.3
Playing ping-pong with the Events module

Programming Event Listeners Dynamically

The ping-pong example demonstrates how event listeners can also become event emitters, but all this logic was created when the script was first run. The Events module also allows you to be dynamic in terms of adding and removing listeners depending on an event or some other logic in your script that happens while your script is running.

By using the Events module, you can add and remove listeners at any point in your script, so you might choose to make your script respond to certain events as they happen or to analyze data that is received in an event to add or remove other listeners accordingly.

In the simple ping-pong example, you can add a second listener after 4 seconds with another `setTimeout` function. This runs the callback function and logs that the second listener has received an event each time a ping event is received:

```
var logPing = function() {
  console.log("Second ping listener got ping");
}
```

```
setTimeout(function(){
  console.log('Added a second ping listener');
  pingPong.on('ping', logPing);
}, 4000);
```

Now when the script is run after 4 seconds, the second listener will be dynamically added and will log that it has received a ping message to the terminal. In reality, you might want to use this to write some logic that responds to a particular scenario based on another event. Event listeners can also be removed by providing a reference to the message and the callback function:

```
pingPong.removeListener('ping', logPing);
```

So if you wanted to remove the dynamically added event listener, you could add another `setTimeout` to remove it after, say, 12 seconds:

```
setTimeout(function(){
  console.log('Removed second ping listener');
  pingPong.removeListener('ping', logPing);
}, 12000);
```

So now when the script is run, there are events that are emitters and also dynamic listeners that are added and removed during the life of the process:

```
Sending first ping
Got ping
Added a second ping listener
Got pong
Got ping
Second ping listener got ping
Got pong
Got ping
Second ping listener got ping
Removed second ping listener
Got pong
Got ping
Got pong
```

For demonstration purposes, this example used `setTimeout` to fire events, but in reality you will use the Events module to respond to I/O and network operations. The Events module is a small but powerful Swiss army knife that lets you approach a problem from the perspective of events.

The full example with listeners that emit events and listeners being added and removed dynamically now looks as follows:

```
var EventEmitter = require('events').EventEmitter;
var pingPong = new EventEmitter();

setTimeout(function(){
```

```
    console.log('Sending first ping');
    pingPong.emit('ping');
}, 2000);

pingPong.on('ping', function() {
    console.log('Got ping');
    setTimeout(function(){
        pingPong.emit('pong');
    }, 2000);
});

pingPong.on('pong', function() {
    console.log('Got pong');
    setTimeout(function(){
        pingPong.emit('ping');
    }, 2000);
});

var logPing = function() {
    console.log("Second ping listener got ping");
}

setTimeout(function(){
    console.log('Added a second ping listener');
    pingPong.on('ping', logPing);
}, 4000);

setTimeout(function(){
    console.log('Removed second ping listener');
    pingPong.removeListener('ping', logPing);
}, 12000);
```

▼ TRY IT YOURSELF

If you have downloaded the code examples for this book, this code is hour18/example05.

Follow these steps to manage events dynamically:

1. Create a new file called app.js and paste in the following content:

```
var EventEmitter = require('events').EventEmitter;
var pingPong = new EventEmitter();

setTimeout(function(){
    console.log('Sending first ping');
    pingPong.emit('ping');
}, 2000);
```

```
pingPong.on('ping', function() {
  console.log('Got ping');
  setTimeout(function(){
    pingPong.emit('pong');
  }, 2000);
});

pingPong.on('pong', function() {
  console.log('Got pong');
  setTimeout(function(){
    pingPong.emit('ping');
  }, 2000);
});

var logPing = function() {
  console.log("Second ping listener got ping");
}

setTimeout(function(){
  console.log('Added a second ping listener');
  pingPong.on('ping', logPing);
}, 4000);

setTimeout(function(){
  console.log('Removed second ping listener');
  pingPong.removeListener('ping', logPing);
}, 12000);
```

2. Start the server:

```
node app.js
```

3. Watch how messages are sent back and forth and how a listener is added and then removed dynamically (see Figure 18.4).

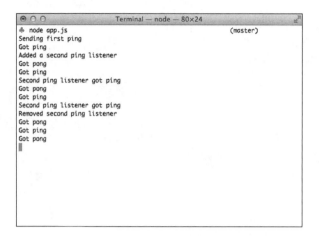

FIGURE 18.4
Adding and removing event listeners dynamically

Summary

In this hour, you were introduced to the Events module and how events are used in Node.js. You played at being a James Bond by creating a self-destructing message and then learned how events are used in many other modules in Node.js. You saw how the HTTP and HTTPS modules use events to receive data and saw an example of this with Twitter's streaming API. You played ping-pong with a Node.js script and saw how event listeners can also emit events to allow scripts to be more intelligent and complex. Finally, you saw that event listeners can be added and removed dynamically.

Q&A

Q. Is there a maximum number of listeners I can have for an event?

A. By default, events will emit a warning if you have more than 10 listeners. You can change this on a per-event basis using `emitter.setMaxListeners(n)`, however.

Q. Why don't things happen in the order they appear in the code?

A. If you program around events, you are turning your script inside out. You no longer program around the order that things appear in your code but around the order that events happen. This is a good thing!

Q. Is there a way to listen to all emitted events?

A. No. You need to create listeners for each event that you want to respond to.

Workshop

This workshop contains quiz questions and exercises to help cement your learning in this hour.

Quiz

1. How is programming around events different?

2. Why are events a good approach for network programming?

3. Why is JavaScript a good fit for the problems that Node.js is trying to solve?

Quiz Answers

1. When you use events, your scripts are no longer executed in the order that they are written in, as is the case with simple sequential scripts. Instead, event listeners are used to respond to events that occur, regardless of when they happen. This is liberating but initially requires a change in thinking about how you approach your code.

2. When your application includes network calls, you are often unable to predict exactly when something will return. As applications become more complex, it becomes much more manageable and efficient to structure code around events. When an event happens, a listener can respond to it!

3. Because JavaScript is an event-driven programming language, it is a great fit for the approach that Node.js takes to network programming. JavaScript allows Node.js to provide an event-driven API that many developers will already be familiar with.

Exercises

1. Read the documentation and examples on Node.js's HTTP module at http://nodejs.org/docs/latest/api/http.html. Can you recognize where the Events module is being used and how events are used?

2. Create a short Node.js script that uses the Events module to emit two different events. Create two event listeners to receive the events.

3. Extend the example that can be found at hour18/example05 to dynamically add and then remove a second listener for the pong event.

The Buffer Module

What You'll Learn in This Hour:

▶ What binary data is

▶ What character encoding is

▶ How to work with binary data

▶ How to work with buffers

A Primer on Binary Data

To understand the Buffer module, you need to understand binary data. If you already have a good handle on this, you can skip this section. If not, read on! A binary digit can be one of two values: 0 or 1. This is also known as a bit (short for binary digit), and this is the atomic unit of data in computer systems. The values 0 and 1 are the simplest way of representing information as the values can only ever be one of two things—0 or 1. This can also be interpreted as true or false and on or off. While this may be considered simple and trivial, using more than one bit allows more complex things to be expressed.

In terms of the way human beings deal with numbers, we have a system that allows numerical values to be expressed using 10 different values:

0 1 2 3 4 5 6 7 8 9

Using these values, we can express numbers by using more than one of these values and combining them together. Because there are 10 values, this system is known as Base 10. Numbers can also be expressed in Binary, but instead of having 10 values to express a number, there are only two—1 and 0. Because there are two values, this is known as Base 2.

BY THE WAY

The Decimal System Is Base 10

The system we use to refer to numbers is commonly referred to as the decimal system as there are 10 numbers, but it can also be referred to as Base 10.

Just like the Base 10 system, the value of a number in Binary (or Base 2) depends on the position starting from the right. A bit's value grows by a power of two as it shifts from the right to the left:

1	1	1	1	1	1	1	1
128	64	32	16	8	4	2	1

Just like the Base 10 system, a binary number in Base 2 depends on the position starting from the right. Values are combined in the same way as the decimal system to represent a value. The following table represents a number of values in the Base 2 system and the equivalent in Base 10:

Base 2	Base 10
0	0
1	1
00	0
01	1
10	2
11	3

Using Base 2, 8 bits all with the value of 1 (or 11111111) is 255. A group of 8 bits is referred to as a byte, and it can be used to store a value that represents a letter or a number. As you just saw, the largest number you can declare with eight bits is 255. With eight values of 0, you can declare a 0, so there are 256 different values you can declare with a byte. Bytes are sometimes also referred to as octets as there are 8 bits, and they form the basis for holding a character of text.

BY THE WAY

4 Bits Are a Nibble

4 bits or half a byte is referred to as a nibble. Because a nibble is four bits, it can have 16 possible values. This can also be referred to as hexadecimal, hex, or Base 16, all because there are 16 possible values!

Binary to Text

Although computing operates on a system of 0s and 1s, humans do not. As such, a number of encoding systems exist to convert binary data to text. One of these is ASCII (American Standard Code for Information Interchange). This is based on the English alphabet and provides a way to encode the alphabetic, numeric, and punctuation characters commonly used in English. The number of possible different characters in ASCII is 128 (0-127). You may recall from learning about the Base 2 system that the number 128 is significant: It is the maximum number that you can declare with 7 bits. This provides a system to declare English language characters. For example, in ASCII, the character 'A' is the number 65 in the decimal system or 1000001 in binary.

ASCII was designed for the English language, but evidently the world does not just use English or English language characters to communicate. In recent years, the encoding of choice for the Web has become UTF-8. This can represent every character in the Unicode set that encompasses the majority of the languages and character sets in use in the world today. UTF-8 uses between 1 and 4 bytes to express characters and is fully backward compatible with ASCII. Characters that are expected to be used frequently are encoded using fewer bytes (usually one), whereas characters that are unusual are encoded using four.

Binary and Node.js

JavaScript was originally designed for browsers and so works well with unicode-encoded strings (human-readable text) but does not handle binary data well. This is a problem for Node.js since it is designed to send and receive data over networks that often will be in binary format. Some examples of where transmitting binary data is needed are

► Sending and receiving data over a TCP connection

► Reading binary data from an image or compressed file

► Reading and writing data from a filesystem

► Dealing with streams of binary data from networks

The Buffer module gives Node.js a way of storing raw data so that it can be used in the context of JavaScript. Whenever you work with moving data in I/O operations in Node.js, it is likely that the Buffer module is being used. For example, when you read a file, Node.js uses a Buffer object to hold the data from the file. You can see this by creating a text file called file.txt, writing some text in it, and then creating a Node.js script to read the file:

```
var fs = require('fs');

fs.readFile('file.txt', function(err,data){
  if (err) throw err;
  console.log(data);
});
```

If you run this script, you see that the data logged is actually a Buffer object:

```
<Buffer 23 23 0a 23 20 55 73 65 72 20 44 61..
```

If you have downloaded the code examples for this book, this code is hour19/example01.

Follow these steps to show a Buffer object:

1. Create a file called app.js and copy the following code into it:

```
var fs = require('fs');

fs.readFile('file.txt', function(err,data){
  if (err) throw err;
  console.log(data);
});
```

2. Create a file called file.txt and add the following content to it:

```
It is the future,
The distant future
It is the distant future,
The year 2000

We are robots
```

3. Run the script:

```
node app.js
```

4. You should see the raw Buffer object printed to the console (see Figure 19.1).

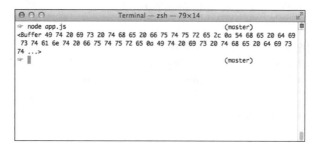

FIGURE 19.1
Showing a raw buffer data from reading a file

In most modules, you must set an encoding to tell Node.js to convert the data into a human-readable format.

To show the data, an encoding must be given as an argument to the fs.readFile() method:

```
var fs = require('fs');
```

```
fs.readFile('file.txt', 'utf8', function(err,data){
  if (err) throw err;
  console.log(data);
});
```

Now rather than the raw buffer, the contents of the file are shown:

```
It is the future,
The distant future
It is the distant future,
The year 2000

We are robots
```

TRY IT YOURSELF ▼

If you have downloaded the code examples for this book, this code is hour19/example02.

Follow these steps to set the encoding for a buffer:

1. Create a file called app.js and copy the following code into it:

   ```
   var fs = require('fs');

   fs.readFile('file.txt', 'utf8', function(err,data){
     if (err) throw err;
     console.log(data);
   });
   ```

2. Create a file called file.txt and add the following content to it:

   ```
   It is the future,
   The distant future
   It is the distant future,
   The year 2000

   We are robots
   ```

3. Run the script:

   ```
   node app.js
   ```

4. You should see the contents of the file rather than the raw buffer printed to the terminal (see Figure 19.2).

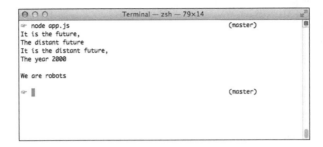

FIGURE 19.2
Showing the file contents after declaring an encoding

BY THE WAY

Characters Can Be Encoded in a Number of Ways

Characters can be encoded and decoded in a number of ways. The most common is UTF-8, and this supports almost all characters in use in the world today. Other encoding formats that you can use in Node.js include ascii, ucs2, base64, and hex.

What Are Buffers in Node.js?

Buffers in Node.js are a way to handle binary data. Because the JavaScript language does not handle binary data well, buffers are actually an allocation of raw memory that Node.js can read and write data to. This allows Node.js to deal with binary data in a sane way instead of having to rely on the JavaScript language that in respect of binary data is deficient.

Buffers are an instance of the Buffer class, and because the Buffer module is global, you can use it without requiring the module. Buffers have a number of options depending on the way they are instantiated. They can take an argument of an integer that represents the number of bytes (or octets) that should be allocated to the buffer. You can also specify the encoding that should be used. The default encoding used is UTF-8, so if you do not specify an encoding, UTF-8 will be used.

To create a new buffer with 8 bytes looks like this:

```
var buffer = new Buffer(8);
```

This instantiates a new Buffer object with 8 bytes of memory:

```
buffer
<Buffer cc cc cc cc cc cc ff 75>
```

If this is written out to the console as a string, it will show a UTF-8 string. Node.js provides the
toString() method to write the buffer out as a string:

```
buffer.toString()
'???????u'
```

Note that you may see different characters than the example, as buffer is a representation of the
raw memory allocated on your machine.

You may also create a new Buffer object and pass in an array of bytes or octets. You may recall
from earlier that 85 equates to the character 'U'. So creating a buffer with the value 85 results in
the UTF-8 encoded contents being the character U:

```
var buffer = new Buffer([85])
buffer.toString('utf-8')
'U'
```

Follow these steps to create a buffer with an array of bytes:

1. Start the Node.js REPL by typing **node** at a console.

2. Initialize a buffer with an octet:

   ```
   var buffer = new Buffer([85])
   ```

3. Convert the buffer to a string:

   ```
   buffer.toString('utf-8')
   ```

4. You should see that the UTF-8 encoded contents of the buffer is 'U'.

You may also add more than one value to the array of octets to build up a string of text:

```
var buffer = new Buffer([79, 72, 65, 73, 33])
buffer.toString('utf-8')
'OHAI!'
```

If you know the string that you want to encode, you can also instantiate a new Buffer object and
pass the string directly into it:

```
var buffer = new Buffer('Look at me mum!')
buffer.toString('utf-8')
'Look at me mum!'
```

Once initialized, buffers cannot be resized, so you should make sure that your buffer size is
enough to hold any data that you are going to throw at it. At the time of writing, the maximum
buffer size is 1GB.

Writing to Buffers

At this point, you have created a buffer with 8 bytes of memory allocated. Unless you like staring at null values, you probably want to write some data into the buffer.

```
var buffer = new Buffer(8)
buffer.write("a", "utf8")
1
```

This writes the character "a" into your buffer, and node returns the number of bytes that were written to the buffer after encoding. The UTF-8 encoding of the letter "a" takes 1 byte, but other characters use more than 1 byte. For example, UTF-8 also has a number of symbols such as the black telephone (☎).

To encode this character takes 3 bytes:

```
var buffer = new Buffer(8)
buffer.write('☎', "utf8")
3
```

> ▼ TRY IT YOURSELF
>
> Follow these steps to initialize a buffer with a string:
>
> 1. Start the Node.js REPL by typing **node** at a console.
>
> 2. Initialize a buffer of 8 bytes:
>    ```
>    var buffer = new Buffer(8)
>    ```
>
> 3. Write a "c" character to the buffer with UTF-8 encoding:
>    ```
>    buffer.write('c', 'utf8')
>    ```
>
> 4. You should see that the encoding took 1 byte.

Appending to Buffers

Buffer objects are often used to buffer data that is received so that all the data can be used once it has been received. This means that when you write to a buffer you need to be able to append data to it. By default, when you write to a buffer, it writes to the first byte, or the start of the buffer. This can be illustrated as follows:

```
var buffer = new Buffer(8);
buffer.write('hi', 'utf8');
buffer.toString();
'hi\u0003H?E?H'
```

```
buffer.write(' there', 'utf8');
buffer.toString();
' thereas'
```

Note that you may see different characters than the example, as Buffer is a representation of the raw memory allocated on your machine.

This is obviously not what you want! When appending to a buffer, you can pass an option offset argument that writes to the buffer at the given byte or octet:

```
buffer.write(' there', 2, 'utf8')
```

WATCH OUT

The Offset Number Starts from 0

Often in computing, counting starts from 0. This is the case with Buffer offsets. If you want your string to be appended at byte 3, the offset will be 2.

Appending to a buffer can now be correctly written as follows:

```
var buffer = new Buffer(8);
buffer.write('hi', 'utf8');
buffer.toString();
'hi\u000\u0000\u0000H?'
buffer.write(' there', 2, 'utf8');
buffer.toString();
'hi there'
```

TRY IT YOURSELF ▼

Follow these steps to append to a buffer:

1. Start the Node.js REPL by typing **node** at a console.

2. Initialize a buffer of 8 bytes:

   ```
   var buffer = new Buffer(8)
   ```

3. Write a string to the buffer with UTF-8 encoding:

   ```
   buffer.write('hi', 'utf8')
   ```

4. Examine the contents of the buffer:

   ```
   buffer.toString()
   ```

5. Write another string to the buffer with an offset:

```
buffer.write(' there', 2, 'utf8')
```

6. Examine the contents of the buffer:

```
buffer.toString()
```

7. You should see that the second string was appended to the first one.

Copying Buffers

Node.js provides a way to copy all or parts of a Buffer object into another Buffer object. You may only copy between Buffer objects that already exist, so you need to create them first. To copy from one buffer to another is as follows, where `buffer` is a Buffer object you want to copy from and `bufferToCopyTo` is a Buffer object you want to copy to:

```
buffer.copy(bufferToCopyTo)
```

Here is the simplest example of copying the entire contents of a buffer into another one of the same size:

```
var buffer1 = new Buffer(8)
buffer1.write('hi there', 'utf8')
var buffer2 = new Buffer(8)
buffer1.copy(buffer2)
buffer2.toString()
'hi there'
```

You may not want to copy all your Buffer object into another one, so you may also specify what you want to copy from your buffer into the target buffer. The Buffer module also allows you to specify where in the target buffer you copy to:

```
buffer.copy(bufferToCopyTo, 2, 3, 8)
```

The second argument specifies which byte that the copying should be written to in the target buffer. The third and fourth arguments specify where the copy should start and stop in the source buffer. This can be illustrated as follows:

```
var buffer1 = new Buffer(8)
buffer1.write('hi there', 'utf8')
var buffer2 = new Buffer(8)
buffer2.write('hi', 'utf8');
buffer1.copy(buffer2, 2, 2, 8)
buffer2.toString()
'hi there'
```

Modifying Strings in Buffers

A pain point that developers often hit is in storing strings of data in buffers that they later need to modify. The Buffer module does not provide methods to modify strings. This makes sense as buffers are designed to hold raw data. If you want to modify strings held within buffers, you should do the following:

► Read the buffer using the `toString()` method.

► Perform any modifications on the String object.

► Write the modified string back to the buffer.

Summary

In this hour, you learned about buffers, one of Node.js's low-level APIs for working with networks and data. You gained a primer into what binary data is and how it powers computing. You learned about how bits can be grouped into bytes (or octets) and be used to represent characters with character encoding. You were introduced to ASCII and UTF-8, two common encoding systems. You then learned how to create, modify, and copy buffers using the Buffer module.

Q&A

Q. **Buffers seem very low-level. Do I need to know this?**

A. If you work with the higher-level parts of the Node.js API, you will not be directly exposed to the Buffer module, even though it is heavily used. If you ever have to work with Streams (covered in Hour 20, "The Stream Module"), you will need to use buffers. Given that buffers are so fundamental to Node.js, it is good to have at least a working understanding of them.

Q. **Which encoding should I use?**

A. Unless you have a good reason not to, use UTF-8. If you do not provide an encoding, Node.js also makes this assumption for you and uses UTF-8.

Q. **What size should I initialize my buffer to?**

A. Try to understand what data you expect to be added to your buffer and how big it is. Buffers allocate raw memory on a computer, so using too much could slow down a system. If you allocate too little, you may lose data.

Q. **Do I have to clean up references to buffer objects?**

A. No. If you drop a reference to a buffer, it will be automatically garbage collected.

Workshop

This workshop contains quiz questions and exercises to help cement your learning in this hour.

Quiz

1. Represent the number 134 in binary.

2. What number does offsetting start from in Node.js buffers?

3. What data encoding format is recommended by default?

Quiz Answers

1. 10000110 (128 + 4 + 2)

2. Offsets start from 0 in Node.js.

3. By default, use UTF-8, which allows almost all languages in use in the world to be encoded.

Exercises

1. Study the list of ASCII characters at http://web.cs.mun.ca/~michael/c/ascii-table.html. Consider how the decimal values relate to the binary representation. Write the binary value of one or more of the characters.

2. Type **node** at a terminal window and initialize a buffer. Try to understand the memory that you have available to work with after you have created the buffer. Add some text to your buffer and then read it out again. Append some text to your buffer.

3. Create a buffer and add the string 'Thas as ancorrect'. Modify the buffer to change the "a" characters to "i" characters. Remember what you learned about modifying strings in buffers!

HOUR 20

The Stream Module

What You'll Learn in This Hour:

▶ What streams are

▶ Creating a readable stream

▶ Creating a writable stream

▶ Piping data between readable and writable streams

A Primer on Streams

In UNIX-type operating systems, streams are a standard concept, and there are three main streams:

▶ Standard input

▶ Standard output

▶ Standard error

Programs can read and write from these streams, and because they are a standard interface, it makes it easy to connect small, discrete programs together. In UNIX-type operating systems, it is possible to redirect these streams, so for example, you can redirect standard input to standard output if you want. It is helpful to understand how data flows between streams, so let's explore this a little more. Suppose that you have a text file called names.txt with a list of names, as follows:

```
Carr, Jimmy
Smith, Arthur
Bailey, Bill
```

The sort utility in UNIX receives lines of text, sorts them, and then returns the sorted version. It expects the data that it will operate on comes from standard input and the result to be sent to standard output. So, to sort the file, you can redirect standard input to the `sort` command, as follows:

```
sort < names.txt
```

When used in the shell, the < symbol (also known as a single guillemet) indicates that whatever is to the right of it should be read and passed as standard input to whatever is to the left of it. In this case, it means the following:

▶ Read the contents of names.txt as standard input.

▶ Redirect standard input to the `sort` command.

If you run this command, you see the results of the contents of names.txt being sent as standard input to the `sort` command:

```
sort < names.txt
Bailey, Bill
Carr, Jimmy
Smith, Arthur
```

Viewing the results in your terminal is actually the result of the `sort` program outputting the result of the data that it received as standard input to standard output, in this case, the terminal. But, you can also redirect standard output. Suppose that you want to have the results of the `sort` command outputted to a file:

```
sort < names.txt > sorted_names.txt
```

Now there is an additional single guillemet that takes the standard output and redirects it to a file. If the file does not exist it will be created, and the standard output will be written to the file. Because the standard output is being redirected, there is no longer anything seen in the terminal. The important thing to think about here is the flow of data. Data is taken from the names.txt file and read as standard input. This is redirected to the `sort` program that performs the sorting and then returns the results as standard output. Finally standard output is redirected to a file.

If you have downloaded the code examples for this book, this code is hour20/example01.

The following steps demonstrate the idea of streams:

1. Create a file called names.txt and copy the following content into it:

```
Carr, Jimmy
Smith, Arthur
Bailey, Bill
```

2. Open a terminal window and sort the file with the following command:

```
sort < names.txt
```

3. You should see the sorted results of the file in the terminal (see Figure 20.1).

4. Sort the file again but this time redirect the output to a file.

```
sort < names.txt > sorted_names.txt
```

5. The file sorted_names.txt should have been created and contain the sorted results of names.txt.

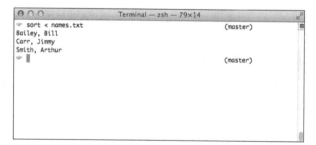

FIGURE 20.1
Redirecting standard input to the `sort` command

Readable Streams

In Hour 19, "The Buffer Module," you learned about buffers and saw how they are a fundamental piece of the architecture of Node.js. If buffers are the way that Node.js handles raw data, streams are usually the way that Node.js moves that data around. Streams in Node.js can be readable and/or writable, and this loosely corresponds to standard input and standard output that you saw earlier, with standard input being readable and standard output being writable. Streams are used in many other modules in Node.js, including HTTP and File System.

You can see this in action in the File System module that uses streams to read and write file data. Suppose that you want to read the list of names that you saw earlier from a file called names.txt so that the data can be used. The File System module allows you to create a readable stream to read this data in. Because the data is streamed, it means you can start acting on the data even before the file has finished being read and as soon as the first bytes of data are received. This is a common pattern in Node.js:

```
var fs = require('fs');
var stream = fs.ReadStream('names.txt');
stream.setEncoding('utf8');
stream.on('data', function(chunk) {
  console.log('read some data')
});
stream.on('close', function () {
  console.log('all the data is read')
});
```

Readable stream listens for events (it is actually an instance of EventEmitter that you learned about in Hour 18, "The Events Module"). In this example, the event data is fired when new data is received. The close event is fired when the file has finished being read. If you run this script, you see the following output:

```
read some data
all the data is read
```

▼ TRY IT YOURSELF

If you have downloaded the code examples for this book, this code is hour20/example02.

To use streams to read a file, follow these steps:

1. Create a file called app.js and copy the following code into it:

    ```
    var fs = require('fs');
    var stream = fs.ReadStream('names.txt');
    stream.setEncoding('utf8');
    stream.on('data', function(chunk) {
      console.log('read some data')
    });
    stream.on('close', function () {
      console.log('all the data is read')
    });
    ```

2. Create a file called names.txt and copy the following content into it:

    ```
    Carr, Jimmy
    Smith, Arthur
    Bailey, Bill
    ```

3. Run the script:

```
node app.js
```

4. You should see the following in the terminal window:

```
read some data
all the data is read
```

This shows that the two events were fired. Some data was received and the file finished being read. But where are the names? This is an important point to note that with streams, you are responsible for using the data in whatever way you want so you have to handle the data when it is received on the data event. If you want to read all the data, you must concatenate it into a variable:

```
var fs = require('fs');
var stream = fs.ReadStream('names.txt');
var data = '';
stream.setEncoding('utf8');
stream.on('data', function(chunk) {
  data += chunk;
  console.log('read some data')
});
stream.on('close', function () {
  console.log('all the data is read')
  console.log(data);
});
```

Now if you run the script, you see the events happening but also the names being shown:

```
read some data
all the data is read
Carr, Jimmy
Smith, Arthur
Bailey, Bill
```

TRY IT YOURSELF ▼

If you have downloaded the code examples for this book, this code is hour20/example03.

Follow these steps to concatenate data from a stream:

1. Create a file called app.js and copy the following code into it:

```
var fs = require('fs');
var stream = fs.ReadStream('names.txt');
var data = '';
stream.setEncoding('utf8');
```

```
stream.on('data', function(chunk) {
  data += chunk;
  console.log('read some data')
});
stream.on('close', function () {
  console.log('all the data is read')
  console.log(data);
});
```

2. Create a file called names.txt and copy the following content into it:

```
Carr, Jimmy
Smith, Arthur
Bailey, Bill
```

3. Run the script:

```
node app.js
```

4. You should see the following in the terminal window (see Figure 20.2):

```
read some data
all the data is read
Carr, Jimmy
Smith, Arthur
Bailey, Bill
```

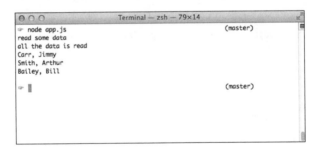

FIGURE 20.2
Reading data with a readable stream

In the case of a list of three names, reading the file is very quick, and there is only one data event. But it may be the case that a file is large and there may be more than one event. This allows developers to do something with the data as soon as it is received rather than wait for an entire file to be read. For example, if a larger text file is read into the readable stream, it gener-ates more than one data event. The website http://www.lipsum.com/ allows generation of Latin text. For the next example, this site is used to generate 1,000 paragraphs and then those paragraphs are copied into a file called latin.txt. As before, a short Node.js script is used to read this file using a readable stream:

```
var fs = require('fs');
var stream = fs.ReadStream('latin.txt');
stream.setEncoding('utf-8');
stream.on('data', function(chunk) {
  console.log('read some data')
});
stream.on('close', function () {
  console.log('all the data is read')
});
```

This time when the script is run, you see more than one data event. Because the file is larger, data is read in when it is received, triggering more than one data event and meaning that it can be used straightaway. Streams make it possible to start operating on data as soon as it is received regardless of how big the file is:

```
read some data
read some data
read some data
all the data is read
```

TRY IT YOURSELF ▼

If you have downloaded the code examples for this book, this code is hour20/example04.

The following steps demonstrate data events:

1. Create a file called app.js and copy the following code into it:

```
var fs = require('fs');
var stream = fs.ReadStream('latin.txt');
stream.setEncoding('utf-8');
stream.on('data', function(chunk) {
  console.log('read some data')
});
stream.on('close', function () {
  console.log('all the data is read')
});
```

2. Visit http://www.lipsum.com/ and generate 1,000 paragraphs of Latin text. Copy the lines into a file called latin.txt.

3. Run the script:

```
node app.js
```

4. You should see the following in the terminal window (see Figure 20.3):

```
read some data
read some data
read some data
all the data is read
```

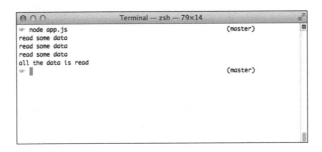

FIGURE 20.3
A readable stream with multiple data events being fired

Writable Streams

As you might expect, you may also create writable streams so that you can write data. This means that, with a simple script, you can now use streams to read a file and write it into another one:

```
var fs = require('fs');
var readableStream = fs.ReadStream('names.txt');
var writableStream = fs.WriteStream('out.txt');

readableStream.setEncoding('utf8');
readableStream.on('data', function(chunk) {
  writableStream.write(chunk);
});
readableStream.on('close', function () {
  writableStream.end();
});
```

Now when a data event is received, the data is written to a writable stream. This is extremely efficient as data is written into the file whenever a data event is received from the readable file, so for large files in particular, the operation performs more quickly than if it had to wait until all the data was read before writing to the file. In essence, this is what streams are. They are an efficient way to move data around networks and filesystems.

If you have downloaded the code examples for this book, this code is hour20/example05.

The following steps show how to use writable streams:

1. Create a file called app.js and copy the following code into it:

```
var fs = require('fs');
var readableStream = fs.ReadStream('names.txt');
var writableStream = fs.WriteStream('out.txt');

readableStream.setEncoding('utf8');
readableStream.on('data', function(chunk) {
  writableStream.write(chunk);
});
readableStream.on('close', function () {
  writableStream.end();
});
```

2. Create a file called names.txt and copy the following content into it:

```
Carr, Jimmy
Smith, Arthur
Bailey, Bill
```

3. Run the script:

```
node app.js
```

4. The contents of names.txt should be copied into out.txt.

Piping Streams

Because piping data between an input and an output is common in Node.js, it also provides a way to connect two readable and writable streams and pipe data between them. This is the pipe() method:

```
var fs = require('fs');
var readableStream = fs.ReadStream('names.txt');
var writableStream = fs.WriteStream('out.txt');
readableStream.pipe(writableStream);
```

The pipe() method takes care of handling events and if necessary pausing and resuming streams, so unless you need to have full control over what happens on events, you should use pipe().

▼ TRY IT YOURSELF

If you have downloaded the code examples for this book, this code is hour20/example06.

Follow these steps to pipe data between readable and writable streams:

1. Create a file called app.js and copy the following code into it:

```
var fs = require('fs');
var readableStream = fs.ReadStream('names.txt');
var writableStream = fs.WriteStream('out.txt');
readableStream.pipe(writableStream);
```

2. Create a file called names.txt and copy the following content into it:

```
Carr, Jimmy
Smith, Arthur
Bailey, Bill
```

3. Run the script:

```
node app.js
```

4. The contents of names.txt should be copied into out.txt.

BY THE WAY

Buffers Are Used to Read and Write Data in Streams

In Hour 19, you learned about buffers in Node.js. Buffers are used to read and write data with streams in Node.js, so having a good understanding of how streams work is well worthwhile.

Streaming MP3s

Streams can also be used in conjunction with the HTTP module that also uses streams for many objects. For this example, you create a streaming MP3 server. The MP3 used is a file from http://www.danosongs.com/. Dan-O is a musician who publishes his music online under a Creative Commons license. The file you will use can be downloaded from http://www.danosongs.com/music/danosongs.com-rapidarc.mp3, and it is also included in the book's code examples.

In the HTTP module, the response object is actually a writable stream. This allows a file to be read as a readable stream and piped through to the writeable stream of the response object just as you saw with copying a file. Because pipe() handles all the necessary pausing and resuming, this allows a streaming MP3 server to be created in a few lines of code:

```
var http = require('http'),
    fs = require('fs');
```

```
http.createServer(function(request, response) {
  var mp3 = 'danosongs.com-rapidarc.mp3';
  var stat = fs.statSync(mp3);

  response.writeHead(200, {
    'Content-Type': 'audio/mpeg',
    'Content-Length': stat.size
  });

  var readableStream = fs.createReadStream(mp3);
  readableStream.pipe(response);

}).listen(3000);
```

The HTTP module should be familiar to you from Hour 5, "HTTP," and using streams allows the MP3 file to read and then pipe out to the response. If you start up the server and browse to port 3000—if your browser supports playing MP3s—you will hear the MP3 being streamed.

Summary

In this hour, you learned one of the more advanced concepts within Node.js: streams. You saw how Node.js streams work similarly to how streams work in UNIX type systems and how they are used in Node.js. You were introduced to how streams are used in the File System module and learned how to read a file using a readable stream. You then saw how to create a writable stream within the File System module and saw how to copy a file in Node.js using streams. You learned how to use the `pipe()` method as a shorthand for moving data between a readable stream and a writable stream. Finally, you saw how to create a streaming MP3 server in a few lines of code and learned how many objects in Node are writable streams, including http.ServerResponse, allowing readable streams to be piped directly into it.

Q&A

Q. What can I use streams for?

A. Streams can be used to create proxy servers, streaming servers, or services that manipulate file uploads like image resizing or video transcoding.

Q. When should I handle events myself and when should I use `pipe()`?

A. You can use `pipe()` to connect a readable stream and a writable stream and this handles pausing and resuming for you. If you need greater control over pausing and resuming, you can handle these events yourself, but for most use cases, `pipe()` takes care of everything for you.

Q. Streams seem more complicated than buffers!

A. Streams are part of the approach that Node.js takes to network programming, so it is important to understand them and how they work. For your day-to-day programming, you will probably use streams (and subsequently buffers) all the time but not be aware of them. As streams are fundamental to how Node.js works, it is important to at least have an overview of how they work.

Workshop

This workshop contains quiz questions and exercises to help cement your learning in this hour.

Quiz

1. Why are streams an efficient way of moving data around?

2. Is it possible to pipe to more than one writable stream?

3. What type of things are streams useful for?

Quiz Answers

1. Because data from streams can be read as soon as it is ready, data can be used before an operation is entirely complete. This means data can get from A to B much more quickly and that developers can start operating on chunks of data as soon as they are ready.

2. Yes. You can pipe data through to multiple streams. An example of where this might be useful is with a file upload that can be piped to a writable stream that uploads to Amazon S3 and another one that saves the file to disk.

3. Streams are useful whenever you want to move data around and need to operate on the data as soon as you can. Examples include an image resizing server, dealing with large text files, or an HTTP server.

Exercises

1. Create a script with the HTTP module to download the following file: http://releases.ubuntu.com/lucid/ubuntu-10.04.4-desktop-i386.iso. Use the data event to log a message to the console each time a data event is received. Note how data is made available as soon as it is received.

2. Create two HTTP servers and proxy traffic from one to the other one using streams.

PART VI

Further Node.js Development

HOUR 21
CoffeeScript

What You'll Learn in This Hour:

▶ What CoffeeScript is and how you can use it

▶ What CoffeeScript offers over native JavaScript

▶ Using classes with CoffeeScript

▶ Some potential issues with using CoffeeScript

What Is CoffeeScript?

CoffeeScript is a pre-compiler for JavaScript written by Jeremy Ashkenas. It is designed with the following goals in mind:

▶ To clean up JavaScript syntax

▶ To provide a number of "goodies" for developers that add new features to JavaScript, taken from Ruby and Python

▶ To make JavaScript easier to use and to expose powerful features of the JavaScript programming language without the need to fully understand the quirks of JavaScript

The term *pre-compiler* means that CoffeeScript is a layer on top of JavaScript that you must compile to output JavaScript. The process is that you write CoffeeScript, compile it, and then get JavaScript out the other end. If you have written programming languages like C, you will be familiar with the idea of compiling source code. If you do not know what compiling is, it will become clear in this hour.

For a quick introduction to CoffeeScript, compare the Node.js Hello World Server.

First in JavaScript:

```
var http = require('http');
http.createServer(function (req, res) {
  res.writeHead(200, {'Content-Type': 'text/plain'});
  res.end('Hello World!\n');
}).listen(3000, "127.0.0.1");
console.log('Server running at http://127.0.0.1:3000/');
```

Then in CoffeeScript:

```
http = require 'http'
http.createServer (req, res) ->
  res.writeHead 200, 'Content-Type': 'text/plain'
  res.end 'Hello, World!\n'
.listen 3000, '127.0.0.1'
console.log 'Server running at http://127.0.0.1:3000/'
```

From first impressions, you can see that CoffeeScript removes things like curly braces and semicolons from the JavaScript version.

You learn about the features of CoffeeScript in this hour, but to start using CoffeeScript, try it in your browser at http://jashkenas.github.com/coffee-script/.

▼ TRY IT YOURSELF

Follow these steps to get started with CoffeeScript:

1. Open a browser and visit http://jashkenas.github.com/coffee-script/.

2. Click Try CoffeeScript. You are now in an interactive editor with CoffeeScript on the left and JavaScript on the right. As you enter CoffeeScript on the left, the equivalent JavaScript is shown on the right.

3. In the left column, type

   ```
   breakfast = 'eggs'
   ```

4. In the right column, the equivalent JavaScript is shown (see Figure 21.1). You should see

   ```
   var breakfast;
   ```

   ```
   breakfast = 'eggs';
   ```

Congratulations! You have just written CoffeeScript and compiled it to JavaScript!

CoffeeScript on the left, compiled JavaScript output on the right.

FIGURE 21.1
Using CoffeeScript in the browser

Installing and Running CoffeeScript

CoffeeScript can be installed via npm. As you may want to use CoffeeScript anywhere on your filesystem, you can install it globally with the -g flag:

```
npm install -g coffee-script
```

Once CoffeeScript is installed, you have the coffee executable available to you on the command line. To check that everything is installed correctly, run the following code from the terminal:

```
coffee --help
```

You should see help text for the coffee command.

CoffeeScript files use the .coffee extension. There are two ways to run a CoffeeScript file with the coffee command. The first is to run the coffee file directly. If you have a CoffeeScript file called app.coffee, you can run it like this:

```
coffee app.coffee
```

The second way to run a CoffeeScript file is to first compile it to native JavaScript and then run the program as normal. To compile a CoffeeScript file, the -c option is used. This creates a JavaScript file from the .coffee file:

```
coffee -c app.coffee
node app.js
```

If you have downloaded the code examples for this book, this code is hour21/example01.

To run CoffeeScript, follow these steps:

1. Create a file called app.coffee and copy the following code into it:

```
http = require 'http'
http.createServer (req, res) ->
  res.writeHead 200, 'Content-Type': 'text/plain'
  res.end 'Hello, World!\n'
.listen 3000, '127.0.0.1'
console.log 'Server running at http://127.0.0.1:3000/'
```

2. Save the file.

3. Assuming you have installed CoffeeScript globally with npm
   (npm install -g coffee-script), start the server with

   ```
   coffee app.coffee
   ```

4. Open a browser at http://127.0.0.1:3000.

5. You should see "Hello, World!"

In the example, you used the coffee command to run a CoffeeScript file directly without pre-compiling it to JavaScript. Within the Node.js community, this is the most common way of using CoffeeScript.

It is also possible to pre-compile CoffeeScript files to JavaScript and then execute the JavaScript files as you would normally.

If you have downloaded the code examples for this book, this code is hour21/example02.

Follow these steps to compile CoffeeScript to JavaScript:

1. Return to the app.coffee file that you created.

2. From the terminal, run the following command:

   ```
   coffee -c app.coffee
   ```

3. Note that a new file is created in the same folder called app.js.

4. Examine the contents of the file app.js.

5. Start the server using the JavaScript file:

   ```
   node app.js
   ```

6. Open a browser at http://127.0.0.1:3000.

7. You should see "Hello, World!"

In this example, rather than running the script directly from CoffeeScript, the file is first pre-compiled to JavaScript. If you examine the JavaScript file that is generated, you will notice that the script looks different from the basic Hello World JavaScript example that you saw in Hour 1, "Introducing Node.js." This is because CoffeeScript applies some opinions about how to best write JavaScript. Generally this is a good thing, but as you learn later in this hour, this is the first of many things that can irritate developers about CoffeeScript.

Why Use a Pre-Compiler?

At this stage, you may well be thinking, "Why do I need this? It adds complexity!" If that's the case, you should read to the end of this hour, see what CoffeeScript can offer you, and then make up your mind!

Some reasons given for using a pre-compiler include

▶ To avoid common syntax errors

▶ To add features to programming languages that are not natively present

▶ To improve code syntax and readability

▶ To take advantage of coding best practices included in a pre-compiler

If you have written CSS, you may have come into contact with a CSS pre-compiler like Sass or LESS. Both of these tools do a similar job to CoffeeScript. They iron out some of the more bumpy parts of using CSS in real life. A great example of this is variables within CSS. CSS has no support for declaring variables, so if you have a color palette, you have to declare the color value every time you want to use it. This is fine in theory until you decide to change the color palette and you have to change the color in multiple places. By using a pre-compiler like Sass, you can set a single variable and then use it over and over again, but just have one single place where the color is set.

In Hour 7, "More on Express," you were introduced to Jade, a template engine. One feature of template engines is that they allow you to pre-compile HTML. If you have ever written HTML by hand, you will have inevitably found a scenario where you forgot to close an HTML tag, causing your layout to be broken. By using an HTML pre-compiler, you can avoid issues like this.

Tools like Sass and Haml both make creating CSS and HTML easier for the developer. You do not need them, but you can choose to use them to improve your productivity. CoffeeScript is similar; it can offer you productivity improvements in return for a little more complexity.

Features of CoffeeScript

This section guides you through the features of CoffeeScript and lets you try examples.

Minimal Syntax

A major feature of CoffeeScript is to provide a minimal syntax version of JavaScript. JavaScript's syntax is often criticized for being too verbose and complex. Specific points that often come up are

- ▶ Semicolons are everywhere and forgetting them introduces errors.
- ▶ You have to declare the function keyword over and over again.
- ▶ Trailing commas can introduce a number of gotchas.
- ▶ Variable scope in JavaScript is easy to get wrong.

Experienced JavaScript programmers would say that many of these accusations are unfair, but for a programmer coming from an object-oriented language like Python or Ruby, these points are commonplace. It is no surprise then that CoffeeScript derives many features of its syntax from Python and Ruby.

To examine how this works, consider the following JavaScript:

```
var cube = function cube(x) {
  return x * x * x;
};
console.log(cube(3));
```

This simple script assigns a function to a variable that cubes the number given to it. To show that it works, it logs the result of 3 cubed to the console.

▼ TRY IT YOURSELF

If you have downloaded the code examples for this book, this code is hour21/example03.

Here's how to cube a number in JavaScript:

1. Create a new file called app.js and paste in the following code:

   ```
   var cube = function cube(x) {
     return x * x * x;
   };
   console.log(cube(3));
   ```

2. From the terminal, run the script:

```
node app.js
```

3. You should see 27.

How does CoffeeScript represent this script?

```
cube = (x) ->
  x * x * x
console.log cube 3
```

That is short compared to the JavaScript! What's happening here?

▶ Semicolons are not required in CoffeeScript.

▶ There is no need to declare variables with var. It is assigned automatically by the = sign.

▶ There is no need for the function keyword. Functions are declared by pointing the arguments to the results with an arrow (->).

▶ There is no need for curly braces. CoffeeScript is white space significant, so by indenting, you infer curly brackets. Indented code equates to {}.

▶ There is no need for a return statement. The last line of a function is automatically returned (like Ruby).

▶ There is no need for brackets to wrap arguments. Anything after a function is assumed to be an argument.

If you want to be super terse, you can even put the function all on one line:

```
cube = (x) -> x * x * x
console.log cube 3
```

If you have downloaded the code examples for this book, this code is hour21/example04.

Here's how to cube a number in CoffeeScript:

1. Create a new file called app.coffee and paste in the following code:

```
cube = (x) -> x * x * x
console.log cube 3
```

2. From the terminal, run the script:

```
coffee app.coffee
```

3. You should see 27.

Conditions and Comparisons

As well as making JavaScript syntax a great deal shorter, CoffeeScript adds a number of new ways to do comparisons. Consider the following JavaScript statement that is a common pattern in JavaScript to check whether a variable exists and is not null:

```
if (typeof happiness !== "undefined" && happiness !== null){
  alert("I am happy!");
}
```

In CoffeeScript, this can be written like this:

```
alert "I am happy!" if happy?
```

CoffeeScript allows conditionals to be placed before and after statements that should be returned and is a language feature that will be familiar to Ruby developers. This is known as prefix and postfix conditionals and is designed to make code read more like natural language. Here are some more CoffeeScript examples:

```
if audience
  sing song

sing song if audience
```

Both of these compile to the following JavaScript:

```
if (audience){
  sing(song);
}
```

CoffeeScript offers a number of aliases for comparisons that further the capability of CoffeeScript syntax to be written more like natural language. Table 21.1 shows a comparison of CoffeeScript and JavaScript operators.

TABLE 21.1 Comparison of CoffeeScript and JavaScript Operators

CoffeeScript	JavaScript
is	===
isnt	!==
not	!
and	&&
or	||
true, yes, on	true
false, no, off	false

CoffeeScript	JavaScript
@, this	this
of	in
in	No JavaScript equivalent

The only one that does not have a JavaScript equivalent is in. This can be used to check for presence in an array. Using these aliases, it is possible to write code like

```
start() if light is on
stop() if light isnt on
```

This code is very close to natural language so the arguments for using this style of programming are

▶ It is easier to read and understand code.

▶ The code is more concise and easier to maintain.

You may not be sold on these reasons, so here is the equivalent JavaScript for comparison:

```
if (light === true) start();
if (light === false) stop();
```

Loops

In JavaScript, for loops are verbose when compared to other languages. Consider this JavaScript:

```
var cheeses = ['Maroilles','Brie de Meaux','Stinking Bishop'];
for(var i=0;i<cheeses.length;i++){
  console.log(cheeses[i]);
}
```

Here, a variable of i is declared to act as a counter for the iteration. For each loop of the iteration, this is increased by 1, and the loop repeats while the variable i is less than the length of the array. This is verbose! CoffeeScript represents the same code like this:

```
for cheese in ['Maroilles', 'Brie de Meaux', 'Stinking Bishop']
  console.log cheese
```

This uses indentation within the loop statement to output each cheese to the console. If compiled to JavaScript, the resulting code is similar, but this would be a good example of where one of the less beautiful parts of JavaScript is abstracted away.

In fact, the example can be just one line of CoffeeScript:

```
console.log food for food in ['Maroilles','Brie de Meaux','Stinking Bishop']
```

▼ TRY IT YOURSELF

If you have downloaded the code examples for this book, this code is hour21/example05.

The following steps show a loop in CoffeeScript:

1. Create a file called app.coffee and copy the following code into it:

   ```
   console.log food for food in ['Maroilles','Brie de Meaux','Stinking Bishop']
   ```

2. Save the file.

3. From the terminal, run the script:

   ```
   coffee app.coffee
   ```

4. You should see a list of cheeses printed in the terminal.

Strings

CoffeeScript adds some string features that make working with strings simpler. Often, when building a string, you want to use a variable within a string. You may have seen JavaScript like this:

```
var beer, order;
beer = "Greene King IPA"
order = "I would like a " + beer;
console.log(order);
```

CoffeeScript supports string interpolation. This means that variables will be automatically expanded within double quotes (note that they will not expand within single quotes). Rewriting the previous example in CoffeeScript results in the following code:

```
beer = "Greene King IPA"
order = "I would like a #{beer}"
console.log order
```

Particularly when you have many different variables that you want to include, this becomes a useful technique.

If you have downloaded the code examples for this book, this code is hour21/example06.

Here's how to use string interpolation in CoffeeScript:

1. Create a file called app.coffee and copy the following code into it:

```coffee
movie = "Willy Wonka & The Chocolate Factory"
string = "My favorite Movie is #{movie}"
console.log string
```

2. Save the file.

3. Change the movie to be your favorite movie.

4. From the terminal, run the script:

```
coffee app.coffee
```

5. You should see your favorite movie printed to the terminal.

CoffeeScript also supports the Heredocs style of string declaration. In native JavaScript, you must escape quotes and apostrophes. The Heredocs style made available via CoffeeScript makes this much more convenient.

In JavaScript, you might write some HTML like this:

```
var html;
html = "<p>\n  My awesome HTML\n</p>";
```

Note that you must use the special \n character to denote a line break. In CoffeeScript, you may write this as you would see it in your HTML:

```
html = """
      <p>
        My awesome HTML
      </p>
      """
```

If you have downloaded the code examples for this book, this code is hour21/example07.

Here's how to use Heredocs In CoffeeScript:

1. Create a file called app.coffee and copy the following code into it:

```
html = """
      <p>
        Hello World!
```

```
    </p>
    """
console.log html
```

2. Save the file.

3. From the terminal, run the script:

   ```
   coffee app.coffee
   ```

4. You should see the HTML outputted with correct indentation and with new lines.

Objects

CoffeeScript supports the creation of objects through YAML (Yet Another Markup Language) style syntax. In JavaScript, an object might be written as follows:

```
var kids;
kids = {
  brother: {
    name: "Max",
    age: 11
  },
  sister: {
    name: "Ida",
    age: 9
  }
}
```

In CoffeeScript, this can be expressed as follows:

```
kids =
  brother:
    name: "Max"
    age:  11
  sister:
    name: "Ida"
    age:  9
```

The object syntax in CoffeeScript offers the removal of curly braces and commas but otherwise closely resembles native JavaScript.

Classes, Inheritance, and super

One of the more difficult parts of JavaScript is prototypal inheritance. For developers used to a more classical implementation of classes in programming, this can be difficult to learn. One of the goodies that CoffeeScript provides is a simple way to create a class structure.

To declare a class, the syntax is as follows:

```
class Car
  constructor: (@name) ->
```

This class can then be instantiated (or created) as follows:

```
car = new Car("Audi")
console.log "Car is a #{car.name}"
```

It is possible to set instance properties on class, too:

```
class Car
  constructor: (@name) ->
  mileage: 81000
```

Class properties can be read after the class is instantiated through dot notation:

```
car = new Car("Audi")
console.log "The #{car.name} has mileage of #{car.mileage}"
```

TRY IT YOURSELF ▼

If you have downloaded the code examples for this book, this code is hour21/example08.

The following steps show class constructors in CoffeeScript:

1. Create a file called app.coffee and copy the following code into it:

   ```
   class Bird
     constructor: (@name) ->
   ```

2. In the same app.coffee file, add the following lines:

   ```
   bird = new Bird("Robin")
   console.log "The bird is a #{bird.name}!"
   ```

3. From the terminal, run the script:

   ```
   coffee app.coffee
   ```

4. You should see the following output:

   ```
   The bird is a Robin!
   ```

Subclassing is used regularly in object-oriented programming where a class inherits from another class. CoffeeScript supports inheritance, meaning it is possible to create classes that inherit properties of the parent class. To inherit from another class, use the `extends` keyword:

```
class Human
  constructor: (@legs = 2) ->
```

```
growLeg: ->
  @legs++

class Horse extends Human
```

In this example, the class describes a human and is constructed with two legs. The class has a function that allows the human to grow a new leg. (You have always wanted to grow some more legs, right?)

Using this class, a second class of Horse is created that inherits from Human. By default, this will have two legs. But it has access to the growLeg function so it is easy to add them:

```
horse = new Horse
horse.growLeg()
horse.growLeg()
```

▼ TRY IT YOURSELF

If you have downloaded the code examples for this book, this code is hour21/example09.

The following steps show how to use classes in CoffeeScript:

1. Create a file called app.coffee and copy the following code into it:

   ```
   class Human
     constructor: (@legs = 2) ->
     growLeg: ->
       @legs++

   class Horse extends Human

   horse = new Horse
   horse.growLeg()
   horse.growLeg()
   console.log "A horse has #{horse.legs} legs"
   ```

2. Save the file.

3. From the terminal, run the script:

   ```
   coffee app.coffee
   ```

4. You should see the following output:

   ```
   A horse has 4 legs
   ```

The final thing to note on classes is the super keyword. This allows a function to be modified within the subclass but also use the implementation in the superclass.

```
class Robot
  makeTea: ->
    console.log 'Making tea.'

class Marvin extends Robot
  makeTea: ->
    console.log 'I have a brain the size of a planet'
    super
```

In this example, the makeTea function is modified in the subclass, but then the super keyword calls the function in the super class.

Note that the subclass is called before the super class.

TRY IT YOURSELF ▼

If you have downloaded the code examples for this book, this code is hour21/example10.

The following steps show how to use subclassing in CoffeeScript:

1. Create a file called app.coffee and copy the following code into it:

```
class Robot
  makeTea: ->
    console.log 'Making tea.'

class Marvin extends Robot
  makeTea: ->
    console.log 'I have a brain the size of a planet'
    super

marvin = new Marvin
marvin.makeTea()
```

2. Save the file.

3. From the terminal, run the script:

```
coffee app.coffee
```

4. You should see the following output:

```
I have a brain the size of a planet
Making tea.
```

CoffeeScript implements just enough of a class structure to provide a useful programming feature. It avoids a developer having to understand prototypal inheritance and provides a clean interface for using classes.

If you are relatively new to JavaScript, compile the example that you just created by running the following code in the terminal:

```
coffee -c app.coffee
```

Examine the resulting app.js file for an example of what CoffeeScript is abstracting for you!

Debugging CoffeeScript

One of the criticisms leveled at CoffeeScript is that it is hard to debug. If you just use JavaScript, the process for debugging an error is

1. Get the line number for the error.

2. Edit the code at the line number.

3. Run the code again.

4. Repeat.

For CoffeeScript, the process is as follows:

1. Get the line number for the error.

2. Find the line number in the JavaScript that CoffeeScript compiled. This can be made more difficult if you are not an experienced JavaScript developer as CoffeeScript is opinionated about the JavaScript it creates.

3. Go to the .coffee file and find the CoffeeScript that relates to the JavaScript line number. There is no CoffeeScript line number available.

4. Edit the code in the .coffee file.

5. Recompile the JavaScript from CoffeeScript.

6. Run the code again.

7. Repeat.

This is clearly much more complex than debugging native JavaScript. For this reason, some developers do not pre-compile CoffeeScript to JavaScript but rather run code directly from the coffee command. If you pre-compile the CoffeeScript to JavaScript, the process is as follows:

```
coffee -c app.coffee
node app.js
```

But, you may also run the script directly and skip the compilation to JavaScript:

```
coffee app.coffee
```

Although this will catch syntax errors, you will still have to debug other issues directly in CoffeeScript, and there are times where you may want to compile to JavaScript to see exactly what is happening.

A few benchmarks are available, but anecdotal reports from CoffeeScript's creator suggest that there is little performance hit in not compiling CoffeeScript to JavaScript.

Reactions to CoffeeScript

In the UK, there is a yeast extract called Marmite that people spread on their toast for breakfast. Marmite causes strong reactions—you either love it or you hate it. Within the Node.js community, the reaction to CoffeeScript is the same. If you want to test this out, drop into the #node.js IRC channel and ask what people think of CoffeeScript. Expect a healthy debate!

For those switching from languages like Python and Ruby, CoffeeScript is generally loved. The syntax is familiar, and there is no need to spend years learning all the quirks of JavaScript. CoffeeScript does all the hard work with a syntax that is familiar, outputting a curated version of JavaScript that avoids many common programming pitfalls.

For those with little programming experience, CoffeeScript can be unpopular. It is another thing to learn in a daunting list of software tools. Particularly for someone who has some experience with JavaScript through jQuery, the additional step to compile to JavaScript can seem slow and unnecessary.

For the experienced JavaScript programmer, reactions can be mixed. These programmers have spent many years understanding the intricacies of JavaScript and many hours of painful debugging! Although CoffeeScript avoids many common JavaScript problems, it outputs opinionated JavaScript that may not be in line with the style of an experienced JavaScript developer. Furthermore, some see CoffeeScript as an irrelevant complication if they are already a highly skilled JavaScript developer. It is often seen as a toy to help inexperienced developers.

In addition to debugging being more complex, it is suggested that by writing your Node.js project in CoffeeScript, it will be much harder to work with other developers. By using CoffeeScript, you are assuming that anyone else on the project will understand CoffeeScript and pre-compiling JavaScript. The accusation is that CoffeeScript adds another barrier for people wanting to collaborate on your project.

Brendan Eich, the creator of JavaScript, wrote the following on his website (http://brendaneich.com/2011/01/harmony-of-my-dreams/):

> CoffeeScript is well done and more convenient to use than JS, provided you buy into the Python-esque significant space and the costs of generating JS from another source language.

This is a telling quote. CoffeeScript is more convenient than JavaScript, but it comes at the cost of learning a new syntax and an extra compilation step.

Summary

In this hour, you learned about CoffeeScript, a pre-compiler for JavaScript. You learned that you can use it with Node.js projects and examined features like syntax, loops, objects, and classes. You learned about the pros and cons of using CoffeeScript as opposed to writing native JavaScript. You covered the productivity boosts that CoffeeScript can offer, issues with debugging and collaborating, and how CoffeeScript sidesteps some of the more difficult parts of the JavaScript programming language.

Q&A

Q. So get off the fence! Should I use CoffeeScript?

A. I am staying on the fence! The short answer is it depends. It depends on your level of JavaScript expertise, whether you are collaborating with other developers who know CoffeeScript, and whether you even like CoffeeScript. CoffeeScript can certainly offer a lot, but it is not without some potential issues.

Q. Is CoffeeScript specific to Node.js?

A. No. CoffeeScript can be used in the browser and within many other programming languages. For example, the 3.1 release of Ruby on Rails introduced CoffeeScript as the default way to write JavaScript within Rails applications. Wherever you can use JavaScript, you can (probably) use CoffeeScript.

Q. Why all the controversy around CoffeeScript?

A. CoffeeScript is a hugely disruptive, yet tiny language. It potentially removes the need for some developers to ever write JavaScript again. For developers who have built a career on writing JavaScript and understanding all the difficult parts of the language, this is a challenge. These developers are certainly going to point out the flaws with CoffeeScript and rightly so. Conversely, for those who do not have a high level of JavaScript experience, CoffeeScript is liberating. It enables access to murky parts of JavaScript that only expert-level programmers understand. These users of CoffeeScript are going to want to write everything in CoffeeScript. This is usually the argument—if you love CoffeeScript, you want to use it for everything. If you see CoffeeScript as a toy and something that potentially challenges years of learning, you are going to hate it.

Workshop

This workshop contains quiz questions and exercises to help cement your learning in this hour.

Quiz

1. What are some of the reasons that CoffeeScript was created?

2. What are some advantages of using CoffeeScript?

3. What are some of the potential issues of using CoffeeScript in a project?

Quiz Answers

1. CoffeeScript was created to abstract some of the more difficult parts of writing applications using JavaScript. It was created to provide developers with a cleaner syntax and add some additional features to JavaScript from other programming languages.

2. By using CoffeeScript, your source code will be more concise. Some may argue that it is easier to understand. You can make use of some features not present in the JavaScript language, so potentially you can solve problems more quickly. If you prefer using CoffeeScript over JavaScript, you will also be a happier developer!

3. Using CoffeeScript commits you to using a pre-compiler in your project. If you are working with other developers, you may find that some hate or even refuse to use CoffeeScript. For less experienced developers, adding a pre-compiler adds another layer to learn.

Exercises

1. Return to http://jashkenas.github.com/coffee-script and click Try CoffeeScript. Experiment with entering CoffeeScript in the left panel and seeing the output in the right panel. Try setting a variable and then creating a simple class to represent an animal. If you get stuck, there are examples on the home page.

2. Write a small web server in CoffeeScript using the Node.js HTTP module. Create three different GET request routes. Run the script using the `coffee` command.

3. To become familiar with larger CoffeeScript projects, visit https://github.com/github/hubot. Examine the CoffeeScript files in the src folder of the project. Try to understand some of the source code and recognize classes being used. Do not worry if you do not understand all the code—it is a complex project! If you want to learn more about CoffeeScript, a free book is available at http://arcturo.github.com/library/coffeescript/.

HOUR 22
Creating Node.js Modules

What You'll Learn in This Hour:

▶ Creating a package.json file for a Node.js module

▶ Testing and developing your module

▶ Adding an executable to your module

▶ Hooking up your project to Travis CI

▶ Publishing your module to the npm registry

Why Create Modules?

In Hour 2, "npm (Node Package Manager)," you learned about npm. This gives you access to a wide range of modules created by third-party developers all around the world. As you become more proficient in Node.js, or your projects become more complex, it is likely that, at some point, you will want to create modules of your own for these reasons:

▶ For convenience and to avoid writing the same code over and over again.

▶ To provide a specific piece of functionality that is not present in the Node.js core. This might be interacting with a third-party API or using WebSockets. In the Streaming Twitter Client that you created in Hour 14, "A Streaming Twitter Client," you used two such modules in nTwitter for interacting with the Twitter API and Socket.IO for WebSockets.

Popular Node.js Modules

To get a better understanding of why you may want to write a module, look at the most popular modules on npm. At the time of writing, the top five modules in the npm registry are

▶ Underscore (https://github.com/documentcloud/underscore)

▶ CoffeeScript (https://github.com/jashkenas/coffee-script)

▶ Request (https://github.com/mikeal/request)

▶ Express (https://github.com/visionmedia/express)

▶ Optimist (https://github.com/substack/node-optimist)

These modules are popular because they address common problems and scenarios that developers face every day when using Node.js or the JavaScript programming language. The most popular module, Underscore, is a Swiss army knife for the JavaScript language itself and is popular with developers as it abstracts away many of the complexities and idiosyncratic parts of the JavaScript programming language. It adds some features that are not natively present in JavaScript. Consider something as simple as a loop in native JavaScript:

```
var numbers = [1,2,3];
for (var i = 0; i < numbers.length; i++) {
  console.log(numbers[i])
}
```

Underscore provides the convience method of "each" to iterate over an array. Many developers consider that using the word "each" is more convenient than the verbosity of the native JavaScript method:

```
var numbers = [1,2,3];
_.each(numbers, function(n){
  console.log(n);
});
```

Request is another module that provides convenience for developers, this time for making HTTP requests. Instead of using Node.js's low-level HTTP client, a simpler and more intuitive interface is available to developers through the module. The popularity of the module illustrates how many developers prefer to use an intuitive abstraction over the native Node.js interface.

Modules can have larger codebases like Express, which provides a framework for creating web applications or can be a single file of code like the Optimist library. Generally, however, modules solve one problem and solve it well. This idea comes from the philosophy behind the UNIX operating system: "Do one thing, and do it well." This approach to software development suggests that it is easier to glue small components together than to attempt to solve all problems with a single approach. The Node.js community follows this philosophy, and you will notice that modules are almost always created to do one thing and do it well. Indeed, many modules themselves depend on other modules, and this is another reason for the popularity of the top five modules from npm; they themselves are used in other modules.

Node.js Modules Often Depend on Other Modules Themselves

Rather than reinvent functionality, many modules include other modules to avoid reinventing the wheel. The most popular modules in the npm registry are often ones frequently used in other modules.

The package.json File

To begin creating Node.js modules, it is a good idea to begin with the package.json file. In previous hours, you used the package.json file to declare the dependencies for creating applications. As a module developer, you now use the package.json file to provide information about your module, including the name, description, and author of the module. The npm command-line utility provides a simple way to start a Node.js module and to create a package.json file. To get started, run the following command from the terminal:

```
npm init
```

This command prompts you for a number of inputs and creates a package.json file that has the minimum amount of information for you to be able to share it. This includes

- ▶ **Package name**—A name for your module

- ▶ **Description**—A description for your module

- ▶ **Package version**—The version of your module

- ▶ **Project homepage**—The website for your module if you have one

- ▶ **Project Git repository**—The Git repository for your module if you have one

- ▶ **Author name**—The author of the module

- ▶ **Author email**—An email address for the author of the module

- ▶ **Author URL**—A website for the author of the module

- ▶ **Main module/entry point**—A main file for the module

- ▶ **Test command**—A command to run tests for the module

- ▶ **Node versions**—Which versions of Node.js the module supports

When these items are entered, the package.json file is shown to you and, if you are happy with it, created. Note that if you are publishing your module to the npm registry, the package names need to be unique, so you may want to search the registry before choosing a name.

DID YOU KNOW?

You Can Save Preferences in ~/.npmrc

You can save many preferences for npm including your author name and home page in a .npmrc file in your home directory. A full list of the options you can set is available at http://npmjs.org/doc/config.html.

▼ TRY IT YOURSELF

If you have downloaded the code examples for this book, this code is hour22/example01.

Follow these steps to create a package.json file:

1. Open a terminal and type the following command:

```
npm init
```

2. For the package name, call it ohaithere.

3. Enter information for all the inputs that you can.

4. Review the information that you have added and respond that you are happy to create the file.

5. Open the package.json in a text editor to review the information that has been added. You should see that a package.json file has been created with the information you submitted.

DID YOU KNOW?

Node.js Modules Are CommonJS Modules

CommonJS is a de facto standard with the purpose of being able to share JavaScript modules between the browser, server, and different JavaScript frameworks. The theory is that you should be able to use CommonJS modules wherever JavaScript is used. This does not always work in practice—especially if you are using Node-specific features—and this has caused some consternation with the CommonJS community. You can read more about CommonJS at http://wiki.commonjs.org/wiki/Modules/1.1.

Folder Structure

No folder structure is enforced for Node.js modules, but many developers use a common pattern that you may want to adhere to. If you choose to use the folder structure suggested below, just use the folders relevant to your project. So if you don't have any documentation, do not use the doc folder! You may also want to add additional folders or files depending on the complexity of your project. For a very small library, you may want to not use any folders at all and place the code for your module in a single index.js file. It is up to you to choose the best approach, but bear in mind that if you are working with other developers, following some kind of convention makes it easier for them to develop with you. A suggested folder structure is as follows:

- ▶ **.gitignore**—List of files to ignore from your Git repository

- ▶ **.npmignore**—List of files to exclude from the npm registry

- ▶ **LICENSE**—License file for the module

- ▶ **README.md**—README file for the module written in the Markdown format

- ▶ **bin**—Folder that holds an executable for the module

- ▶ **doc**—Folder that holds documentation for the module

- ▶ **examples**—Folder to hold practical examples of how to use the module

- ▶ **lib**—Folder to hold the code for the module

- ▶ **man**—Folder to hold any man pages for the module

- ▶ **package.json**—JSON file describing the module

- ▶ **src**—Folder to hold source files, often used for CoffeeScript files

- ▶ **test**—Folder to hold tests for the module

If you have downloaded the code examples for this book, the folder structure is available as hour22/example02.

DID YOU KNOW?

.npmignore and .gitignore Are Complementary
If you want to keep files out of the npm registry, add them to the .npmignore file. If a module has no .npmignore file, but does have a .gitignore, then npm uses the contents of the .gitignore file for what to ignore in the registry. If you want to exclude some files from Git but not from the npm registry, use both a .gitignore file and a .npmignore file.

Developing and Testing Your Module

Now that your module is set up, you can start developing it. To assist with development, npm comes with a utility to install the module that you are developing globally on your machine. If you created the package.json file, you can run the `npm link` command from the same directory and the module is installed globally on your machine. Note that the module name is taken from the name that you gave it in the package.json file:

```
npm link
/usr/local/lib/node_modules/ohaithere ->
➥/Users/george/code/nodejsbook.io.examples/hour22/example03
```

This creates a global link for your module on your computer so you are now able to start Node from the terminal and require your module just as would any other that you have installed on your system. The module that you develop in this hour is simple. It has a single function of hello() that returns a string saying Hello from the ohaithere module.

Now that the module is linked, you can create the module:

1. If you are following the suggested convention, add a new file into the lib folder and give the file the same name as your module. In this case, a file called ohaithere.js is added to the lib folder.

2. Once the new file has been added, you can amend the package.json file to note the entry point for the module:

```
"main" : "./lib/ohaithere.js"
```

3. Building on the Test Driven Development (TDD) approach that you learned in Hour 10, "Testing Node.js Applications," you first write a test for this functionality and then write some code to make the test pass. A new folder called test is created to hold tests for the module. For the test, you want to test that the hello() function returns a certain string. Using Node.js's native assert module, the test looks like this:

```
var assert = require ('assert'),
    ohaithere = require('../lib/ohaithere.js');

/**
 * Test that hello() returns the correct string
 */
assert.equal(
  ohaithere.hello(),
  'Hello from the ohaithere module',
  'Expected "Hello from the ohaithere module". Got "' + ohaithere.hello() +
➥'"'
)
```

4. Copy this example and add it to the test folder as ohaithere.js. Note that after the assert module, the main file for the module that you are developing is included.

5. The package.json file is able to register how tests should be run on the application. This enables tests to be run by the npm test command. To register how to run tests for the module, the following is added to the package.json file:

```
"scripts": {
  "test": "node ./test/ohaithere.js"
}
```

6. When this is complete, you can run the tests with `npm test`:

```
npm test

> ohaithere@0.0.0 test /Users/george/code/nodejsbook.io.examples/hour22/
➥example03
> node ./test/ohaithere.js

node.js:201
        throw e; // process.nextTick error, or 'error' event on first tick
        ^
TypeError: Object #<Object> has no method 'hello'
```

7. You see that the test fails, as you have not yet implemented the `hello` method. To do that, add the following to the lib/ohaithere.js file:

```
exports.hello = function() {
  var message = "Hello from the ohaithere module";
  return message;
};
```

8. If you run the tests again, you should see that the tests pass!

Note here that the word "exports" is used. This is used to expose the function to the external or public scope of the module, making it accessible to anyone who wants to use the module. This is the pattern to use if you have a series of functions that you want to make public to users of your module. If you have private functions that you only want to use within your module, then just declare them as normal functions. They will not be accessible outside your module. If you are programming in an object-oriented or prototype-based style, making parts of your module public is slightly different. This is covered shortly.

TRY IT YOURSELF ▼

If you have downloaded the code examples for this book, the code is hour22/example03.

The following steps demonstrate how to develop a module using a test-driven approach:

1. Building on Example 1 where you created a package.json file, create lib and test folders alongside the package.json file.

2. Within the lib folder, create an empty file called ohaithere.js.

3. Add a main declaration to your package.json file to read as follows:

```
"main" : "./lib/ohaithere.js"
```

4. Within the test folder, create a file called ohaithere.js and add the following content:

```
var assert = require ('assert'),
    ohaithere = require('../lib/ohaithere.js');

/**
 * Test that hello() returns the correct string
 */
assert.equal(
  ohaithere.hello(),
  'Hello from the ohaithere module',
  'Expected "Hello from the ohaithere module". Got "' + ohaithere.hello() +
'"'
)
```

5. Add the following to the package.json file to let npm know where to find tests:

```
"scripts": {
  "test": "node ./test/ohaithere.js"
}
```

6. Run the tests from the root folder of your module by running the following command in the terminal. You should see that the tests fail:

```
npm test
```

7. Open the lib/ohaithere.js file and add the following code:

```
exports.hello = function() {
  var message = "Hello from the ohaithere module";
  return message;
};
```

8. Run the tests again. You should see that they pass.

An example of using Mocha to test modules is also available as hour22/example04.

Adding an Executable

Executables are commands that you can run directly from the terminal. For example, the command npm is an executable. If you are following the suggested convention, executable files are added to a bin folder within a module. In this case, a file called ohaithere.js is created to call the hello() function and log the output to the console:

```
#!/usr/bin/env node
var ohaithere = require("../lib/ohaithere");
console.log (ohaithere.hello());
```

The first line is known as a *shebang*. This tells an operating system how to run the file (in this case, to use Node.js). Once this file has been added, the package.json file can be updated to declare that there is an executable in the module and note where to find it:

```
"bin" : { "ohaithere" : "./bin/ohaithere.js" }
```

This tells npm that there is an `ohaithere` executable and that it can be found at ./bin/ohaithere.js. If the executable is the same name as your module, the syntax is shorter because you can leave out the name of the command:

```
"bin": "./bin/ohaithere.js"
```

After adding these files, you must run npm `link` again to link the new executable into your system:

```
npm link
```

```
/usr/local/bin/ohaithere -> /usr/local/lib/node_modules/ohaithere/bin/ohaithere.js
/usr/local/lib/node_modules/ohaithere -> /Users/george/code/nodejsbook.io.examples/
➥hour22/example05
```

Now, you can run the `ohaithere` command from anywhere on your system and see the output in your terminal!

TRY IT YOURSELF ▼

If you have downloaded the code examples for this book, this code is hour22/example05.

Follow these steps to add an executable to a module:

1. Building on Example 3, add a folder called bin to the module.

2. Within the bin folder, create a file called ohaithere.js and add the following content:

   ```
   #!/usr/bin/env node
   var ohaithere = require("../lib/ohaithere");
   console.log (ohaithere.hello());
   ```

3. Amend the package.json file to include a declaration for the executable:

   ```
   "bin": "./bin/ohaithere.js"
   ```

4. Run npm `link` from the root folder of your module to link the executable into your system:

   ```
   npm link
   ```

5. From the terminal, run the `ohaithere` command:

   ```
   ohaithere
   ```

6. You should see "Hello from the ohaithere module."

Using Object-Oriented or Prototype-Based Programming

Many developers like to use an object-oriented or prototype-based style of programming to better organize code and to manage the scope of variables and methods. The ohaithere module is currently just a single method made public using `exports`:

```
exports.hello = function() {
  var message = "Hello from the ohaithere module";
  return message;
};
```

If this code was written in a prototype-based style, then this would become a method within an object:

```
module.exports = new Ohaithere;

function Ohaithere(){}

Ohaithere.prototype.hello = function(){
  var message = "Hello from the ohaithere module";
  return message;
};
```

If you are using an object-oriented programming style, you must use `module.exports` instead of `exports`. What `exports` actually does is collect properties and attach them to `module.exports` if `module.exports` does not have anything attached to it already. If, however, you are creating your own object to organize and scope your code, you should attach directly to `module.exports`. Note that you are then responsible for defining the scope of methods within your object.

Because JavaScript is a flexible language, you will come across many different programming styles within the Node.js community. Some developers, like marak (Marak Squires) and the developers that work at Nodejitsu, simply use `exports` and functions. Other developers, like mikeal (Mikeal Rogers), use a prototypal-based style and `module.exports`. Furthermore, some developers like substack (James Halliday) use the `this` keyword to create privileged methods within an object:

```
module.exports = new Ohaithere;

function Ohaithere(){
  this.hello = function(){
    var message = "Hello from the ohaithere module";
    return message;
  };
}
```

Often, any of these techniques can be used in parallel. The rule here is that if you use an object-oriented style of JavaScript programming, you must use `module.exports` to export your object and use programmatic techniques to make methods private or public. If you are just using a functional style of programming, you can use `exports` to make a method public or declare a function without `exports` to make it private.

TRY IT YOURSELF ▼

If you have downloaded the code examples for this book, this code is hour22/example06. There is also an example of using privileged methods available as hour22/example07.

The following steps show you how to write modules with a prototypal style:

1. Building on Example 5, open the lib/ohaithere.js file and change the content to use a prototypal-based programming style.

```
module.exports = new Ohaithere;

function Ohaithere(){}

Ohaithere.prototype.hello = function(){
  var message = "Hello from the ohaithere module";
  return message;
};
```

2. From the root of your module, run the test tests. You should see that they pass.

Sharing Code Via GitHub

Within the Node.js community, most developers publish modules as open-source software and frequently collaborate using GitHub. GitHub is a web application for source code collaboration created around Git. Git is a distributed revision control system that is preferred by the Node.js community and is subsequently used heavily in collaboration via GitHub. If you are happy to open source your code, you should strongly consider using Git and GitHub to share your source code. GitHub is free for open source projects and provides a number of tools to help you manage your project including an issue tracker and a wiki. If you are new to Git or GitHub, there is a comprehensive guide to getting started available at http://help.github.com/. If you choose to use GitHub, you can add further information to your package.json file. First, if you are storing source code on GitHub, you can let npm know where your repository is

```
"repository": {
  "type": "git",
  "url": "https://github.com/yourusername/yourproject.git"
}
```

If you are using GitHub to track bugs and issues, you may also specify this in the package.json file. Many larger projects have mailing lists, and this can also be included within the bugs section:

```
"bugs": {
  "email": "yourproject@googlegroups.com",
  "url": "http://github.com/shapeshed/ohaithere/issues"
}
```

You can view the GitHub repository for this example at http://github.com/shapeshed/ohaithere (see Figure 22.1).

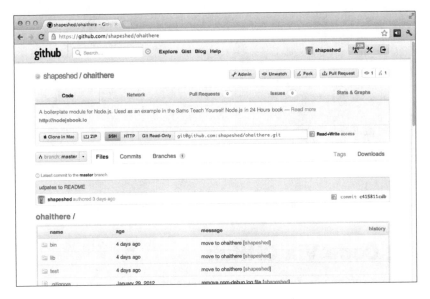

FIGURE 22.1
Publishing your module to GitHub

Using Travis CI

A popular tool within the Node.js community is Travis CI (http://travis-ci.org/). This is a free cloud-based, distributed Continuous Integration server. In this context, Continuous Integration means that your tests are run every time there is a change to your codebase. So, every time you push into your GitHub repository, Travis CI runs your tests and can report to you if there is a problem. This can increase the stability of your code, as if there are any issues with your tests, you are certain to know about it.

To use Travis CI, you need the following:

▶ A GitHub account (you can sign up for free at http://github.com).

▶ Your source code must be in a GitHub repository.

To begin using Travis CI, you must sign into the Travis CI site with your GitHub details (see Figure 22.2). Once this is complete, follow the link to your profile in the top right-hand corner.

FIGURE 22.2
Logging in to Travis CI

You see your list of GitHub repositories (see Figure 22.3). To use a repository with Travis CI, you must first turn it on by flicking the switch.

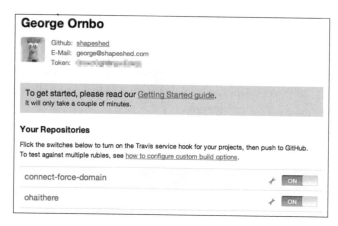

FIGURE 22.3
Enabling repositories for use with Travis CI

In another browser, open the GitHub repository for your project and click the Admin button. Next, follow the link to Service Hooks on the left. Scroll down and find Travis in the list (see Figure 22.4). Click Travis and scroll up to the top. You see that some pieces of information are requested:

▶ **Domain**—Enter **travis-ci.org**.

▶ **User**—Enter your GitHub username.

▶ **Token**—Enter the token from your Travis CI profile.

▶ **Active**—Check this box.

FIGURE 22.4
Adding Travis CI to your GitHub repository

The final step is to create a file within your project that tells Travis CI what to test and how to run the tests within your project. This is a .yml (Yet Another Markup Language) file that declares that the code should be tested against versions 0.4, 0.6, and 0.7 of Node.js:

```
language: node_js
node_js:
  - 0.4
  - 0.6
  - 0.7
```

Save this file to the root of your project as .travis.yml. Now when you push the update to GitHub, your tests will be run on Travis CI. An excellent feature of Travis CI is that you can show the status of the Continuous Integration test on your README page by adding the following snippet of markdown:

```
[![Build Status](https://secure.travis-
➥ci.org/yourgithubuser/yourproject.png)](http://travis-ci.org/yourgithubuser/
➥yourproject)
```

If you visit http://travis-ci.org just after you have pushed to GitHub, you should see your tests being run (see Figure 22.5).

FIGURE 22.5
Tests being run on Travis CI

Publishing to npm

To date, you have done a lot of work on your module! You have

▶ Created a package.json file

▶ Created tests for how the module should work

▶ Added code to make the module work how you expect it to

▶ Added an executable to the module

▶ Added the project to GitHub

▶ Hooked the project up to Travis CI for Continuous Integration testing

The last thing to do is to publish your module to the npm registry. The way this works is that your code is compressed into a tarball and sent to the npm registry servers where it is stored so that it may be installed and used by other developers (see Figure 22.6). To publish to the registry, you must have an account. To create an account, run the following command:

```
npm adduser
```

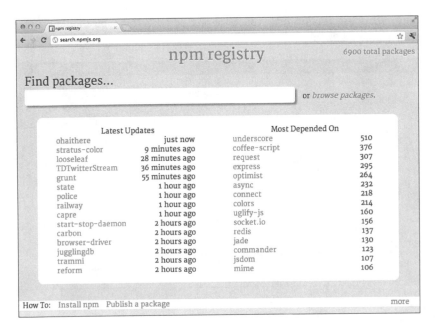

FIGURE 22.6
Publishing your module to the npm registry

You are prompted for a username, password, and email address. Once you have successfully authenticated, you can publish your module. From the root folder of your module, run the following command:

```
npm publish
```

This sends a copy of your module to the registry servers. If everything was successful, you will not see any output, but you can check the npm registry website to see that it was published successfully. If you want to publish an update in the future, you can amend your code and then run the `npm version` command followed by the number of the new version. So, if your current version is 0.0.1, you can issue a minor version update with the following command:

```
npm version 0.0.2
```

This increments the version number in your package.json file and, if you are using a Git repository, also creates a commit message for you with the new version number. When you are ready, run the following from the root of your module:

```
npm publish
```

Publicizing Your Module

You spent a long time crafting your module, so it is time to let people know about it! You can publicize your module in a few places:

▶ Via the Node.js Google Groups mailing list at http://groups.google.com/group/nodejs

▶ Via IRC on irc.freenode.net in the #node.js channel

▶ Via Twitter using the #nodejs hashtag

Summary

In this hour, you learned how to create Node.js modules. You learned how to create a package.json file and then discovered how to develop and test your module. You added an executable to your module and then learned about sharing code with other developers. You saw how to integrate Travis CI with your project and finally how to publish your module to the npm registry.

Q&A

Q. I am just getting started with Node.js. Should I worry about creating modules?

A. If you have a problem in your development that is coming up over and over again, the first thing to do is to check the npm registry. It may be that another developer has already created a module. If there is no module and you think you have the coding skill, you should absolutely create a module! It is a great way to contribute to the community!

Q. Do modules that implement abstractions slow performance?

A. While abstractions make it easier to implement features, they are often at the cost of performance. In the underscore example earlier in this hour, you saw how underscore's each method can be used instead of JavaScript's more verbose for. The performance of underscore is slower than using native JavaScript in this case. You can run tests to show this here, http://jsperf.com/jquery-each-vs-for-loop/58. Unless performance is paramount, this is likely to be unimportant, but keep in mind that creating your own interface to native code can impact performance.

Q. If a module already exists but does not do exactly what I want it to, should I create my own?

A. Sometimes, you may find that a module already exists but does not exactly match your requirements. In this scenario, you can consider adding your requirements to the existing module. If the source code is in GitHub, you can fork the existing module, add your code, and then send the module author a pull request. At the very least, consider contacting the module author before you create an entirely new module.

Q. **Do I have to open-source my module?**

A. No. Although most developers publish modules under an Open Source license, you do not have to. You may want to create modules just for yourself or a team you are working with.

Workshop

This workshop contains quiz questions and exercises to help cement your learning in this hour.

Quiz

1. **How can you search for existing npm modules?**

2. **What command do you use to install your module globally on your machine while you are developing it?**

3. **How can you get help on using npm?**

Quiz Answers

1. You can search for an existing npm module by using `npm search` from the command line or by using the web interface at http://search.npmjs.org/.

2. The command is `npm link` and this installs your module globally on your machine. If you want to unlink the module, run `npm unlink`.

3. You can find help on npm by running `man npm`. For individual commands, you can run `npm help link` to get comprehensive information on the command that you want to run.

Exercises

1. Add another method to the module called "goodbye". This should print a message saying goodbye.

2. Browse the source code of some popular modules in the npm registry. Try to understand the coding style and recognize where `exports` and `module.exports` are used.

3. Publish your module as a project on GitHub.

4. Hook your project up to Travis CI.

Creating Middleware with Connect

What You'll Learn in This Hour:

▶ What Middleware is

▶ How you can use Middleware with Connect and Express

▶ What you can use Middleware for in Connect and Express applications

▶ What Middleware can offer developers

What Is Middleware?

In the context of Node.js, Middleware is a way to filter a request and response in your application by adding a thin layer between the client and your application logic (see Figure 23.1). It provides a simple way to separate concerns within your application and can lead to more maintainable code, a better security model, and code reuse across projects. The idea is relatively simple, but it offers a great deal of power and flexibility to developers.

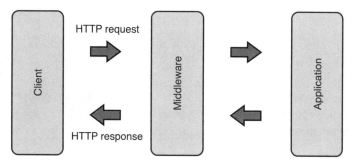

FIGURE 23.1
How Middleware works

Some examples of Middleware include

▶ Cleaning up HTML markup by indenting and reformatting content

▶ Automatically adding Google Analytics code to HTTP responses

▶ Fully featured authentication libraries

▶ Error and exception notifiers that post to third-party services or send emails

▶ Loggers that log data on a web application

▶ Monitoring the performance of an application

In Node.js, the web server and application are the same process so Middleware is not supported natively by Node.js, but a third-party module called Connect adds support for Middleware to Node's HTTP module. This allows developers to add a Middleware layer on top of their Connect or Express applications that can manipulate an HTTP request and response.

Middleware in Connect

Connect is a module for Node.js that provides a Middleware framework and allows developers to create Middleware for applications created with Connect. Express, the web framework you were introduced to in Hour 6, "Introducing Express," is created on top of the Connect module, so you can also use Middleware within Express applications, too.

Connect wraps the Server, ServerRequest, and ServerResponse objects from Node's HTTP module to add Middleware functionality. Middleware in Connect is simply a function that takes the request, response objects, and a next callback as arguments. You can think of Middleware as a list of functions that a request must flow through before hitting the application logic. The most basic example of Middleware is a function that simply passes the request along:

```
function nothingMiddleware(req, res, next) {
  next()
}
```

When the next() callback is invoked, the Middleware is complete and the request is passed to the next piece of Middleware or through to the application layer if there is no more Middleware. This example is pretty pointless as it does nothing more than pass on the request, but the point to note is that once inside the Middleware function, it is possible to manipulate the processing of a request. To illustrate this, here is a Hello World server in Connect. This is the same server that you saw in Hour 1, "Introducing Node.js," but the server now uses Connect so that Middleware can be added to it:

```
var connect = require('connect'),
    http = require('http');

var app = connect()
  .use(helloWorld)

function helloWorld(req, res){
```

```
    res.writeHead(200, {'Content-Type': 'text/plain'});
    res.end('Hi! Hello World');
}

http.Server(app).listen(3000);
```

If you have downloaded the code examples for this book, this code is hour23/example01.

A basic middleware example is shown in the following steps:

1. Create a file called app.js and copy the following code into it:

```
var connect = require('connect'),
    http = require('http');

var app = connect()
  .use(helloWorld)

function helloWorld(req, res){
  res.writeHead(200, {'Content-Type': 'text/plain'});
  res.end('Hi! Hello World');
}

http.Server(app).listen(3000);
```

2. Create a package.json file with the following content:

```
{
  "name": "middleware",
  "version": "0.0.0",
  "dependencies": {
    "connect" : "2.0.1"
  }
}
```

3. Install the dependencies:

```
npm install
```

4. Start the server:

```
node app.js
```

5. Open a web browser at http://0.0.0.0:3000.

6. You should see Hi! Hello World in your browser.

At this point, there is nothing different from the functionality available with Node's HTTP module. But wrapping the HTTP module with Connect enables Middleware to be added to the standard HTTP module.

Note that in the example, Node's HTTP module is being used and that the Connect application is passed into http.Server. The Hello World response is actually a piece of Middleware itself, too.

Middleware is added to the Connect application by mounting it within the Connect server. Middleware can be mounted for the entire application or just specific routes and is chained together in the order that it is declared. In the following example, Middleware is mounted in the Connect application and is used to respond to all requests:

```
var app = connect()
  .use(connect.favicon());
  .use(connect.logger());
  .use(connect.static(__dirname + '/public')); .
```

By using Middleware, a request is passed along until a response is returned. In the following example, the first piece of Middleware, nothingMiddleware, simply passes through to helloWorld, which returns the response. By using res.end, the processing of the request finishes as the response is sent. If you can understand how a request flows through Middleware in this example, you will begin to understand what Middleware can offer to developers:

```
var connect = require('connect'),
    http = require('http');

var app = connect()
  .use(nothingMiddleware)
  .use(helloWorld)

function nothingMiddleware(req, res, next) {
  next()
}

function helloWorld(req, res){
  res.writeHead(200, {'Content-Type': 'text/plain'});
  res.end('Hi! Hello World');
}

http.Server(app).listen(3000);
```

Middleware can be used to manipulate a request and response. In the following example, some Middleware is used to add a custom header to any response that the application sends:

```
var connect = require('connect'),
    http = require('http');
```

```
var app = connect()
  .use(addHeader)
  .use(helloWorld)

function addHeader(req, res, next) {
  res.setHeader('X-Custom-Header', 'My header content')
  next();
}
function helloWorld(req, res){
  res.writeHead(200, {'Content-Type': 'text/plain'});
  res.end('Hi! Hello World');
}

http.Server(app).listen(3000);
```

Within the `addHeader` function, the response object is altered to add an extra header before it is passed through to the `helloWorld`. This is a simple example of using Middleware to amend a response without going into your application code. Because Middleware can also be extracted into modules, it allows developers to reuse specific pieces of functionality across different projects.

 TRY IT YOURSELF ▼

If you have downloaded the code examples for this book, this code is hour23/example02.

Follow these steps to add a custom header with Middleware:

1. Create a file called app.js and copy the following code into it:

```
var connect = require('connect'),
    http = require('http');

var app = connect()
  .use(addHeader)
  .use(helloWorld)

function addHeader(req, res, next) {
  res.setHeader('X-Custom-Header', 'My header content')
  next();
}
function helloWorld(req, res){
  res.writeHead(200, {'Content-Type': 'text/plain'});
  res.end('Hi! Hello World');
}

http.Server(app).listen(3000);
```

2. Create a package.json file with the following content:

```
{
  "name": "middleware",
  "version": "0.0.0",
  "dependencies": {
    "connect" : "2.0.1"
  }
}
```

3. Install the dependencies:

```
npm install
```

4. Start the server:

```
node app.js
```

5. Make a cURL request to your server and examine the headers. If you do not have cURL on your system, you can open the page in Google Chrome and use the HTTP headers extension:

```
curl -i http://0.0.0.0:3000
```

6. You should see that the Middleware has added a custom header to the response (see Figure 23.2).

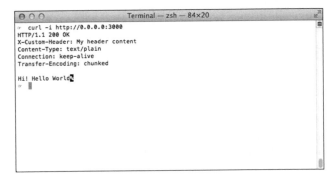

FIGURE 23.2
Adding a custom header with Middleware

Now that you understand a little more of what Middleware is, you can begin to think of potential uses for Middleware. Although Connect is a Middleware framework, it ships with some useful Middleware for commonly used scenarios that can give you a good insight into what Middleware is good for. These include

▶ A logger for logging information to a file

▶ Basic authentication to provide username and password protection to a page or site

▶ A cookie parser

▶ Cross-site request forgery protection

These are all good examples of Middleware where the requirement is to do something with a request or response that is independent of your application code. As Middleware can be encapsulated in a Node.js module, this can make your application more modular and maintainable. The following is an example from Connect's source code and is the Middleware for converting HTTP requests from one sort to another. This is often used for making PUT requests from forms in a web browser. Forms in most web browsers only support making GET or POST requests, but many APIs expect a PUT request. This is a good example of how Middleware can be used to manipulate the request before it hits the application code:

```
module.exports = function methodOverride(key){
  key = key || "_method";
  return function methodOverride(req, res, next) {
    req.originalMethod = req.originalMethod || req.method;

    // req.body
    if (req.body && key in req.body) {
      req.method = req.body[key].toUpperCase();
      delete req.body[key];
    // check X-HTTP-Method-Override
    } else if (req.headers['x-http-method-override']) {
      req.method = req.headers['x-http-method-override'].toUpperCase();
    }

    next();
  };
};
```

This Middleware is similar to the examples that you saw earlier in this hour in that the methodOverride function takes a request, response, and a next callback as arguments. The Middleware manipulates the native Node.js method request.method to change the type of request. The code checks req.body._method, and if it is found uses it to swap out the HTTP request method. This allows developers to create RESTful web forms. With just a few lines of code, this Middleware provides an excellent workaround for a limitation of web forms and allows RESTful web services to be used with HTML forms.

Access Control with Middleware

Middleware is a good candidate for managing access control. Many applications place access control logic directly in application code. By extracting access control to a Middleware layer, you are able to control access to your application before you hit application logic. Many developers consider this a more secure and elegant solution. In the following example, suppose that you want to limit access to a website based on the time of day. If the time is between 9 in the morning and 5 at night, then the website should be open. If it is outside those times, then the website is closed. One way of writing some Middleware for this scenario looks as follows:

```
function nineToFive(req, res, next) {
  var currentHour = new Date().getHours();
  if (currentHour < 9 || currentHour > 17) {
    res.writeHead(503, {'Content-Type': 'text/plain'});
    res.end('We are closed. Come back between 0900 and 1700.');
  } else {
    next();
  }
}
```

As the request flows through this Middleware, the current time is checked to see whether it is outside the 9–5 working hours of the website. If it is outside these hours, then a 503 HTTP response is returned to indicate that the service is temporarily unavailable. The usage of res.end finishes the processing and returns the response to the client. If the current time is not outside 9–5, then the request is passed through to the next piece of Middleware. Here is a full example of this Middleware:

```
var connect = require('connect'),
    http = require('http');

var app = connect()
  .use(nineToFive)
  .use(helloWorld)

function nineToFive(req, res, next) {
  var currentHour = new Date().getHours();
  if (currentHour < 9 || currentHour > 17) {
    res.writeHead(503, {'Content-Type': 'text/plain'});
    res.end('We are closed. Come back between 0900 and 1700.');
  } else {
    next();
  }
}

function helloWorld(req,res){
  res.writeHead(200, {'Content-Type': 'text/plain'});
```

```
  res.end('Hi! We are open!');
}

http.Server(app).listen(3000);
```

If you have downloaded the code examples for this book, this code is hour23/example03.

Follow these steps to use access control with Middleware:

1. Create a file called app.js and copy the following code into it:

```
var connect = require('connect'),
    http = require('http');

var app = connect()
  .use(nineToFive)
  .use(helloWorld)

function nineToFive(req, res, next) {
  var currentHour = new Date().getHours();
  if (currentHour < 9 || currentHour > 17) {
    res.writeHead(503, {'Content-Type': 'text/plain'});
    res.end('We are closed. Come back between 0900 and 1700.');
  } else {
    next();
  }
}

function helloWorld(req,res){
  res.writeHead(200, {'Content-Type': 'text/plain'});
  res.end('Hi! We are open!');
}

http.Server(app).listen(3000);
```

2. Create a package.json file with the following content:

```
{
  "name": "middleware",
  "version": "0.0.0",
  "dependencies": {
    "connect" : "2.0.1"
  }
}
```

3. Install the dependencies:

   ```
   npm install
   ```

   4. Start the server:

   ```
   node app.js
   ```

   5. Open a browser at http://0.0.0.0:3000.

   6. If you are viewing the page between 9 in the morning and 5 at night, you should see
   "Hi! We are open!" (see Figure 23.3). If not, you should see "We are closed. Come back
   between 0900 and 1700."

   7. Try stopping the server, amending the hours, restarting the server, and opening the page
   again so you can see how it works.

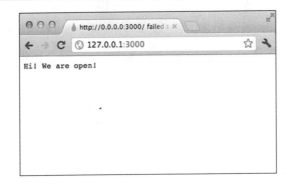

FIGURE 23.3
Time-based access with Middleware

Limiting Access by IP Address

When clients make requests to a Node.js server, it is possible to find the IP address that the
request is originating from in `req.connection.remoteAddress`, where `req` is the request
object. This can be used to create some Middleware that filters access to an application based
on the originating IP address of the request. In this example, you see how to make Middleware
more flexible by allowing arguments to be passed in:

```
function filterByIp(ips){
  var ips = ips || [];
  return function (req, res, next){
    if (ips.indexOf(req.connection.remoteAddress) == -1) {
```

```
    res.writeHead(401, {'Content-Type': 'text/plain'});
    res.write('Sorry. You are not allowed to access this server');
    res.end();
  } else {
    next();
  }
 };
};
```

If the request ip address is not found in the array of allowed IP addresses, then a 401 response
is returned to the client to indicate that they are not authorized to access the server. Calling
res.end() ensures that the request is finished. If the IP address is found in the list of whitelisted
IP addresses, then the request is passed through. In the following example, the Node.js server is
only accessible from 127.0.0.1:

```
var connect = require('connect'),
    http = require('http');

var app = connect()
  .use(filterByIp(['127.0.0.1']))
  .use(helloWorld)

function filterByIp(ips){
  var ips = ips || [];
  return function (req, res, next){
    if (ips.indexOf(req.connection.remoteAddress) == -1) {
      res.writeHead(401, {'Content-Type': 'text/plain'});
      res.write('Sorry. You are not allowed to access this server');
      res.end();
    } else {
      next();
    }
  };
};

function helloWorld(req,res){
  res.writeHead(200, {'Content-Type': 'text/plain'});
  res.end('You can view this!');
}

http.Server(app).listen(3000);
```

▼ TRY IT YOURSELF

If you have downloaded the code examples for this book, this code is hour23/example04.

Follow these steps to use Middleware to filter by IP addresses:

1. Create a file called app.js and copy the following code into it:

```
var connect = require('connect'),
    http = require('http');

var app = connect()
  .use(filterByIp(['127.0.0.1']))
  .use(helloWorld)

function filterByIp(ips){
  var ips = ips || [];
  return function (req, res, next){
    if (ips.indexOf(req.connection.remoteAddress) == -1) {
      res.writeHead(401, {'Content-Type': 'text/plain'});
      res.write('Sorry. You are not allowed to access this server');
      res.end();
    } else {
      next();
    }
  };
};

function helloWorld(req,res){
  res.writeHead(200, {'Content-Type': 'text/plain'});
  res.end('You can view this!');
}

http.Server(app).listen(3000);
```

2. Create a package.json file with the following content:

```
{
  "name": "middleware",
  "version": "0.0.0",
  "dependencies": {
    "connect" : "2.0.1"
  }
}
```

3. Install the dependencies:

```
npm install
```

4. Start the server:

```
node app.js
```

5. Open a browser at http://0.0.0.0:3000.

6. You should see that you can access the server.

7. Stop the server and change the IP address on line five of the script to 127.0.0.2.

8. Start the server again:

```
node app.js
```

9. Open a browser at http://0.0.0.0:3000.

10. You should see that you can no longer access the server (see Figure 23.4).

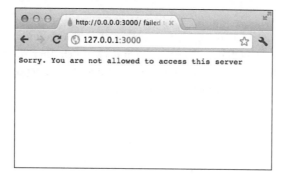

FIGURE 23.4
IP-based access with Middleware

Forcing Users onto a Single Domain

With many Platform as a Service (PaaS) providers, you are able to add custom domains to applications. So for example, an application hosted on the Heroku platform might be assigned the
URL of http://smooth-light-324.herokuapp.com/. You might want to serve the site from your own
domain name (let's say it is fooboo.com), so you could use the Custom Domains add-on and
set up a CNAME record for fooboo.com so that the site will be served from your domain. At this
point, the site will be accessible from two domains:

▶ http://smooth-light324.herokuapp.com

▶ http://fooboo.com

If you are just testing something, this may be okay, but if the site is in production, you should really direct all traffic to a single domain as this can be detrimental for SEO (Search Engine Optimization). Google has stated publicly that duplicate content can be penalized and encourages web developers to use 301 redirects to redirect requests where the same content exists on multiple domains. By using Middleware, you can write a small piece of code to solve this problem:

```
function forceDomain(domain){
  var domain = domain || false;
  return function (req, res, next){
    if (domain && (req.headers.host != domain)){
      res.writeHead(301, {"Location": 'http://' + domain + req.url});
      res.end();
    } else {
      next();
    }
  };
};
```

In this example, the Middleware accepts an argument of a domain and then checks this against the request headers to see whether this matches. If it does match, then the request is passed through. If it fails to match, then the request is redirected to the correct domain with a 301 response code. A full example for this Middleware is as follows:

```
var connect = require('connect'),
    http = require('http');

var app = connect()
  .use(forceDomain('127.0.0.1:3000'))
  .use(helloWorld)

function forceDomain(domain){
  domain = domain || false;
  return function (req, res, next){
    if (domain && (req.headers.host != domain)){
      res.writeHead(301, {"Location": 'http://' + domain + req.url});
      res.end();
    } else {
      next();
    }
  };
};

function helloWorld(req,res){
  res.writeHead(200, {'Content-Type': 'text/plain'});
  res.end('Hello World');
}

http.Server(app).listen(3000);
```

BY THE WAY

301 Redirects Users and Search Engines

A 301 status code indicates a permanent redirect and lets search engines know that one resource is now permanently redirected to another. For users, they are seamlessly redirected to the new resource.

TRY IT YOURSELF ▼

If you have downloaded the code examples for this book, this code is hour23/example05.

Follow these steps to force a single domain with Middleware:

1. Create a file called app.js and copy the following code into it:

```
var connect = require('connect'),
    http = require('http');

var app = connect()
  .use(forceDomain('127.0.0.1:3000'))
  .use(helloWorld)

function forceDomain(domain){
  domain = domain || false;
  return function (req, res, next){
    if (domain && (req.headers.host != domain)){
      res.writeHead(301, {"Location": 'http://' + domain + req.url});
      res.end();
    } else {
      next();
    }
  };
};

function helloWorld(req,res){
  res.writeHead(200, {'Content-Type': 'text/plain'});
  res.end('Hello World');
}

http.Server(app).listen(3000);
```

2. Create a package.json file with the following content:

```
{
  "name": "middleware",
  "version": "0.0.0",
  "dependencies": {
    "connect" : "2.0.1"
  }
}
```

3. Install the dependencies:

```
npm install
```

4. Start the server:

```
node app.js
```

5. Open a browser at http://0.0.0.0:3000.

6. You should see in your address bar that you are redirected to http://127.0.0.1:3000.

Summary

In this hour, you were introduced to Middleware. You saw how it is possible to use Middleware with Connect to manipulate a request and response without hitting your application code. You learned how Middleware is a thin layer between the client and your application that offers a lot of power. You saw how to add headers to a response, limit access based on time, limit access based on IP address, and how to force all users onto a single domain. During the course of these examples, you learned how to pass arguments to Middleware and how a request can flow through Middleware.

Q&A

Q. **Should I use Middleware all the time?**

A. Middleware is great for manipulating a request and response. It should be considered as separate from your application, so where you are doing things like crunching data or querying a database, this should not be in Middleware.

Q. **Is the order of Middleware important?**

A. Yes. A request will flow through Middleware in the order that it is declared in. As you add more Middleware to your application, you should be aware of this as it can lead to unexpected results if Middleware is declared in the wrong order.

Q. Can I use Middleware outside Connect and Express?

A. JSGI is another way of using Middleware with Node.js, and a module exists to use this with Node.js. For more information, see https://github.com/persvr/jsgi-node. You can also write Middleware without a framework, although this is beyond the scope of this hour.

Workshop

This workshop contains quiz questions and exercises to help cement your learning in this hour.

Quiz

1. What types of things is Middleware useful for?

2. What options are available for ending a piece of Middleware?

3. Is Connect the only way you can use Middleware in Node.js?

Quiz Answers

1. Middleware is useful for things like authentication, logging, caching exception notifiers, and redirection. It is a thin layer that sits in front of your application logic that can manipulate the request and response.

2. You can call `next()` to pass the request and response objects onto the next piece of Middleware (or the application logic if it is the last one). You can use `res.end()` to return the response.

3. No. Connect makes it very easy to create Middleware, but you can also use JSGI or write your own.

Exercises

1. Create a Middleware function for Connect that logs the browser version to the console. Hint: This is available through `req.headers['user-agent']`.

2. Read the source code of the Middleware that ships with the Connect library at https://github.com/senchalabs/connect/tree/master/lib/middleware. Try to understand how a request is being manipulated.

3. Explore the Middleware that is listed on the Node.js Wiki at https://github.com/joyent/node/wiki/modules#wiki-middleware. Try to understand what some of these modules are doing and read the source code of one or more projects.

Using Node.js with Backbone.js

What You'll Learn in This Hour:

▶ What Backbone.js is

▶ How you can use Node.js with Backbone.js

▶ Creating a simple single-page application with Node.js and Backbone.js

▶ Create a simple Backbone.js view

What Is Backbone.js?

Backbone.js is a front-end JavaScript framework for creating modern, browser-based web applications. It is designed to help developers create desktop type applications in the browser. It can be used to create single-page applications or applications that have URLs. It is designed to integrate with either jQuery or Zepto and allows developers to create applications that do not require the page to refresh when users update data.

As browsers have become more capable, developers have pushed more of their application logic into the browser, relying on Ajax to send and receive updates to the server. This allows users to enjoy a very fast experience, rivaling the speed of desktop applications. On the server side, developers have been able to use mature frameworks like Rails or Django to create web applications, but until recently there was little available for creating rich client-side web applications.

Backbone.js is one framework that aims to help developers create rich client-side web applications using JavaScript. It achieves this through providing a structure to a JavaScript-heavy application and makes it vastly easier for developers to build and maintain client-side JavaScript applications.

One of the exciting things about using Node.js is that it brings JavaScript to the server side and brings all of the capabilities of an event-driven dynamic language to network programming. The idea that you can use JavaScript to create the client and the server allows JavaScript developers to become "full stack" developers. This means that a JavaScript developer can create a server and rich client. Good news if you are a JavaScript developer! Furthermore, by using a data store like MongoDB or CouchDB, you can even use JavaScript to store and interact with your data. In this context, your entire application could be created using JavaScript from the server to database to the client.

If you are creating Node.js applications, it is likely that at some point you will want to create a rich JavaScript-based client for your Node.js server. As Backbone.js is a framework for client-side applications it expects that it will communicate with a server-side application. By default, it expects this to be a JSON-based API very similar to the type you learned to create in Hour 15, "JSON APIs." Node.js is an excellent choice for the server side of a Backbone.js application as it is lightweight, fast, and JavaScript!

In this hour, you learn how to create the server-side element of a Backbone.js application and gain an overview of how Backbone.js works.

BY THE WAY

The Creator of Backbone.js Also Created Underscore.js and CoffeeScript

Backbone.js was created by Jeremy Ashkenas. He also created Underscore.js, a library that augments the JavaScript language itself and is also used in Backbone.js. Jeremy Ashkenas also created CoffeeScript, the JavaScript preprocessor that you were introduced to in Hour 21, "CoffeeScript."

How Backbone.js Works

To understand how to use Node.js with Backbone.js, you first need to understand how Backbone.js approaches client-side web applications. Backbone.js structures data in applications around Models and Collections. If you have worked with a web application framework like Rails or Django, these concepts may be familiar to you. If you have not used these frameworks, this can be explained by thinking about a simple Backbone.js application: a to-do list.

Within a to-do list, Backbone.js thinks of a task (or to-do item) as a Model and the list of tasks as a Collection of the tasks. Put simply, a Model is a single item and a Collection is a group of items. In a to-do type application, a single task is a Model and all the tasks is a Collection.

Backbone.js expects to interact with a server-side JSON API using HTTP and the same GET, POST, PUT, and DELETE requests that you were introduced to in Hour 15. By default, Backbone.js expects routes to follow RESTful conventions. With an API endpoint of /api/tasks, the routes are as follows:

▶ GET /api/tasks: get all tasks

▶ GET /api/tasks/:id: get a single task

▶ POST /api/tasks: create a new task

▶ PUT /api/tasks/:id: update a task

▶ DELETE /api/tasks/:id: delete a task

WATCH OUT

MongoDB Must Be Running for These Examples

To work through these examples, you need a MongoDB server to be running on your machine. If you need a refresher for this, consult Hour 15.

Using MongoDB and Express, a simple API can be created for Backbone.js to interact with. The Express application will have the following folder structure:

```
.
├── app.js
├── package.json
├── public
│   ├── javascripts
│   │   └── application.js
│   └── stylesheets
│       └── style.css
└── views
    └── index.jade
```

The application uses Mongojs to interact with MongoDB, so the package.json file looks as follows:

```
{
  "name":"backbone_example",
  "version":"0.0.1",
  "private":true,
  "dependencies":{
    "express":"2.5.8",
    "mongojs":"0.4.3",
    "jade":"0.22.0"
  }
}
```

The main app.js file is a simple Express application that serves as an API to the Backbone.js client and also serves a single HTML page. This is similar to the JSON-based API that you saw in Hour 15:

```
var express = require('express'),
    db = require("mongojs").connect('backbone_tasks', ['tasks']);

var app = module.exports = express.createServer();
```

```
app.use(express.bodyParser());
app.use(express.static(__dirname + '/public'));
app.use(express.errorHandler({dumpExceptions: true, showStack: true}));

app.get('/', function(req, res){
  res.render('index.jade', {
    layout: false
  });
});

app.get('/api/tasks', function(req, res){
  db.tasks.find().sort({ $natural: -1 }, function(err, tasks) {
    res.json(tasks);
  });
});

app.get('/api/tasks/:id', function(req, res){
  db.tasks.findOne( { _id: db.ObjectId(req.params.id) } , function(err, task) {
    res.json(task);
  });
});

app.post('/api/tasks', function(req, res){
  db.tasks.save(req.body, function(err, task) {
    res.json(task, 201);
  });
});

app.put('/api/tasks/:id', function(req, res){
  db.tasks.update( { _id: db.ObjectId(req.params.id) }, { $set: { title: req.body.
title } }, function(err, task) {
    res.json(200);
  });
});

app.del('/api/tasks/:id', function(req, res){
  db.tasks.remove( { _id: db.ObjectId(req.params.id) }, function(err) {
    res.send();
  });
});

app.listen(3000);
```

This includes the necessary routes for Backbone.js and a single HTML page that serves as the Backbone.js client for the application. The following is added to the index.jade file:

```
!!! 5
html
```

```
head
   title Node.js / Backbone.js Example
   link(rel='stylesheet', href='/stylesheets/style.css')
body
   h1 Tasks
   div#tasks
   script(src='https://ajax.googleapis.com/ajax/libs/jquery/1.7.1/jquery.min.js')
   script(src='http://cdnjs.cloudflare.com/ajax/libs/underscore.js/1.3.1/
➥ underscore-min.js')
   script(src='http://cdnjs.cloudflare.com/ajax/libs/backbone.js/0.9.1/backbone-
➥ min.js')
   script(src='/javascripts/application.js')
```

This includes jQuery, Underscore.js, Backbone.js, and a link to an application.js file where the Backbone.js code will go. Finally, the application.js file will have the following content:

```
var App = {};

App.Task = Backbone.Model.extend({
   idAttribute: "_id",
});

App.Tasks = Backbone.Collection.extend({
   model: App.Task,
   url: '/api/tasks'
});
```

In this code, an empty App object is declared. This is to namespace the Backbone.js application to reduce the risk of any variable collisions with other libraries. Next, a Backbone.js model is declared, and because MongoDB is being used, the idAttribute is set correctly to be "_id". Finally, a Backbone.js collection is declared, referencing the model that was just created and setting the URL to send and receive data from. Backbone.js takes care of all the GET, POST, PUT, and DELETE methods behind the scenes, so this is all you need.

A skeleton Backbone.js is now ready, so assuming MongoDB is installed and running on your machine, you can now start the Node.js server and open a browser at http://0.0.0.0:3000. At this stage, there is no view from the application other than a placeholder page, but to gain an understanding of how Backbone.js works, you can begin to interact with the Node.js server from the JavaScript console in the browser.

With the Node.js server running, open a JavaScript console in your browser so you can begin interacting with the Node.js API. You can create a new task from the JavaScript console by running the following code:

```
var tasks = new App.Tasks;
tasks.create({ title: "Test Task" });
```

You will see in the console that Backbone.js handles posting the data for you (it uses jQuery for this) and posts it to the Node.js API. Backbone.js also handles the response.

▼ TRY IT YOURSELF

If you have downloaded the code examples for this book, this code is hour24/example01.

The following steps show a basic Backbone application:

1. Create an Express project with the following structure:

```
.
├── app.js
├── package.json
├── public
│   ├── javascripts
│   │   └── application.js
│   └── stylesheets
│       └── style.css
└── views
    └── index.jade
```

2. Within the package.json file, add the following content:

```
{
    "name":"backbone_example",
    "version":"0.0.1",
    "private":true,
    "dependencies":{
        "express":"2.5.8",
        "mongojs":"0.4.3",
        "jade":"0.22.0"
    }
}
```

3. Within the app.js file, add the following content:

```
var express = require('express'),
    db = require("mongojs").connect('backbone_tasks', ['tasks']);

var app = module.exports = express.createServer();
app.use(express.bodyParser());
app.use(express.static(__dirname + '/public'));
app.use(express.errorHandler({dumpExceptions: true, showStack: true}));

app.get('/', function(req, res){
  res.render('index.jade', {
    layout: false
```

```
    });
  });

  app.get('/api/tasks', function(req, res){
    db.tasks.find().sort({ $natural: -1 }, function(err, tasks) {
      res.json(tasks);
    });
  });

  app.get('/api/tasks/:id', function(req, res){
    db.tasks.findOne( { _id: db.ObjectId(req.params.id) } , function(err, task)
  {
      res.json(task);
    });
  });

  app.post('/api/tasks', function(req, res){
    db.tasks.save(req.body, function(err, task) {
      res.json(task, 201);
    });
  });

  app.put('/api/tasks/:id', function(req, res){
    db.tasks.update( { _id: db.ObjectId(req.params.id) }, { $set: { title: req.
  body.title } }, function(err, task) {
      res.json(200);
    });
  });

  app.del('/api/tasks/:id', function(req, res){
    db.tasks.remove( { _id: db.ObjectId(req.params.id) }, function(err) {
      res.send();
    });
  });

  app.listen(3000);
```

4. Within the index.jade file, add the following content:

```
!!! 5
html
  head
    title Node.js / Backbone.js Example
    link(rel='stylesheet', href='/stylesheets/style.css')
  body
    h1 Tasks
    div#tasks
    script(src='https://ajax.googleapis.com/ajax/libs/jquery/1.7.1/jquery.min.
➥js')
```

```
    script(src='http://cdnjs.cloudflare.com/ajax/libs/underscore.js/1.3.1/
 underscore-min.js')
    script(src='http://cdnjs.cloudflare.com/ajax/libs/backbone.js/0.9.1/
 backbone-min.js')
    script(src='/javascripts/application.js')
```

5. Within the application.js file, add the following content:

```
var App = {};

App.Task = Backbone.Model.extend({
  idAttribute: "_id",
});

App.Tasks = Backbone.Collection.extend({
  model: App.Task,
  url: '/api/tasks'
});
```

6. Install the required dependencies:

```
npm install
```

7. Start the server by running the following from a terminal:

```
node app.js
```

8. Open a browser with a JavaScript console at http://127.0.0.1:3000.

9. Open the JavaScript console and enter the following; then press Return to run the code:

```
var tasks = new App.Tasks;
tasks.create({ title: "Test Task" });
```

10. You should see that Backbone.js sends the data to the server and that a new task is created (see Figure 24.1).

FIGURE 24.1
Interacting with Backbone.js from the JavaScript console

A Simple Backbone.js View

Backbone.js has the concept of views that allow users to see and interact with the data in your application. Backbone.js uses templates in much the same way that server-side frameworks do. These are snippets of code that data is dynamically written to. The concept is similar to what you have already seen with Jade in Express, but this time it is all in the browser! You can use a range of template languages with Backbone.js. For this example, Underscore.js templates are used. For the purposes of the view, the following is required:

▶ A form to allow users to submit tasks

▶ An unordered list to hold the list of tasks (or collection)

▶ A list item template to hold each task

Using Underscore.js templates, these can be created and added to the index.jade file to look like this:

```
script(id='task_form', type='text/template')
  | <form action='' id='task-form'>
  |   <fieldset>
```

```
        |        <legend>Add a task</legend>
        |        <input type='text' name='title' class='task-title' />
        |        <input type='submit' value='Submit' />
        |     </fieldset>
        |  </form>
script(id='task_template', type='text/template')
        |  <li data-id="<%= task.id %>">
        |    <%= task.get('title') %>
        |  </li>
script(id='tasks_template', type='text/template')
        |  <%= task_form() %>
        |  <ul>
        |    <% _.each(tasks, function(task){ %>
        |      <%= task_template({ task: task }) %>
        |    <% }); %>
        |  </ul>
```

Note that the type of `'text/template'` is used to allow Backbone.js to find these templates and use them. Much like server-side templates, data is expected to be passed into these templates and will be displayed dynamically. To allow any data from the Node.js server to be passed to Backbone.js, a query is made to MongoDB when the page is first loaded. Although this could be done from the client side, the recommended approach is to perform this on the server side. The Express route for the index page within the app.js file is now amended to include the query and pass the data to the index.jade template:

```
app.get('/', function(req, res){
  db.tasks.find().sort({ $natural: -1 }, function(err, tasks) {
    res.render('index.jade', {
      tasks: JSON.stringify(tasks),
      layout: false
    });
  });
});
```

Within the index.jade file, this data can now be made available to Backbone.js by adding a script tag with the data received from the server at the end of the file:

```
script
  var tasks = new App.Tasks;
  tasks.reset(!{tasks});
```

The Backbone.js view can now be created within the application.js file:

```
App.TasksView = Backbone.View.extend({
  el: $("#tasks"),
  initialize: function() {
    this.task_form = _.template($('#task_form').html());
```

```
    this.tasks_template = _.template($('#tasks_template').html());
    this.task_template = _.template($('#task_template').html());
    this.render();
  },
  render: function() {
    $(this.el).html(this.tasks_template({
      task_form: this.task_form,
      tasks: this.collection.models,
      task_template: this.task_template
    }));
  }
});
```

Backbone.js views must target an element with the HTML structure so the empty div with the id of 'tasks' is declared as the target. This means that Backbone.js generates the output and then injects it into this HTML element.

The view is then initialized within the initialize function. Anything within the initialize function will be run when the view is instatiated so it can be thought of as a setup stage for the view. Within the initialize function, the templates that were just created are referenced to build the view. Note at the end of the initialize function, the render() method is called. This causes Backbone.js to render the templates into the view and show them within the HTML.

The render method writes the templates in the specified page element. The view is now set up, but to use a view, it must be instantiated. A common pattern within Backbone.js is to have an init function that completes anything required for an application to start. In this case, all that is required is for the TasksView to be instantiated and for the tasks to be passed in so the data can be displayed. This can be added to the end of the application.js file:

```
App.init = function() {
  new App.TasksView({ collection: tasks });
}
```

Finally, the script tag at the end of the index.jade file can be amended to call the init function and start the Backbone.js application:

```
script
  var tasks = new App.Tasks;
  tasks.reset(!{tasks});
  $(function() {
    App.init();
  });
```

WATCH OUT
***
Watch Out for Browser Caching

As you work through these examples, you may find that your browser caches client-side JavaScript between examples. You may find it useful to clear your browser cache between working on each example.
***

▼ TRY IT YOURSELF

If you have downloaded the code examples for this book, this code is hour24/example02.

Follow these steps to add a Backbone.js view:

1. Building on the previous example open the index.jade file and add the following after the `div#tasks` tag:

```
script(id='task_form', type='text/template')
  | <form action='' id='task-form'>
  |   <fieldset>
  |     <legend>Add a task</legend>
  |     <input type='text' name='title' class='task-title' />
  |     <input type='submit' value='Submit' />
  |   </fieldset>
  | </form>
script(id='task_template', type='text/template')
  | <li data-id="<%= task.id %>">
  |   <%= task.get('title') %>
  | </li>
script(id='tasks_template', type='text/template')
  | <%= task_form() %>
  | <ul>
  |   <% _.each(tasks, function(task){ %>
  |     <%= task_template({ task: task }) %>
  |   <% }); %>
  | </ul>
```

2. Amend the Express route that serves the index page to look like this:

```
app.get('/', function(req, res){
  db.tasks.find().sort({ $natural: -1 }, function(err, tasks) {
    res.render('index.jade', {
      tasks: JSON.stringify(tasks),
      layout: false
    });
  });
});
```

3. Add the Backbone view and the `init` function to the application.js file:

```
App.TasksView = Backbone.View.extend({
  el: $("#tasks"),
  initialize: function() {
    this.task_form = _.template($('#task_form').html());
    this.tasks_template = _.template($('#tasks_template').html());
    this.task_template = _.template($('#task_template').html());
    this.render();
  },
  render: function() {
    $(this.el).html(this.tasks_template({
      task_form: this.task_form,
      tasks: this.collection.models,
      task_template: this.task_template
    }));
  }
});
App.init = function() {
  new App.TasksView({ collection: tasks });
}
```

4. To give Backbone.js access to the data from the server, add the following to the end of the index.jade file:

```
script
  var tasks = new App.Tasks;
  tasks.reset(!{tasks});
  $(function() {
    App.init();
  });
```

5. Start the Node.js server:

```
node app.js
```

6. Open a browser with a JavaScript console at http://127.0.0.1:3000.

7. You should see any tasks that you added in the previous examples displayed on the page.

Creating Records with Backbone.js

The example currently has a form, but this needs to be wired up to Backbone.js so that the data can be sent to the server and written to the page. Within a Backbone.js view, it is possible to set up events and functions that should be called when events happen. In this case, the desired functionality is that a submitted task is posted to the server when the form is submitted and also written to the HTML. Backbone is optimistic about data being written to the server, so by default, it assumes data has been successfully sent to the API. The event that triggers a task being created is the form being submitted, and this calls a `createTask` function:

```
events : {
  'submit form' : 'createTask'
},
createTask: function (event) {
  event.preventDefault();
  var taskTitleInput = $('.task-title');
  var taskTitle = taskTitleInput.val();
  tasks.create({ title: taskTitle }, {
    success: function(task){
      $('#tasks ul')
        .prepend("<li>" + taskTitle" + "</li>");
      taskTitleInput.val('');
    }
  });
}
```

The `createTask` function first captures the submit event and prevents the form from being submitted. Next, using jQuery selectors, the value that the user entered is captured, and then a task is created through Backbone.js using the `create` method on the Tasks collection. If this is successful, the task is written to the HTML using jQuery.

▼ TRY IT YOURSELF

If you have downloaded the code examples for this book, this code is hour04/example03.

Follow these steps to create records through Backbone.js:

1. Building on the previous example, add the following to the `TasksView` block in application.js:

```
events : {
  'submit form' : 'createTask'
},
createTask: function (event) {
  event.preventDefault();
  var taskTitleInput = $('.task-title');
  var taskTitle = taskTitleInput.val();
  tasks.create({ title: taskTitle }, {
    success: function(task){
      $('#tasks ul')
        .prepend("<li data-id=" + task.id + ">" + taskTitle + "
➥ <button>Done!</button></li>");
      taskTitleInput.val('');
```

```
      }
    });
  }
```

2. Run the script:

   ```
   node app.js
   ```

3. Open a browser with a JavaScript console at http://127.0.0.1:3000.

4. Enter a task into the input and click the Submit button.

5. You should see your task is written to the page.

6. Refresh the browser window.

7. You should see the task that you just created is still on the page (see Figure 24.2).

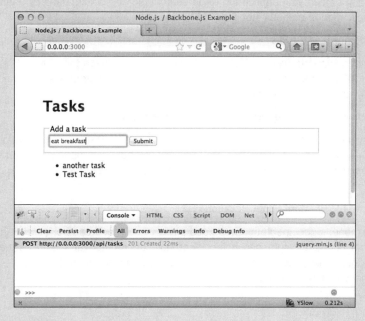

FIGURE 24.2
Adding records through a Backbone.js view

Backbone.js comes with a range of features including data validation and error handling that is a little beyond the scope of a book on Node.js. A fuller example, including deletion of tasks, is available for you to explore and run in this book's code examples as hour24/example04.

Summary

In this hour, you learned how to use Node.js as an API for Backbone.js, a client-side framework for creating rich JavaScript applications in the browser. You learned how the entire application stack can be JavaScript with Node.js on the server, MongoDB as the data store, and Backbone.js on the client side. You were introduced to Backbone.js and learned how to create a Model, Collection, and a View and saw how to use Backbone.js to create a basic single-page application.

Q&A

Q. **When should I use a single-page application?**

A. A single-page application means that the user never refreshes the page once the page has loaded. If you need your application to be searchable and bookmarked by users, a single-page application is probably not a good choice.

Q. **Can Backbone.js use URLs?**

A. Backbone.js supports using URLs in applications too and uses the HTML5 History API to allow the URL in the browser windows to be updated. For older browsers, Backbone.js gracefully falls back to the fragment version of the URL.

Q. **Is using JavaScript for the entire application a good idea?**

A. For many browser-based applications, using JavaScript for the entire application is a great idea. But as always, it depends on what your application is trying to do. If you want to create a desktop-type application for the browser, using JavaScript for the server, data store, and client is an excellent choice.

Q. **Where can I learn more about Backbone.js?**

A. The Backbone.js documentation is a good place to start and can be found at http://documentcloud.github.com/backbone/. A number of commercial screencasts are available at PeepCode https://peepcode.com/products/backbone-js and http://backbonescreencasts.com/.

Workshop

This workshop contains quiz questions and exercises to help cement your learning in this hour.

Quiz

1. Is Backbone.js just for single-page applications?

2. Is Backbone.js the only framework for creating rich client-side applications?

3. Do you need to use Node.js as the server for Backbone.js applications?

Quiz Answers

1. No. Although Backbone.js excels at creating single-page applications, it provides many features to allow client-side applications to interact with a server. Depending on your application and requirements, jQuery or just plain JavaScript may be enough, though.

2. No. There are many client-side frameworks for creating desktop-type applications in the browser. Some of these include Spine.js and Ember.js. A good comparison of client-side frameworks can be found at http://codebrief.com/2012/01/the-top-10-javascript-mvc-frameworks-reviewed/.

3. No. Backbone.js is agnostic to the server application. Node.js makes a great choice, though!

Exercises

1. Add some validation to the Node.js API so that a task cannot be submitted without a title.

2. Write some tests for the Node.js API to ensure that Backbone.js can interact with the API as expected.

3. Add the capability to delete a task. The solution is available in the book's code examples as hour24/example04.

Index

L

layout files (Express), 97-98

lightweight frameworks, 73

limiting access by IP address, 407-409

listening for events, 321-320

Live HTTP Headers add-on, 62-64

local module installation, 21-22

local variables (Express), 99-101

locating modules, 19-21

loops

    CoffeeScript, 368-370

    in Jade, 83-85

lovehateometer, creating, 252-262

M

managing events dynamically, 325-327

McConnell, Charlie, 241

messaging

    in chat server application, 229-231

    in Socket.IO, 202-208

Middleware, 399-400

    access control, 406-414

        forcing users onto single domain, 410-414

        limiting access by IP address, 407-409

    custom headers, adding, 404

mixins, Jade, 87-89

Mocha, 163-166

modifying strings in buffers, 343

modules, 15-16, 381-383

    assert module, 152-155

    Buffer module, 333-337

    Cluster module, 311-312

    creating, 381

    developing, 385-387

    documentation, 22-23

        locating, 22-23

    Events module, 317

    executables, adding, 387-389

    folder structure, 384-385

    HTTP, 59-69

    installing, 17

        global installation, 22

        local installation, 21-22

    locating, 19-21

    Process module, 291-293

        exiting, 293

    publicizing, 397

    requiring, 17-18

    Socket.IO, 189-191

        bi-directional data, 202-208

        data, broadcasting to clients, 197-203

        data, sending from server to clients, 192-198

        example of, 191-194

        and Express, 213-214

STDIO, 136-140

Stream module, 345-346

    MP3s, streaming, 354-355

testing, 385-387

third-party, 18

URL, 67

websites, 381-383

MongoDB, 109-131

    connecting to, 113-114

    create view, 118-121

    edit view, 120-125

    flash messages, 126-130

    index view, 117-119

    input data, validating, 130-131

    installing, 110-112

    tasks, deleting, 126-127

    Twitter Bootstrap, 116-117

MP3s, streaming, 354-355

N

network programming frameworks, 54

networked I/O, unpredictability of, 33-34

nibbles, 334

nicknames, adding (chat server application), 214-231

Node Inspector, 144-147

Node.js, installing, 9-10

Node.js debugger, 141-143

SAMS

REGISTER

THIS PRODUCT

informit.com/register

Register the Addison-Wesley, Exam Cram, Prentice Hall, Que, and Sams products you own to unlock great benefits.

To begin the registration process, simply go to **informit.com/register** to sign in or create an account. You will then be prompted to enter the 10- or 13-digit ISBN that appears on the back cover of your product.

Registering your products can unlock the following benefits:

- Access to supplemental content, including bonus chapters, source code, or project files.
- A coupon to be used on your next purchase.

Registration benefits vary by product. Benefits will be listed on your Account page under Registered Products.